All HE Wanted

Aphrodite Jones

Copyright © 2016 by Aphrodite Jones, AphroditeJonesBooks.
All rights reserved.

No part of this book may be used or reproduced by any means, graphic, electronic, or mechanical, including photocopying, recording, taping or by any information storage retrieval system without the written permission of the publisher except in the case of brief quotations embodied in critical articles and reviews.

*For Brandon
and for all those sisters and brothers out there
who deserve sexual freedom*

APHRODITE JONES

AUTHOR'S NOTE

The idea of changing the title of an existing book is something very foreign, yet in this case, I feel it's justified and even necessary. The story I told in *All She Wanted* is a chronicle of one of the first known transgender hate crimes in America and though I'm not sure I realized how important it was at the time, I did understand that in Falls City, Nebraska, a movement was being born. Still, it took me over twenty years to get it through my head that this book should have been entitled *All HE Wanted*, because Brandon was a transgender person and was always a he on the inside, even though he had female parts on the outside. These days, with the transgender movement in the spotlight, I finally had to admit to myself that I really did not "get it." Twenty years ago, I didn't understand the truth behind being transgender, and for that, I sincerely apologize.

The funny thing is that back in time, in 1995, not many people cared to "get" the notion of being transgender. It was something that was being ignored by the public, and the national news didn't cover this transgender murder case—not really at all. It was amazing to note that Falls City was Ground Zero to transgender activists who descended there from all parts of America, yet at the time that Teena Brandon's killers were convicted of triple homicide and a transgender hate crime, not one national TV news source reported it. I was stunned that there was no coverage on CNN, no coverage on any broadcast network. Locally, the convictions hit newspapers in Lincoln and Omaha, but national TV news coverage was focused on the O.J. Simpson trial and all the antics it entailed. The tabloid show, *A Current Affair*, did a short piece on the Brandon case, and that was about it.

I am thankful to know that if an LGBT murder happened today, for sure it would be headline news and covered non-stop. Let's face it, being transgender has become a hot-button topic. If nothing else, it shows we've come a long way in our efforts to understand and accept different forms of sexual identity. Even if we haven't come far enough, people today have a more sincere concern for the LGBT community. It's a start.

But back then, when I was researching and writing about the world of Brandon Teena/Teena Brandon in the mid-1990's, Brandon was actually considered to be perverted or perverse instead of transgender. For Falls City folks, the idea of someone being transgender was not a concept people could wrap their brains around. I say this because I heard people shouting lewd things to the transgender people who came to the courthouse during the murder trials. I say this because Falls City officials held press conferences stating that "this is not a hate crime." In fact, local law enforcement completely denied that Brandon was a transgender person and one called him an "it" before the homicides went down. To be fair, this intolerance was not shared by everyone in the area, but it certainly was prevalent.

When I wrote *All She Wanted*, I now look back and realize that in some small way, I myself had become a part of the story. I had become so outraged by the hate crime, and yet I could not tell it in a way that was unbiased by my traditional views of gender identity. To others around me, the attitude was that I could not, or would not, get the Brandon story right. Especially to activists, because I was not "one of them," I was deemed unfit to tell the tale. I was living a conundrum, and I sometimes thought maybe they were right. I had a struggle on my hands.

As I took notes and observed, as much as I tried to understand the nature of a transgender/transsexual person, I was considered an outcast and not given access to transgender people's thoughts or feelings. People from the transgender activist movement treated me like an unwanted outsider and most of the trans activists even made it a point to show they despised me. Why? Because I was telling the story from the perspective of Teena Brandon's family, because I was calling Teena a SHE and not a HE. To them, it was the ultimate insult. To me, it was the physical fact. Teena was in transition when she was murdered. She had taken no hormones. She had had no sexual re-assignment surgery. Teena Brandon was logged as a "female" in all the police reports that involved her murder and rape, so, on a practical level as a crime writer, I had to deal with the facts from a legal perspective.

For me, the thing that made the case particularly difficult to cover was that Brandon lived as both sexes. Brandon may have been known as Brandon Teena in Falls City, but back at home in Lincoln with her family, she became Teena Brandon again. It became a problem in the narrative of *All She Wanted* because I had to refer to Brandon as a she – and also as a he. As I wrote the book, I felt like I was always walking on eggshells to keep all the necessary elements of the story in check. I researched this book for almost two years and as time moved on it became painfully clear to me that each group didn't trust me as a writer. Whether it was the local townsfolk of Falls City, the law enforcement officials in Nebraska, or the transgender activists of the day, people felt I didn't know what I was doing. In the end, I hope I proved them wrong.

****

People may not realize that back when Brandon was killed, on December 31, 1993, the concept of being transgender did not exist in the minds of the mainstream public. In fact, the word "transgender" was not yet a part of our cultural vocabulary, and the phrase LGBT did not exist in America at all. Instead, what did exist was a gay and lesbian community that did not accept transgender people as being "a part" of them. It was a very strange time in the world of sexual rights. Perhaps that's why I dedicated my book to Brandon, and "for all those sisters and brothers out there who deserve sexual freedom."

The fact is, when Brandon was unmasked as a female, when Brandon was raped and degraded by two young thugs, she was warned not to report the incident, or she would be killed. But she reported it anyway. Brandon was still in transition, and had no choice but to report being raped as a female, which in the end, became the impetus for her murder.

So it was Teena Brandon who went to the police. Not Brandon Teena. It was Teena Brandon's homicide, along with the homicides of Lisa Lambert and Phillip Devine, that were chronicled in the court transcripts and in the few newspapers that covered the murders. Only in death did Brandon become known as "Brandon Teena," a transgender person. And years later, it was only after my book, and the subsequent film, *Boys Don't Cry*, that Brandon became widely known and accepted as the victim of a transgender hate crime. It's tragic that in life, Brandon was never accepted as a male by anyone other than girls he "fooled." No one really understood that he was always a HE – not me, not his family, not anyone in his world.

How could this be? Well for starters, back in the early 1990's no one other than activists really talked about such things. At worst, Brandon was considered a freak. At best, Brandon was considered a person with a gender identity crisis. The idea of being "transgender" was a fuzzy and vague concept to the mainstream. I recall vividly how confused I was when I met with a group called "Transgender Menace," which was an organization involved in fighting gender oppression at a time when Gay and Lesbian literature did not include the word transgender. To be sure, this was still the dark ages of the transgender revolution.

On May 14, 1995, the day before the triple murder trial of Teena Brandon, Lisa Lambert, and Phillip DeVine, a group of gay and transgender folks gathered in Kansas City to hear leaders of the "trans community" speak about the transgender movement. They were transgender Warriors who were fighting to put their voice on the map. The event was held at the All Souls Unitarian Universalist Church and about a hundred and fifty people were in attendance.

Unfortunately for me, when I was asked to take the podium to address the group, I made the mistake of starting my speech with the comment that Brandon was not a HE, that she was a SHE, and that she was a part of a triple homicide in Nebraska. I wanted the group to acknowledge the fact that three people were murdered, and furthermore that Brandon was never given the chance to become a HE, to have gender re-assignment surgery.

But, boy, looking back, I was so stupid to start my presentation with that comment. Of course in hindsight, I see how ridiculous this statement was. At the time, I didn't understand that Brandon was always a HE, born in a female body. Nor did I see that this activist group had not travelled to Kansas City for details about three murders, for details about Brandon's female body parts, or about the rape she suffered. They were there to hold up "Brandon Teena" as a symbol of hate crimes against transgender people — and they certainly let me know it. I realized my error just as soon as I opened my mouth, but by then, I was already being heckled and was escorted off the stage by people who were so outraged, they wrote nasty things about me on the Internet for years to come. At the time, I wondered if I could ever live it down. I never did.

When my book came out a year later, it was banned in Falls City for being "perverse" and it was considered so controversial in Lincoln, Nebraska, that I was assigned security guards at Borders because the bookstore anticipated a riot. But sadly, when *All She Wanted* hit bookstands, there was no riot, there was no commotion at all, because the transgender activists didn't show up. Through their silence, they made it clear that they thought my book was irrelevant.

For over twenty years, even though *All She Wanted* is the only book to cover the "Brandon Teena" case, nobody in the transgender activist community will acknowledge it. It seems kind of crazy to me that trans people would not care to have the real story of Brandon read by the mainstream. But that's how it's been.

In full disclosure, over the same twenty-plus years, I've received a good deal of mail from people thanking me for "outing" this story, for giving them a true account of a murder case that somehow helped them to understand what they were feeling as a transgender person. People wrote to thank me for having the courage to write about a subject that no one in the mass media seemed to care about at the time. They said my book made a difference. And that, after all, is what I really care about.

To this day, people ask me why my book, *All She Wanted*, is not associated with the film *Boys Don't Cry*. The answer is a bit complicated but

I'll try to boil it down. Back in 1995, I was the first to bring the story of "Brandon Teena" to Hollywood, where I optioned it to Diane Keaton who attached a young Drew Barrymore to star as Brandon. But unbeknownst to me, there were other forces at work with the same idea in mind. A production company called Killer Films had already joined forces with a brilliant young director and they were quickly moving ahead with their version of the Brandon Teena story in the film *Boys Don't Cry*. I later sued 20th Century Fox, and Fox Searchlight decided to settle with me after a court in California ruled that I had an actionable claim. Even though I ultimately received a cash settlement from 20th Century Fox, the studio refused to acknowledge my book in the film credits.

Such is life in Hollywood.

When *Boys Don't Cry* screened at Sundance in 1999, it made Hilary Swank an instant superstar, won her an Oscar for Best Actress, and put the word "transgender" into the mainstream. In the end, it seemed to me that nothing could have been better than an Oscar to shed light on such a dark and disturbing hate crime. That was the most important thing.

Today, with the help of people like Caitlyn Jenner and Chaz Bono, transgender issues are front and center. Still, for all the attention and buzz that these stars get in today's media, it certainly doesn't mean mainstream people have accepted transgender people for who they are. I pray that after all these years, after so much struggle and continuous hate crimes and suffering, the misunderstanding of transgender people will slowly but surely disappear. Let's not forget that Brandon was bullied and battered and killed for being transgendered, and even as I write this, countless victims of transgender hate crimes still hang in the balance.

Finally, above all else, I want people to know this:

> Brandon was not a freak.
> Brandon was not an "it."
> Brandon was someone denied his true sexual identity.

That was all HE wanted.

APHRODITE JONES

ACKNOWLEDGMENTS

Of all those who helped me, there are a few persons I *must* single out, particularly the Brandon family—JoAnn and Tammy—and their attorneys, Steve Berry and Mike Hansen, who cooperated fully and unabashedly. Also the Tisdel sisters, Lana and Leslie, as well as the handful of Brandon's other girlfriends featured in this book, who opened up their hearts and souls without expecting anything in return.

I owe thanks to Judge Robert Finn and to court reporter Kathie Garman, who made it possible for me to obtain the transcripts and the legal documentation absolutely critical to a work such as this. And since there's so much technical support involved in a true crime book, I'd be remiss if I didn't also acknowledge Kerry Lane, M.D., who freely provided his medical expertise and assisted me with gender research. In addition, I thank my hardworking transcribers: Pamela Willfinger, Louis Flores, Peggy Henderson, and Donna Norton—and especially Pamela, because she bitched the least and worked the most. You are people who will always be precious to me. Then there are my fellow writers: Darcy O'Brien, Mike McGrady, Jack Olsen, Vicki Hendricks, and above all, Paul Levine, who shared trade secrets and gave me continuing sustenance in ways only a writer can appreciate. And I've got to mention the ever-brilliant Diane Keaton and her associate Bill Robinson, who, along with a team of people from the William Morris Agency and my attorney, Robert Youdelman, thought enough of this book to want to see it turned into a major motion picture.

On a different note, I have been asked by certain of my close friends—some of you who've believed in me when the chips were really down, some of you who are relatively new to me, to perhaps mention *names*. The thing is, I just can't single anybody out. I'd have to list a score of people (you who are) connected to me whose loving energy and enthusiasm in seeing me through this book is something I consider the greatest blessing of all. I will, though, send a huge kiss to my Security Guy for being a crime stopper, for making me feel safe and sure, and for showing me love.

In the past, I have thanked my sister Janet for her devotion and loyalty and kindheartedness—she has really kept me sane. Today, I should really take the chance to thank the rest of my family—my aunts, uncles and cousins, and — particularly my cousin Vickie Lynne and my brother-in-law Joey—you've all been there in times of need. Without you, I don't know how I would have come this far.

And *of course*, I thank the two people who've been behind this book in a very big way: my agent, Matt Bialer, and my editor, Tom Miller. It was almost two years ago that Matt started pushing me to go to Nebraska. I can't say how glad I that he did. He had seen the significance of this project *long before* I did, and even though I had been prodded by certain friends in the media, as well as my close buddies in Iowa, it was Matt who convinced me to do this book, so I really owe him one. Regarding my editor, Tom—sometimes a slave driver but always a sweetheart—his concern in following the progress of this work certainly went beyond the call of duty. I want people to realize that his knowledge and his character shine through this book from cover to cover.

Finally, I must give thanks to my readers because *you* are the thing that keeps me going late at night when I'm stuck in front of my computer screen and sometimes pulling my hair out. Your kind devotion reminds me that, yes, you actually *care* — maybe more than I'll ever know.

"We fix our eyes, not on what is seen, but on what is unseen. For what is seen is temporary, but what is unseen is eternal."

2 Corinthians 4:17

PART ONE

GUT FEELINGS

APHRODITE JONES

PROLOGUE

IT WAS ONLY A MATTER OF SECONDS BEFORE THEY were through the house and in the back bedroom. Lisa was dialing the phone when the two guys entered, her hands shaking, feeling fear in every bone. One guy had a gun pointed at her. He took the phone out of Lisa's hands and calmly hung it up. She heard the other one asking her, "Where's Brandon at?"

But they didn't have to wait for an answer. They saw some movement on the floor, under a blanket at the foot of the bed, and one of them reached down and grabbed Brandon's arm. He picked Brandon up and threw her next to Lisa on the waterbed, keeping the gun pointed at them all the while. The two guys were drunk and cursing—it was John and Tom, and they were just breathing fire.

From the other bedroom, Phillip could hear this chaotic screaming match, topped off with the wailing of Lisa's eight month-old baby in a crib at his mother's side. Phillip lay there frozen.

There was an unnatural calm for a second, then Tom went over to try to quiet the infant, Tanner, who was now on his knees, hanging on the edge of the crib. Tom looked in the crib, hoping to find something that would pacify the child, but there was really no time for that. Tanner's screams just got louder, so Tom picked the boy up.

"Tom, please don't hurt my baby," Lisa begged.

Then a shot rang out. Then another. Brandon was hit, and her body slumped back on the bed, her knees dangling off the side.

"Tom, why are you doing this?" Lisa screamed. "Give me my baby!"

Tom handed Tanner to her because he noticed that Brandon's body was twitching.

Brandon needed to be finished off.

One of them pulled out a knife. As the guy opened it, he reached down with his left hand, grabbed Brandon's right shoulder, and pulled her toward him. He was close enough to feel her breath as he pushed the knife toward her, making sure Brandon was dead Lisa had Tanner next to her chest, holding her hand around the baby to help him sit up. It was all happening so fast. One of them moved away from the bed, and the other raised his arm with the pistol and shot Lisa in the stomach. It was a graze wound. It made Lisa jump and scream, but she could live through it.

Toni asked Lisa to hand the baby back over, and she did it without much of a fight. She watched Tom put the boy back in his crib and pleaded for her child's life. John was busy messing with the sliding mechanism on the gun. It had jammed, and he was trying to move the mechanism back and forth to get it to work again.

"Is anyone else in the house?" one of them asked "Phil's in the other room." John disappeared for a minute, on his way to Phillip.

"How bad were you hit?" Tom asked.

Lisa pulled up the bottom of her shirt and showed him a bullet hole. She was bleeding, and it was obvious she was in a lot of pain. In the background, Tom could hear loud hysteria. It was Phillip and John making their way through the living room to the back bedroom.

They stopped at the doorway, John holding Phil up alongside of him, Phil half leaning on the door.

"It doesn't have to be this way, man. I won't tell anyone," Phillip shrieked.

One of them moved closer to Lisa. He raised the gun and hit her in the right eye. The girl's pretty head jerked back, and she went completely limp.

"Let's get out of here," Tom whispered.

Phillip was now screaming wildly, saying anything to get them to listen.

"Shut the fuck up!" John barked.

For a minute, Phil calmed down, and John led the way out to the living room. When Tom and Phil got to the entryway, Phillip put his hand on Tom's shoulder, pleading with him, "Look, man, I didn't see anything. I won't tell nobody nothing. I'm not even from around here. I won't tell, man, I swear."

Tom listened as he escorted Phillip to the couch and ordered him to sit down. Then Tom moved back toward John.

Pistol fire rang out. It looked like a hit, and Phil slumped back into the couch. There was a second shot fired, and Phil slid down the couch, partly hunched on the floor.

Like lightning, John went back to Lisa's room. He tried firing the gun, but it jammed again, and he had to play with the mechanism once more. Tom was right behind him. By the time Tom stepped in the bedroom, the gun was back in working order.

Two or three more shots went off.

Tom motioned to John as he picked up a live round he saw near the bed. "Come on, let's get the fuck out of here," he said.

They shut the lights, retrieving two spent casings off the living room floor before they exited the house. Tom got behind the wheel, and John gave him directions to travel an alternate route. They drove along the Morrill Road and crossed down into Kansas before returning to Nebraska, arriving back home to Falls City in the frozen dead of night.

Just as they hit the outskirts of town, one of them threw a neatly wrapped package into the Nemaha River, knowing it would be downstream by sunrise. It was the gun, the clips, and the folding knife, cautiously encased in a pair of golden gloves.

APHRODITE JONES

1

WHEN THEY GOT OUT OF THE CAR, JOHN LOTTER AND Tom Nissen weren't that drunk anymore, and they were thinking straight. They decided that Kandi, and Rhonda would lie and say they heard them come home somewhere around 1:00 AM that morning. They had their alibi.

Actually it was just after 3:00 AM., December 31, 1993, when the two young men drove down Chase Street, pulled around to the back of Tom's house, and knocked on the door of the tiny one-story place.

Kandi, pregnant with her third child, was lying in bed listening to the baby's heartbeat when she heard them back there. Wearily, she waltzed by Rhonda, who was sound asleep on the living room floor. It was strange that her husband would knock to get into his own house. She never knew him to use the back door as an entryway because they always kept the front door unlocked. She didn't know why Tom was making her get up out of bed at that hour, especially when she was almost into her eighth month.

But Kandi never questioned her husband. They had a don't-ask, don't-tell kind of marriage. Her first child, Bobbie, was conceived before Tom came into the picture, and even after there was a paternity test, Tom felt he could never be sure about who the father was. She said her second girl, Tiffany, was Tom's, but he wasn't so sure he believed her. Same with the baby Kandi was carrying now. Tom started cheating on Kandi just days after they married, so he always guessed she would do the same. Now, two years later, the two of them hardly bothered to keep track of each other.

So Kandi didn't say much when Tom walked in with his hands in his pockets and asked her to go get the jug of Clorox out from under the sink. All she knew was that Tom had something on his hands and he wanted her to help him wash it off. John stood behind them at the sink and watched as Kandi poured the bleach while Tom scrubbed. Kandi didn't see what was there. She didn't care; she just wanted to get back to bed.

By the time Tom took off his black jacket and blue flannel shirt and went into the living room to smoke a cigarette, John was already in there talking with Rhonda, getting her to agree that if the cops ever asked, she would say they came in somewhere between 12:30 and 1:00 AM. Kandi joined the threesome in the living room and nodded yes, she would cover for them.

"Check to see if there's any blood on my shirt," Tom ordered. "What do you mean by that?" his wife asked.

But there was no response. Kandi looked for blood, but she didn't find any. Tom went in the bathroom for a few minutes and got sick. When he came out, he found John and Rhonda passed out on the floor. He joined Kandi in the bed and told her their problems were solved. She had no idea what he was talking about and just rolled over.

Just shortly after 10:00 AM that same day, about the same time that everyone in the Nissen house was waking up, a volunteer member of the Humbolt Rescue Squad got a call from the Richardson County Sheriff's Office reporting some deaths at the old Frank Rist place. When the dispatcher said it was two bodies, a grandmother and a baby, the rescue team went into a tailspin. Those kinds of things never happened in places like folksy Humbolt, Nebraska.

Dr. Stephen Stripe had also received a call that morning, a report that two women and a baby were killed at a farmhouse south of Humbolt. Stripe had expected it to be an easy day since it was New Year's Eve, but within minutes, he too was in the ambulance headed down Highway 105. Deputy Ray Harrod radioed to say he was just thirty seconds behind them, that the ambulance should wait before approaching the crime scene.

Harrod entered the residence with his gun drawn and immediately came upon a young African-American male leaning against a couch with an exit wound to the top right side of his head, an entrance wound to the jaw, and a heavy coffee table over his legs. The rescue worker touched the right side of the male's neck to check for carotid pulse and found none. He noticed there was little blowout from the wound. He looked around carefully for a gun, thinking it could have been a murder/suicide.

It was Anna Mae Lambert, Lisa's mother, Tanner's grandmother, who initially discovered the scene. She was there, sitting at the dining room table, feeding Tanner a bottle of formula when the deputy and ambulance squad arrived. She remembered the exact time she got there that morning—10:05—because she looked at the digital clock in her car before she walked up on the porch and was kind of looking around to see where Lisa's dog was. She was not paying attention to the front door at first. She did not realize it had been broken into.

Anna Mae had knocked twice on the outside door, the screen door, and she could hear her grandson crying inside the house. As she stepped inside, seeing the young man dead on the floor, she could only think the worst.

Lisa is probably dead in the bedroom, she thought.

When she got back there, she found Tanner very wet and cold, his little eyes bloodshot. He had been crying for God knows how long. As she picked Tanner up out of the crib, Anna Mae turned to her left and saw her daughter lying on the waterbed. She saw blood running from the side of Lisa's mouth, and there was someone else on the bed. Anna Mae couldn't tell if the person was a male or a female; she didn't know who it was.

She grabbed the phone, which was on the floor next to the dresser; went in the dining room; reached for the phone book; and called the Humbolt Police Department She got disconnected the first time and had to call the police back, identifying herself as Anna Lambert and telling them the location of Lisa Lambert's house. After she hung up the phone, she went into the kitchen, opened the refrigerator with a towel, and found an open can of formula, then went through all the cupboards and finally found a bottle.

She quickly warmed it in the microwave, sat back down at the dining room table, and, while feeding Tanner, called the police again. It seemed like a long time since she had first dialed the police department, and she wondered if anyone was coming out there. As she was banging up the phone, the ambulance arrived.

A uniformed officer, someone she did not recognize, told Anna that she had to get out of the house. Dr. Stripe examined the baby, and Tanner seemed to be in good shape with the exception of a soiled diaper, but it was still necessary for Anna and Tanner to be taken by ambulance to the Humbolt Hospital.

At approximately 10:22 AM., December 31, 1993, Investigator Jack Wyant of the Nebraska State Patrol was contacted by the dispatcher of the Richardson County Sheriff's Office and was informed that Sheriff Charles Laux was en route to Humbolt, Nebraska, where three bodies were found. Wyant waited ten minutes and called Laux at the crime scene, discovering that the bodies had been shot execution style, that no weapon was located in the house. Laux identified the dead females as Lisa Lambert and Teena Brandon.

The sheriff told Investigator Wyant that Teena Brandon was a female who had reported being raped on December 25, 1993, that there were two local suspects still under investigation.

Wyant asked Sheriff Laux to have his department locate the suspects, jumped in the mobile evidence collection van, and made the drive from Lincoln to Humbolt in under two hours.

When he got there, he was met at the edge of the driveway by the sheriff and the Richardson County attorney. He was shown tire tracks east of the front porch, and it was evident that the wheels had spun out of the place. Since he could find no delineation of a tread whatsoever, an accident reconstructionist would have to be called in.

There was one lone footprint, possibly a tennis shoe, partially visible in the tracks. It was not defined enough for a cast to be made. It could barely be seen with the naked eye.

2

TO EVERYONE AT THE SCENE, THE FARMHOUSE SEEMED far too neat for there to have been any kind of struggle. With the exception of the coffee table, there was nothing really upset inside. The collage of photos hanging on the paneled wall in the living room remained perfectly in place. Behind the crib in the bedroom, Mickey Mouse and Pluto hung on cheery green—and-white-patterned wallpaper. The Graco baby swing sat undisturbed next to the door that led to the back porch. The back screen door was still locked from the inside, and that area was largely untouched. Someone's denim jacket was strewn on one of the chairs in the dining room. There were little green, red, yellow, and orange Christmas lights strung up behind the dining room table, a Christmas stocking over by the front door, and a Christmas tree jug in the kitchen that read Happy Holidays sitting near boxes of Honeycombs and Captain Crunch.

Dr. Stephanie Stripe, Stephen's wife, had checked for a heartbeat in all three victims. She knew Lisa Lambert well, but could hardly recognize her because of the massive bruising to Lambert's face.

Another woman at the scene, Shannon Frankhauser, gossiped a bit with other rescue workers, retelling the piece of the puzzle she had been aware of for some time: the victim, Teena Brandon, was *one and the same person* as the cute, polite young man people in Humbolt knew as Brandon. Brandon was not the cute boy they had seen around town for the last month or two; Brandon was actually this murdered female in bed with Lisa.

Investigator Jack Wyant examined the solid-core door, the main entrance to the house, noting that the interior molding of the door edge was forced away from the wall. On the carpet directly in front of the door was a large amount of plaster from behind the molding. The door could have been kicked open, although since no outline of any foot could be seen, Wyant considered the possibility that the door had been forced open with a shoulder.

The scene at the sofa was remarkable in that there appeared to be no signs of violence anywhere else in the living room. The male victim, sitting on the floor with a large wooden coffee table on his lap, had a prosthesis on his right leg, which was partially covered by a boot. A large amount of blood appeared on the victim's white turtleneck shirt, and later on, Wyant pulled away the top portion of the collar, discovering a small bullet hole in the neck. There were no defensive wounds to be found on the male anywhere. The veteran investigator believed that the wooden leg, which extended from below the knee, possibly forced the coffee table to rise so that when the victim came to his final resting place, the table then crashed down on top of him. The only piece of evidence collected in that room was a single red spot that appeared on the carpet, located just to the south of the front door, near a radio stand.

Directly behind the northeast corner of the sofa was a doorway leading into a bedroom where the mate to the boot on the male victim's prosthesis was found under some sweat clothes lying on the floor. A wallet was found, and the male was identified as Phillip DeVine, a name that no one at the scene recognized. The bed appeared to have been slept in; however, the top quilt had been pulled up.

From there, Wyant proceeded into the northwest bedroom. Right in front of him was a baby crib with infant clothes and a small blue sweatshirt hanging on one of the corner posts. As he entered the room further, he noticed that one of the doors of a large closet was slid to the north. He later learned that Deputy Harrod, in searching for the suspects, had opened that door.

The blue shag carpet in Lisa's bedroom was wet, and both bodies were soaked. A bullet had also punctured the waterbed, causing it to leak, so there was blood diluted with water everywhere. There were a few tracks on the rug in the bedroom, said to belong to the grandmother, Deputy Harrod, and the ambulance attendant who had removed a blanket from the crib for the baby, but these faint footprints were being washed away by leaking water as Wyant stood there. The blood and water mixed.

Teena Brandon was observed lying on her back crossways along the lower segment of the bed, her body clothed in a sweatshirt and sweatshorts. Lisa Lambert's body was partially under the covers with her head on a pillow. Brandon's knees were on the top east edge of the waterbed. Her feet, in pinkish-white socks, were dangling over the edge. It was apparent that her right foot was touching the floor at one time because the right sock was pinkish in color, probably a result of the sock soaking up the water diluted with blood.

An immense amount of blood could be seen on Brandon's front abdomen, and though Wyant didn't want to disturb the body, he very lightly lifted up the bottom of her sweatshirt and observed a jagged wound on Brandon's hands, which were up at her sides, had blood on them; at some point she probably clenched her stomach.

Under Brandon's chin was one small round hole, and it looked like there was gunpowder on the lower section of her face, chin, and neck. Wyant surmised that Brandon's body could have been standing to the side of the bed, facing east when she was shot, that she most likely would have sat down at the time and simply fallen backward on the bed. He noted a fracture in the left side of her skull, which indicated she had been hit by some type of object—clearly blows were struck.

The wound in Lambert's right eye was observed, with blood running down from her eye to the bed and also running down from the right corner of her mouth. Later during the crime scene search when Wyant pulled the bed sheets away from Lambert, after Brandon was removed from the bed, he realized Lambert's legs were mainly under the covers of the east division of the bed and not underneath Brandon as he originally thought. Wyant believed that Lambert was sitting up in the bed when she was first wounded, the shots causing her to fall backward.

During the course of the search, Wyant requested technicians from the Latent Fingerprint Lab to process the crime scene, which was done using both normal and laser methods.

Wyant followed proper protocol, first making notes, then taking photographs of the entire area. Before, during, and after, measurements were taken. The evidence casings, one live cartridge, one spent bullet, a cigarette lighter and ashtray, and two possible blood spots were all systematically collected, bagged, tagged, and kept in Wyant's custody until everything was submitted to the Nebraska State Patrol Criminalistics Lab for analysis.

Sheriff Laux was put in charge of taking care of the bodies. Since the Richardson County attorney, Doug Merz, had already been to the farmhouse and had gone back to his office to pursue suspects and arrest warrants, Laux decided to make the half-hour drive down to Falls City to talk to Merz in person about where and when he wanted the bodies moved.

At approximately 3:00 PM that same day, Investigator Roger Chrans was transported to Humbolt from Beatrice, Nebraska, where he was met by Trooper Mark Williams, Investigator Wanda Townsend, Investigator Jud McKinstry, Investigator Ron Osborne, and Investigator Jack Wyant, all of the Nebraska State Patrol. Technically, Wyant was in charge of the processing of the crime scene itself, but it was Roger Chrans who became the lead investigator in the triple homicide. Basically, it was now his case.

Also present was Deputy Tom Olberding of the Richardson County Sheriff's office, who informed Chrans and the rest of the state police at the scene of Teena Brandon's rape allegation, mentioning the Sheriff's office continuing sexual assault investigation of suspects John Lotter and Marvin Thomas Nissen, aka Tom Nissen. As they stood there at the Humbolt farmhouse, Olberding told them sexual assault warrants were in the process of being issued for these two by county attorney Meiz.

Chrans didn't waste any time. By 3:40 PM he was out of there, on his way to assist the Sheriff's Office and the Falls City Police Department in the arrests of Lotter and Nissen.

Laux arrived back in Humbolt at 6:30 that evening and spent over an hour loading the three bodies, bagged up, sealed up, into his vehicle. He transported them to the Douglas County Hospital in Omaha and stayed in the city overnight to be there for the autopsies, which would begin first thing the next morning, New Year's Day.

3

EARLIER THAT AFTERNOON, AROUND 2:30 ON DECEMBER 31, while police investigators were busy documenting the Humbolt murder scene, two young blondes had shown up at the end of Lisa Lambert's driveway looking for someone named Phil—they said Phil owed them gas money. They were sisters, Lana and Leslie Tisdel, and they had crossed over the yellow crime scene tape, trying to find out what was going on.

The minute they stepped foot on the property, the two fair-skinned women were unofficially questioned, and then each was separately interviewed. Investigator Wanda Townsend took twenty-one-year-old Leslie Tisdel into the patrol car first. Leslie told the investigator she and Lana had come out to the farmhouse simply to return some of Brandon's and Phillip's belongings.

Leslie was dating Phillip DeVine, she said; they were both students at the Job Corps in Denison, Iowa. They had met in November. Leslie had returned home to Falls City on December 7, and Phillip had decided to follow her. They wanted to spend Christmas together. DeVine had arrived in Omaha via bus on December 14; Leslie, Lisa Lambert, and Teena Brandon had all gone together to pick him up at the station.

At the scene, Leslie mentioned that she and Phillip had gotten into a big fight, that she had driven Phillip to Humbolt the day before, on December 30. She said they were arguing over their relationship, that Phillip wanted to become more involved but she wanted to take it slow. Leslie thought Phil was the jealous type, that he wanted to possess her. Leslie had a long history of abusive relationships; she didn't know a good thing when she had it. She didn't appreciate Phil, so when DeVine decided to go off with Brandon to stay at Lambert's, Leslie drove the two of them up there, racing the car as fast as she could. She dropped them off around 6:00 in the morning and watched DeVine and Brandon walk to the front door. Lisa Lambert was waiting for them.

Even though Leslie said she had only known Lambert for two months, she considered Lisa a good friend. She hadn't spoken to Lisa, however, since December 14, the day they had picked Phillip up in Omaha. Leslie told

Officer Townsend that she drove off the morning of December 30, without ever entering the Lambert residence.

To Leslie's knowledge, John Lotter and Tom Nissen knew Phillip DeVine because the three of them had gone out drinking in Falls City on at least one occasion. DeVine was introduced to Brandon through her, Leslie said; her sister, Lana, had dated Brandon for approximately a week, and while they were dating, Brandon lived at their residence in Falls City, where Phillip also stayed. Brandon's real name was Teena Ray Brandon, Leslie said. She explained that Brandon acted like she was a man, but in reality she was female.

When Lana got in the cruiser, she told Townsend that the last time she saw Brandon was the afternoon before, approximately 4:00 PM on December 30. At that time, Brandon and Phillip had driven down from Humbolt in Lisa's car—they were at her house briefly to pick up some of their things. Lana said she knew Teena Brandon because she dated him for about a week or two; she believed they started dating around the beginning of December.

In her initial interview, Lana Tisdel gave an account of her whereabouts on the evening of December 30, 1993, saying she was home until about 5:30 PM., at which time she and Leslie went to the Hinky Dinky supermarket to pick up spaghetti, then went over to their dad's and ate supper. On their way home, around 7:00 PM., they were pulled over by a city police officer for a broken headlight and were detained for fifteen minutes. About an hour later, toward 8:15, Lana went to see her friend and neighbor Teeni Armfield.

Teeni wasn't there, so Lana tried again at 9:00 with no luck. She left a note on Armfield's door.

At approximately 10:00 PM, Linda Gutierres, Lana's mom, asked her to take her cousin Jason home. On her way back from Jason's, Lana stopped off at Tom Nissen's to talk with her aunt, Gutierres's baby sister, Melissa Wisdom. Lana went there to tell Missy that Linda wanted her home no later than 10:30. Lana spoke to Missy out on the Nissen front porch because Kandi refused to let Lana into her house. Kandi hated Lana's guts—why, she wasn't sure.

Lana said she had seen both Nissen and Lotter around 1:00 AM that morning, December 31. The two of them had come to her mom's house—they said they bad walked there, which seemed strange to her—and they told her mother Linda that they bad been drinking all day in a nearby Nebraska town called Rulo. They were pretty drunk, Lana thought, but no more than they usually were.

The last time Lana saw the two of them was about 12:30 PM that very day, an hour or so before she headed over to Humbolt. At that time, Lotter came into her house for about five or six minutes. He was there to return some of Brandon's clothing. Nissen stayed in the car. She saw him sitting out there alone.

Lana told the officer that she had called out to the Lambert residence earlier that morning, December 31, around 11:00 AM., and had talked to a woman she thought was Lisa.

A female answered the phone, Lana reported. Lana told "Lisa" that she and Leslie were on their way out to visit.

The female voice said, "OK."

The interviews at the crime scene with Lana and Leslie Tisdel were over in less than an hour. In talking to Townsend, both girls mentioned that Teena Brandon had been raped on Christmas. Each believed John Lotter and Tom Nissen were responsible.

4

ROGER CHRANS ARRIVED AT THE FALLS CITY POLICE DEPARTMENT at around 4:15 on December 31, in the middle of a briefing. Members of the city police, along with Deputy Tom Olberding, were in the lineup room making arrangements to handle the arrests of John Lotter and Marvin Thomas Nissen for sexual assault and kidnapping. Roger Chrans and Jud McKinstry of the state police were there, technically, to provide backup. The sexual assault and kidnapping charges had already been filed against Lotter and Nissen with the Falls City Police Department and the Richardson County Sheriff's Office on December 25, 1993. Now, in the course of the briefing, Assistant Police Chief John Caveizagie determined that there was probable cause to bring them in on these charges. County attorney Doug Merz was issuing warrants.

Minutes before the law enforcement briefing, someone from the Falls City Police Department had driven by the Nissen house and spotted the Lotter car parked out front.

In the lineup room, assignments were quickly being given out, because nightfall was approaching, and these two were definite flight risks. It didn't take long to decide which officer was doing what, safety-wise, and who has covering what area. In no time, Chrans and McKinstry were positioned two houses north of Nissen's on an intersecting street, J Street, waiting in Investigator McKinstry's patrol unit The Nissen residence, 1815 Chase Street, was well within their view. They watched as Assistant Chief Caveizagie and Patrolman Greg Cowan knocked on the front door.

Immediately, they saw Nissen come out of the house and be placed on the ground. Chrans got out of McKinstry's vehicle with his gun drawn, he saw Lotter step out of the house and positioned on the ground next to Nissen.

The two suspects were very close to each other, and they were talking, an unsafe situation for officers in any kind of felony arrest, so Chrans approached both individuals with his gun pointed at them, identified himself, and told them to look at him instead of looking at each other. The whole thing seemed to happen in slow motion, but within ten minutes from the time of arrival at Chase Street, Nissen and Lotter were out on the front lawn being taken into custody.

At 10:15 that night, New Year's Eve, Marvin Thomas Nissen was formally interviewed by Falls by Investigator Keith Hayes and Nebraska State Patrol Investigator Roger Chrans.

Tom Nissen was read the Miranda warnings, signed the NSP 708 form, and waived his rights. He wanted to talk.

At first, Nissen said he and Lotter had gone out to Humbolt because Lotter wanted to scare Brandon.

Chrans told Nissen that he believed both he and John Lotter were involved in the murders, that he had information that the gun used in the homicides was taken from the house of Bill Bennett, Lotter's friend. Chrans also informed Nissen that he knew Rhonda McKenzie was told to lie about what time Lotter got home and that Nissen himself told his wife, Kandi, to lie as well. When Kandi's name was mentioned, Nissen stared at the floor and became teary eyed. Nissen began his first statement by relating his whereabouts early in the evening of December 30, from the time he and John Lotter drove from Falls City to Nissen's mother's house in Rulo. After they stopped at his mother's, he and Lotter went drinking at Camp Rulo, a local hangout, stopped over at the Old Tyme Bar for a drink, then went back to "Camp," where they stayed until closing time, around midnight. The two of them returned to Nissen's house around 12:30 or 1:00 in the morning. Kandi and Rhonda were there. Nissen ate a sandwich and grabbed a case of beer, and then he and Lotter took off. Lotter drove around a little bit and stopped at Eddie Bennett's house. John said he wanted to take a piss. Nissen told Hayes and Chrans that at some time in the past John made a comment to him that Eddie had a gun. Tom stayed in the car, shifting position over to the driver's side. John was in and out of Eddie's in a matter of minutes. According to Tom, John directed him to drive to Lana and Leslie Tisdel's place on 21st Street, and on the way there, John pulled a box out of his pocket and showed Tom a small black handgun that looked like a .25. There was a clip in the gun and a second clip in the box, which had two or three bullets in it. John made the comment that he wanted to take care of Brandon. Tom claimed he didn't know exactly what Lotter meant by that. "Who is Brandon?" Chrans asked. "Teena Brandon." Nissen said that when they got to Lana's, he talked to Linda and asked her if Missy made it home all right. He didn't remember what time they stopped there; he thought they were there for about five minutes.

Nissen then drove them to Humbolt. He turned up Lisa Lambert's driveway and noticed that the car clock said 2:00 AM. He told investigators there were no lights on in the house. Tom didn't know what John was going to do.

"I don't want anyone hurt but Brandon," Tom said as they stepped out of the car.

"Yeah, right," John said.

"You better be careful because someone in there may have a bigger gun than you do," Tom warned.

Nissen told police that both he and Lotter were wearing gloves as they approached the front door, that he held the screen door open as John knocked, getting no answer. Lotter then kicked the door several times until it opened. At this time, Nissen immediately dropped to his knees, thinking there might be some gunshots coming from the house.

Once inside, Lotter made his way to the back bedroom where he shot Brandon and "some other girl." Then Lotter shot Phil; Nissen didn't remember how many times the gun was fired. When he was finished, Lotter turned to Nissen, telling him, "Nobody narked on me and got away with it."

At ten minutes after January 1, 1994, Investigator Chrans and Sergeant Ron Osborne attempted to talk to John Lotter in his cell in the Richardson County Jail. Lotter was read his rights, and Chrans advised him that Tom Nissen had implicated him in the shooting deaths of three people in Humbolt, claiming that Lotter was the shooter, the gun getter.

Lotter didn't feel like talking. He wanted a lawyer. The only comment John made was "I can't believe Tom said that stuff about me."

PART TWO

SEXUALLY SPEAKING

5

JOANN BRANDON WAS WIDOWED YOUNG—SHE HAD married when she was just a child— and she was carrying Teena when she got the news that her husband, Pat, died in a car crash.

He had gone fishing and was driving home in his convertible with the top down. The car flipped over three times and went up over a bridge. JoAnn heard about the accident over the radio, but of course she didn't relate it to the car Pat was in—that was, until she saw her sister-in-law, Molly, talking to a state trooper in their living room.

When the trooper handed JoAnn a wallet, she kept telling him he was lying, that the wallet didn't prove anything, she just wouldn't believe it. Then the trooper handed her Pat's wedding ring, something be never took off, and she just fell apart. Here they were, two kids still in puppy love, then all at once it was over.

JoAnn was petite, sweet sixteen, with strong model-like features—the high cheekbones, the almond-shaped face, the wide-set eyes that looked *through* people rather than at them. She was beautiful and she knew it. She had an attitude about herself that way. She had long desired a career as a model, had even modeled children's clothes for local department store catalogs, but now she was puffy, bloated, and depressed, mourning the loss of her handsome young husband, having to face motherhood alone. She and her oldest girl, Tammy, a toddler at the time, moved from a two-bedroom mobile home off Cornhusker Highway to her mom's place on the other side of Lincoln. Somehow they would have to make it.

JoAnn had been used to living without a man around the house—her father deserted her when she was just seven, and her mother never spoke of him much. All JoAnn knew was that he once worked for the police force in Omaha, that he was considered to be classified as a *genius*, that he supposedly became a medical doctor, had remarried, and started a whole new life out on the West Coast somewhere. She had no contact with the man after her seventh birthday party.

The only thing JoAnn remembered about him—he was probably in kindergarten when this occurred—was that a neighbor had come over to tell her mom something awful: her dad bad given the little neighbor girl, the girl that was her baby-sitter, an engagement ring. As JoAnn was sitting on the front steps, she watched the baby-sitter's father pull a small diamond ring from his pocket as proof. In overhearing the conversation between her mother and gentleman neighbor, she discovered that her dad had given out several engagement rings around town. At the tender age of five or maybe six, JoAnn decided that she didn't trust men. She figured they all lied.

JoAnn's brother Allen was just a tiny baby then, and her other brothers, Billy and Michael, never went to try to find their dad—they were hardly old enough to figure out how to go about it. JoAnn's mom was supposed to be getting child support but she wasn't, so Francis Brayman learned a skill at a training school in Lincoln called Manpower, worked at Ward's Department Store for a long time, and then Deitze Music, a landmark in downtown Lincoln, as a bookkeeper and payroll clerk. She was able to keep food on the table without asking any of her kids to work and even able to afford to send them all to Catholic school.

Back in the sixties, when JoAnn was growing up, she didn't much follow the hippie movement, she had a serious and determined approach to life. She wanted a career, she wanted to be the chief executive of a fashion company, she wanted to *be* somebody. JoAnn wanted glamour and riches and never talked about having kids. Now, in the early seventies, Frances had to quit Deitze Music to help her daughter in the wake of Pat Brandon's death: he was killed in April of 1972, and JoAnn delivered Teena in December of that year. JoAnn was having a really rough pregnancy and had been depressed for quite some time. When Teena was conceived, she and Pat had just moved back from his father's place in Oregon, where she had been so homesick, JoAnn went from a weight of 114 down to 83 pounds.

Two weeks after the car crash, things got so bad that Francis checked JoAnn into the hospital and had her treated by a psychiatrist. At one point, JoAnn even suggested the *unthinkable* for a Catholic girl in those days: getting an abortion. She had so much trouble during Tammy's delivery, she felt she just couldn't handle it a second time. But JoAnn's doctor was Catholic too, and he wouldn't even consider the idea. Almost as instantaneously as she had suggested it, JoAnn did a 180° turnaround and decided she would do whatever it took to have Teena, and she fought really hard to have her baby.

"I was having a lot of problems," JoAnn recalls. "I started having a lot of pain with Teena when I was going into my third month, so I went back to the doctors. They thought maybe it was a tubal pregnancy, and they went down in the vaginal area and looked. It was my uterus, it wasn't tipped back, and the doctor told me it was a miracle that I even got pregnant."

Then in her fifth month, the baby wasn't growing sufficiently, so the doctors put JoAnn back in the hospital for a couple of weeks once more. JoAnn was too young and too scared to ask many questions. She listened to the doctors and accepted their treatments as gospel, something she would later regret.

"They gave me hormone shots or something, and they were so thick, a thick serum. They would give one in each cheek and pretty soon you couldn't sit either way in bed," JoAnn explained. "I went through this for two weeks, and then she started to grow and I didn't *seem* to have more problems."

When she was pregnant with Tammy, JoAnn had been able to go to the state fair in her regular blue jeans and a pullover, even into her eighth month. With Teena, however, she blew up and got fat for the first time in her life, eating onion rings, chipped ice, french fries—any junk food she could get her hands on. At just five feet three inches, she weighed 138, which made her feel tremendous and unnatural. JoAnn was uncomfortable with all that weight, especially because Teena was way overdue. Teena was late coming—forever coming.

"I was running around trying to do everything to induce this labor that you can imagine," JoAnn remembers. "I mean, I was moving furniture around the house, I'd jog around the block, I scrubbed and waxed my car, and nothing was working. It was like, come on, *please*."

On December 12, when she went into false labor for the fourth time, her doctor decided it was time to induce her.

It was a natural childbirth until the head was out; the last thing JoAnn remembered was begging for gas. When she woke up in the intensive care unit, she thought she was in heaven, her head spinning as she looked at a circle of people standing around her dressed in white.

JoAnn really didn't know how bad off she was. All she knew was that the staff wouldn't let her see Teena, that she had all these tubes in her, that they had to cut her rings off her fingers because her hands were so swollen. Her mother-in-law, Doris, walked in the room and started bawling when she heard a nurse say they didn't expect the young woman to make it through the night.

But JoAnn did make it through and was allowed to see her baby the next day for the first time.

"They wouldn't let me touch her; they just brought her up and showed her to me," JoAnn remembers. Joe had a staph infection and wasn't allowed to touch Teena for five days. She blamed the hospital for the infection, believing that someone screwed up in the operating room. She really didn't know for sure why she was so sick, and she never got a sufficient answer from anyone.

When little Tammy came to see her in the visiting room, the toddler wouldn't talk to her mom at first. Finally, little Tammy blurted, "Don't you bring that baby home!" Luckily, by the time JoAnn arrived at her mom's with Teena, all that sibling rivalry vanished. Tammy considered Teena *her* baby, and that was it.

Their grandfather on their father's side was a full-blooded Sioux Indian, so Teena, like Tammy, was an exotic-looking infant. To JoAnn, she almost looked black, even though it was only her hair that was dark. Teena was beautiful, blessed with the bluest Irish eyes. Though she was a bit scrawny at first, she would blossom and become an adorable little girl.

JoAnn clung dearly to Teena, the final product of her love with Patrick. She didn't breast-feed because the doctor told her it would make her breasts sag—besides, she had tried with Tammy, and it drew blood. With Teena, JoAnn went for Pampers and bottles all the way.

Teena was a really good baby—she pretty much slept through the night—but she tended to be sick. She caught bronchitis and pneumonia when she was fifteen months and had to be put in an oxygen tent in the emergency room. JoAnn was such an overly concerned mother that the hospital staff had to ask her to leave because the stress was making JoAnn's asthma flare up and creating an unhealthy situation for both mother and child.

That was a fact of life JoAnn just had to learn to live with. Teena was forever catching a fever, a flu—it was always something. When the girl was in the second grade, she came down with mono. In looking back, JoAnn reflected, "It just seemed like Tammy was my healthy child and Teena was my sick child."

At first there was no father figure for the girls, but JoAnn's brothers were around, and they helped out to a certain extent. It would be a couple of years before JoAnn got remarried. By then, Teena was a toddler, and she called JoAnn's second husband "Daddy" practically from the minute she laid eyes on him, which is why JoAnn agreed to wed this man, Jug, in the first place. When JoAnn met Jug, it was early September. By the middle of that month, he bought her a ring. He was just crazy about her, couldn't do enough for her. On October 4, a justice of the peace pronounced them man and wife.

But JoAnn really didn't want to marry Jug—she wasn't in love with him. She tried to get out of the wedding, then decided to go through with it in a haphazard kind of way. In the judge's chambers, when JoAnn was asked to say, "I do," she paused long enough for Jug's dad to stand up and ask, "JoAnn, would you please say *yes*?" For the reception, Jug's parents took the newlyweds to the Moose's Lodge on Cornhusker Highway. Afterward, when she thought about what she had done, JoAnn went in the bathroom and cried for two hours.

Apparently her tears weren't in vain, because she was very unhappy in their marriage and eventually divorced Jug. Although Jug put her on a pedestal and treated her like gold, she says he also became possessive to the point of no return. Jug's friends were always trying to come on to JoAnn, and Jug would blame *her* even though she was doing nothing more than trying to be polite.

"He and I were not compatible as a couple," JoAnn reminisced. "I married him for all the wrong reasons, which wasn't fair to him, but he was a good stepfather. He did love the girls, and they loved him."

On JoAnn and Jug's wedding day, Teena was just twenty-two months and Tammy was going on five. They moved from their grandmother's place in Havelock to a duplex in Airpark and from the very get go, the two girls had Jug wrapped around their little fingers. In his eyes, they were his two sweet angels who could do no wrong. He spoiled them completely.

6

JUG WAS THE ONLY FATHER TEENA EVER KNEW. IN TAMMY'S case, she was just old enough to remember her real dad, but with Teena, JoAnn decided to let her think it was Jug until she got a bit older when she could understand these things better.

In any case, both girls called him Dad, and he was the head of the household long enough—about five years—to be a meaningful person in their lives. Tammy and Teena never paid much attention to the rocky relationship between their parents; all they cared about was having fun. Their father taught them important things like how to ride bikes without training wheels and how to roller skate. He did everything he was supposed to do, including taking them trick-or-treating and dressing up as Santa Claus.

He also took the girls on trips—he'd take them camping and show them what Nebraska was really like, the three of them walking the same trails as Crazy Horse, Sitting Bull, and Red Cloud. JoAnn wasn't as much of an outdoors type, so for the most part, she'd forgo these big adventures and tag along when they went to places like Worlds of Fun, an amusement park in Kansas City, where things were *civilized*.

The girls especially loved to visit Jug's sister Cheryl in Grand Island, which they did at least three or four times a year. It was one of their favorite adventures because Cheryl and her husband lived on a big farm, close to the center of Nebraska, where it was totally rural, and the kids would get to ride horses, watch cows, and play with an old English setter. Tammy remembers watching the dog eating frogs and foaming at the mouth.

With a step-dad to provide for them, Teena and Tammy each had their own room. They were exact opposites—Tammy's was entirely decorated and Teena's was anything but. Tammy had knickknacks displayed everywhere, mostly stuffed animals and doll stuff. Teena collected things—stop signs, beer signs, whatever—and squirreled them away. Teena was a definite tomboy, which seemed strange sometimes, at least to Tammy.

"She took a lunch box full of garden snakes and threw them in my face, scared the crap out of me," Tammy remembers. "She thought it was hilarious. She laughed at me for three hours about that. She always used to pick up dead bugs and shove them in my face. She knew I was a fraidy cat so she'd try to scare me—she would purposely do it."

It wouldn't be stretching things to say they were the all-American family, especially in the seventies, when the pace of childhood was slower and *The Brady Bunch* was a larger role model for people than anyone wanted to admit. For the Brandon girls, those years proved to be a wonderful family affair, the best they would ever know as kids.

Every Saturday morning, they watched cartoons—Scooby Doo was Teena's favorite—and they had cable, so they'd get to watch kid movies and also R-rated things that they weren't supposed to see. Tammy recalls many weekends the two of them spent playing house down in their basement, using boxes, card tables, and sheets to create tents. They both had dolls, but Tammy was the only one who actually played with them. Teena had a doll that when it peed, it would get a little red rash on its bottom, but she tired of it just as quickly as she did all of her other dollies and mostly played with sturdy things like Tinker-toys and Lincoln Logs. She liked to construct and destroy. She liked radios and walkie-talkies and spent hours taking them apart and putting them back together to see how they worked.

When they played house, Teena would always sneak up on Tammy and scare her. Teena wasn't interested in pretending to cook or anything like that. She wasn't like Tammy when it came to any kind of girly stuff. For instance, Tammy wore frilly little flowered dresses and lace ankle socks; Teena was always in T-shirts, jogging shorts, and unsightly boy's tube socks, the kind trimmed with red and blue stripes.

Tammy loved to get dressed up; she always tried to wear makeup to school. Teena never wore makeup except maybe once or twice when Tammy tried it on her for school plays, the little Christmas pageants Teena was in. That was during Teena's kindergarten and early schooldays when she sometimes wore dresses because she was forced to.

"Mom pretty much made her wear dresses to school, and she hated them," Tammy remembers. "She just felt uncomfortable, she'd tell Mom, '*I don't like 'em,*' and she'd argue with my mom all morning about it, but for her pictures, she'd have to wear a dress."

"Teena was a real tomboy, but yet she could go either way," JoAnn explained. "When she was at Saint Mary's and got to the point where she didn't want to wear dresses anymore, I asked her, '*What's wrong?*'"

"Well, Mom, when you walk up those steps, those boys can look right up your dress, and they're *cold*," Teena told her.

JoAnn knew a lot of girls who didn't wear dresses—for starters, her sister-in-law Molly was one—so she never attached any significance to it. She herself wore jeans a lot, she set her own pace when it came to style, so she thought Teena was just being her own person. Yes, Teena was the biggest tomboy, but then, so was JoAnn when she was that age. As long as Teena would agree to wear a dress on occasion and would go along with having her hair curled now and then, JoAnn didn't question her daughter's ways.

But Tammy didn't always understand her kid sister, especially Teena's wild imagination and the things she would dream of doing, like the times Teena used to play priest, where she'd use Kool-Aid for communion, put a little bathrobe over herself, and get everyone around her to take part in a mass.

"The church was really significant to her. We went to Catholic school, and I think they kind of brainwash you in kindergarten on being priests and nuns. They always bring in priests and nuns to talk about how they got the calling and how you'll know if you have the calling," Tammy remembers.

"Teena never wanted to be a nun, she always wanted to be a priest, and I thought it was funny because I had to participate in her masses, and I'd get really bored half the time, 'cause she'd read from the Bible and make us sing. I thought it was just a game she played, then every once in a while she'd say, 'Oh, I want to be a *priest* someday.' But we never really went into depth about it, 'cause back then, how many women did you ever hear about that were priests?"

Back then, Tammy considered it all a joke and just laughed it off.

JoAnn and Jug became good friends after their divorce, at least for a while. In fact, they were much better friends than they had been in the course of their five-plus-year marriage. Luckily, they didn't have any children of their own to worry about, so the split was rather final. JoAnn wanted it that way. She didn't want kids with Jug. She had gone on the Pill even with the knowledge that Jug had been tested for a low sperm count, because, as JoAnn bluntly put it, "I told him I didn't want any ugly children."

They had been wed in 1974, JoAnn was out of the marriage by 1980, and the experience left such a bad taste in her mouth she never had any desire to marry again.

Even though she was happy to be free, things were difficult for her at first and even more so for Tammy and Teena. With Jug around, JoAnn didn't work, so she'd be home when the girls got home from school; they would seldom walk into an empty house. JoAnn was good at being domestic. She would prepare dinner every night, all the kids' favorites—a lot of tacos and spaghetti—and she'd have fun with her kids. Sometimes they'd have food fights, sometimes they'd scramble on the floor wrestling. Life was easygoing.

In the course of their marriage, Jug had bought her a '65 Mustang, had nursed her through a four-year period where she was in and out of traction due to a car accident, and had bought her a relatively new house out in Belmont, which they furnished according to JoAnn's taste. But none of it mattered. They had tried counseling, they had tried everything, and they couldn't put the cracked egg back together again. JoAnn had already filed for divorce twice. By the third time, when she and Jug were unofficially separated, he called her on the phone, hoping she'd beg him to come back.

"I guess if you're not gonna give in, we just might as well let this go through," Jug finally told her.

"This is what I've been tellin' ya all along," she snapped back. "It's not gonna change, it's not gonna be any different. I'm not gonna change how I am. I want *out*."

In the end, Jug told one of her brothers that he would always love JoAnn, but he would never marry another pretty girl.

Tammy and Teena had been collecting Social Security since their dad's death, and according to JoAnn, that's what the three of them lived on after she and Jug sold their house.

Of course, their grandmother Francis wanted them all to move back home with her, but JoAnn wanted her own place with her children. She was still young and needed to explore without being questioned. Even though she was only in her early twenties, she felt she could handle things pretty well, financially and otherwise.

Teena was doubly destroyed by the divorce because it occurred just about the same time she discovered that Jug wasn't her real dad. Now she had two fathers missing from her life and no way to claim either one of them.

JoAnn's lawyer suggested that if Jug wanted visitation rights, he should pay child support, but Jug wouldn't agree to that and JoAnn decided he had a right to see them regardless—she wanted what was best for her children—so the girls would go every other weekend and spend time with him, still being treated like little princesses. But things were changing. By then, Jug had started dating Debbie, a lovely young woman who was rather strict and conservative— the antithesis of JoAnn.

"When they got the divorce, Teena was more depressed than I was, you could just tell," Tammy said. "Our stepdad didn't have to see us; he really wanted to. When we were able to go and see him, Teena was always excited, but she couldn't see him as often, and she'd get upset on the days that he was supposed to see us but couldn't because of work."

Things were tough even when they did visit Jug, because now Debbie was there all the time, trying to act like their mom, which was *not* the thing to do. She gave Tammy literature on menstruation, which Tammy already knew about; she bought the girls clothes from Goodwill, which they felt was degrading. Although she tried, Debbie just didn't get it right, and JoAnn was beginning to notice a visible negative effect on her daughters.

For one thing, Teena started having nightmares. JoAnn tried to find out what was bothering her, but Teena was closemouthed about it, at least at first. JoAnn knew Debbie was threatened by Jug's relationship with the girls; she felt that Debbie viewed the whole thing as an unwanted attachment to his ex-wife. JoAnn sensed Jug's woman was jealous of her, but she couldn't understand why. In JoAnn's eyes, she had thrown Jug away. If she wanted him, she could have kept him, but she *didn't* want him, so there was no reason for Debbie's insecurities. Still, JoAnn thought, Debbie was taking her hostility out on the girls.

Eventually, JoAnn got to the bottom of it: Debbie was scolding the girls, trying to impose her standards on them, changing the rules JoAnn had worked so hard to define.

After one particularly unpleasant scene between Teena and Debbie, JoAnn called Jug and gave him an ultimatum: it would be either the kids or Debbie.

"He made the choice to stay with his girlfriend and not see the kids, which devastated Teena. I always thought it bothered her, but she would say no, no, no, no, no," JoAnn remembers.

"We just quit seeing each other. There was no discussion," Tammy recalls. "Mom told us he was going to marry this person, she said he needed to go on with his life. I understood that; Teena didn't."

"She just detested him after that. I always talked about him, but Teena would never answer me back. She was really hurt. We would discuss past events, but he would never be mentioned, at least not by her. It was like he died."

7

THERE WAS NO LINE OF MEN WAITING FOR JOANN'S hand, which was fine with her. She wanted it that way. She was having too much fun going out to discos with her sister-in-law, Molly-after all, it was still the seventies. She and Molly were both busy taking college classes at Southeast Community, and for a while, they were meeting people at the Grove, the local pool hall and meat market, where almost every young person in Lincoln went at the time, especially in the summer. Molly can still picture the two of them doing the funky chicken.

In those days, Molly Brandon wore her hair parted straight down the middle, and she kept it long, very long, which seemed to accentuate her Native American heritage and beautiful high cheekbones. Half white, Molly had a stick-thin figure, dark skin, and distinct features that made her pleasantly exotic, and she was constantly hit on by men without her even trying. Molly wasn't one for makeup and disco dresses; she lived in turtlenecks and bell-bottom jeans. Molly worked for the city doing hard labor jobs most of her life; she was in construction, she ran bulldozers, she worked at the railroad and the city dump. She was not one for a desk job, where you had to wear any kind of pantyhose.

She doesn't want to remember her childhood, especially the time period before her brother Pat got killed—Molly claims a lot of that time is a blur. She just knows that in the Brandon house, it was her and her brothers, Mike, Joe, and Patrick, and they were on their own pretty much. They too had been deserted by their father. Their mom, Doris, supported them by working at the VFW Club in Lincoln.

She remembers growing up in a racially mixed area in Lincoln, on Starr Street, a good neighborhood at the time, where she mostly hung around her brothers and their buddies, playing touch football. She says her brother Pat was earning money digging ditches at about the time JoAnn came into the scene, that JoAnn stayed at the Brandon house quite a bit, that she was a quiet and shy girl who seemed to fit in with the family right away. The three of them went to junior high together—Molly, Pat, and JoAnn—and in Molly's eyes, even though life wasn't a bed of roses, things were more wholesome back then.

"There was never any trouble, you know; there was just the typical bullies around and stuff," Molly recalled. "But there was never any bad trouble that I can remember. I'd say half of my junior high was white, the other half was Indian or black. There was never anything big going on racially. It was a long time ago. Not like today where there's gangs up here from Omaha, kids doing drive-by shootings and carjackings."

Molly thinks she blocked out a lot of things because she was traumatized by her parents' divorce. Molly was just eleven years old when that happened. At that time, she dropped out of school for a while, became more of a loner, and was having really bad headaches and fainting spells.

"Mom had two jobs then; she was working days and nights. Dad was gone, and it hurt me and I was upset," Molly explained. "I didn't want to know why he left, but I had my suspicions. Maybe it was because Mom worked too much, and he didn't want her to work."

Eventually Doris found a new boyfriend, but it was someone who didn't like to be around kids, so Doris wasn't home much. According to Molly, she and her siblings did a lot of drinking and partying in their mother's absence. They were all drinking at young ages, and now Molly regrets it.

"My mom didn't come home a lot. She'd come home from work to make sure we were okay, then she'd go to her boyfriend's house. I choose not to remember a lot of things because maybe I'm resentful," Molly admitted. "I resent some of the choices I made when there was no one around to supervise or take care of us. I cleaned house, did most everything. My mom would make sure we had food or cook something and we'd heat it up or she'd buy us pizza. I was in counseling one time and they wanted me to ask my mother why they divorced, but I never did. I never had the heart to want to know why he left."

At some point, not long after JoAnn's divorce from Jug, when she realized she couldn't make ends meet on her own, JoAnn was happy to find a haven with Doris and Molly back on Starr Street. That was a time before Molly had kids of her own to worry about, so she lavished her attention on JoAnn's girls, taking them with her to the downtown State Theater, mainly to Walt Disney movies. Tammy and Teena were her favorites in the family, and Molly spent a lot of her free time playing with them, particularly at the Pioneer and Peter Pan parks in Lincoln. Pioneer was Teena's pick because they had wild animals you could feed—deer, elk, and buffalo. Teena would watch them and just squeal with delight.

As Tammy and Teena grew up, eventually moving into their grandmother Frances's trailer on the Cornhusker highway with JoAnn, Molly still remained close. She didn't just baby-sit the girls, she hung out with them. She loved them like little sisters.

"We used to drive around and yell out the windows at people," Molly remembered. "Tammy and Teena and I would always goof around and yell, '*nice legs*!' things like that, at men. Then we'd keep on driving so no one would see us. We used to drive with the stereo up and just sing at the top of our lungs and laugh and stuff. We used to have a lot of fun."

Back in those early days, no one noticed anything unusual about Teena when it came to liking boys.

Teena had boyfriends all through grade school. She and Jeff Rollinson were boyfriend and girlfriend from kindergarten; JoAnn used to joke with Jeff's mom about how hyper their kids would be if they ever got married. As she got older, Teena would point out cute guys on the street, although there were none that she mentioned being interested in—at least not to her mother. Tammy caught Teena French-kissing a redheaded boy in the hallway once, but it was just one time.

How many boys Tammy liked, how many Teena liked, it didn't matter. If Teena wasn't overly interested in boys, JoAnn didn't find it unusual. She didn't worry about that kind of thing.

As a mom, she was most concerned about Teena's progress in school, about tracking her studies. Thankfully, Teena was a good student. She had a sunny disposition and a desire to learn. At the age of twelve, Teena was given the Best of the Bunch award by her teacher, Mrs. Greg. Nothing could have pleased JoAnn more.

Both girls went to Sacred Heart Elementary, the same Catholic school JoAnn attended as a girl. She had given her daughters their choice, and they wanted to go to parochial school. Of course, JoAnn liked the idea. She found the structured experience to be a good learning environment, and she wanted both of her daughters to have a firm knowledge of church traditions, to have a strong moral code.

JoAnn was practical about life—she taught her daughters right from wrong, she instilled in them a work ethic, and she made sure both girls knew how to handle money, opening a Squirrel Club savings account for each at First National Lincoln. For a while, Teena saved her pennies and diligently made deposits of five or ten dollars a week. JoAnn has saved the cardboard savings book all these years, just a reminder of the good little girl Teena was.

JoAnn may have never checked and probably never asked, but Teena's savings book was actually listed in the name of Teen R. Brandon. Somewhere along the line, Teena decided to officially call herself Teen.

Over the years, it would be a name that would pop up here and there, in the least likely of places—places like—Humbolt.

8

AT THAT ROCKY STAGE, WHEN THEY WERE BOTH ON THE verge of puberty, Teena met Sara Gapp at a basketball game in Saint Theresa's gym. Sara had been in a big fight with her mother that day: she had gotten sick in church and missed communion so she was being punished for it; she said she had been hit with a bread board.

Saint Mary's, where Teena went, was a rival school to Saint Theresa's, but that didn't stop Teena from walking right up to Sara and introducing herself.

"Can I sit by you?" she asked.

"Sure," Sara told her, moving over slightly to make room on the bleachers.

Sara, a dark-haired beauty with full cheeks, thick eyebrows, and wide brown eyes, had a natural sexiness about her. Something in her expression reminded Teena of sultry young girls in magazines. Something about her clicked with Teena.

The two girls went outside during halftime and just started opening up. Teena was twelve, Sara was just a few months younger, and right away their discussion got serious.

"We were still children then. We talked about my mom, what my mom would do to me," Sarah remembered. "There was a lot of abuse that went on at my mom's house. My mom has no feelings. She uses religion as, like, her stand for everything. It's her excuse."

"If I even made a peep in church, I'd get ten swats with a breadboard. If I put my hands in the way, she'd hit me in the head. She'd hit me in the arms, she'd hit me in the legs, she'd hit anything that was open. There was constant abuse. I mean, from the time I was about seven years old, I was being called a slut. I didn't even know what a slut was."

That very first night with Teena, Sara was so upset she even hinted about some kind of incest in the Gapp family, but she mostly talked about what fanatic Catholics they were and the problems that caused. Her life was steeped in church events, in church behavior, in the Catholic way. She confided that her family put on a big religious act, but in reality, none of them openly talked to each other much. The Gapps weren't close with each other at all.

"Our house was so bad that my mom built an altar on our piano in our living room. There was a bunch of candles, a crucifix, a statue of Mary, rosaries, stuff like that," Sara explained. "Every time we had to walk through that room, we had to get on our knees and kiss the floor or we got twenty whacks with the breadboard and were sent to our room for the rest of the night."

"I ain't bullshitting. Every day you had to do it. And then finally all of us started walking out in the dead of winter with no shoes just to walk around the house so we wouldn't pass by the altar. We were all getting sick, and my mom's like, '*You're going to hell*?' Our house was like a psycho place. I mean, you didn't want to go over there."

Teena listened to all this. She was a great listener. She always knew the right moment to speak. She sat there and heard Sara's sob story without ever interrupting. She knew where Sara was coming from, and when her new buddy finished the stream of complaints, Teena looked up with compassionate eyes, softly wiping Sara's tears away.

"I told her about the hitting, about the things my mom said to me, and about the way it made me feel. My mom was telling me I was worthless, stuff like that," Sara recalled. "I know how you feel, you aren't the only one," Teena said, and she began to describe what was happening between her and a male relative.

"She told me that one of her relatives was doing something to her that she didn't like. She just kinda said that, you know, he would kinda just whip this thing out and kinda play with it a little bit. She said he'd do all these weird things with it. Basically jack.

"Being girls, we really don't know how guys jack, so it's gonna be weird to us, and she said occasionally he'd have her touch him and then he would play with her and tell her, '*oh, you like it.*'"

"*You know this feels good*," he would insist. "*You know you don't want me to stop.*"

"And I was just sitting back, going 'Oh, Lord,' 'cause I couldn't even imagine something like that could feel good, that anyone could like it," Sara continued. "At the time I didn't even know what sex was. That's how sheltered my life had been. I mean, they didn't teach it in school I didn't know. My mom told me that babies come out of your belly button. Your belly button grows and the baby pops out."

After Teena told Sara her bit, Sara felt a little stupid, like her problems were nothing in comparison. That night, they talked for hours, never returning to the ball game. Teena and Sara quickly became close and eventually became best friends, like sisters. They swore each other to secrecy about their family problems, promising that they'd never tell a soul, and for years, neither one did.

"At that point in time, she didn't want anyone to know about what had happened. She didn't want the guy mad at her, you know, if people found out, if he got in trouble," Sara remembered "She was embarrassed. No matter what he did to her, she still loved him. I couldn't understand it because after everything I went through with my mom, I hated her. I wanted her dead."

A year later, they both wound up at Pius X High School in an exclusive area of Lincoln, surrounded by big mansions, sunken gardens, and cascade fountains. Neither of them came from that kind of well-manicured world; they had only known the back streets and neon strips of the city. Now they were two fresh-faced kids cruising around rows of handsome white-columned and Tudor houses, taking in the golf courses and wide range of luxury of the leisure class, totally oblivious to the gaze of the marble-eyed statue of Pope Pius X they passed in the main hallway of their school.

Even though JoAnn bad scrimped and saved to send her two daughters there, she wasn't kept very well informed about what they actually *did* at Pius socially. Like many moms of her day, JoAnn was out of touch with her teenagers and was leery of talking to either of her girls about sex, about protection, or anything like that.

"I've never been really good with the birds and bees. I have to admit I wasn't really good about sitting down and talking about the birds and the bees with them, but it was not something that was ever done with me, so I didn't know how to approach it," JoAnn would later reflect, "except for those little films you see in school."

"I explained Teena's period to her. She knew she had it, but she didn't like it, she didn't like cramps, she didn't like dealing with it," JoAnn recalled.

"I *hate* it, Mom," Teena would whine.

"Well, you know, that's part of life," JoAnn would tell her.

Teena just never related to these things the way, for instance, Tammy did. And since Teena didn't care to know, Tammy wasn't about to tell her sister the facts of life. The first time Teena saw a douche, her sister told her it was mouthwash.

"At that time she wore bras and female briefs. There was nothing abnormal," JoAnn explained. "She told me she didn't want to go through childbirth; she would adopt if she ever had children. I don't know why she said that, but now I have my own theories after being in counseling with her."

To say that Teena didn't care much for Pius's strict environment would be the understatement of the year. Teena made fun of the place and mocked it every chance she got. When school toilet bowl seats came up missing, it was Teena Brandon who was responsible. According to her dearest friends, she was always pulling pranks, always running around like a maniac.

The dress code in Pius wasn't exactly a uniform, but it was strict enough—girls' skirts had to touch the top of their knees, boys couldn't have hair touching their collars, and guys couldn't wear mustaches, beards, or earrings. No sweatshirts or jeans were allowed for either sex. It was a preppy place, filled with khaki slacks and button-down shirts.

But Teena was cool—she didn't quite break the rules, but she didn't quite conform either. She always wore slacks, sometimes with a tie. No one could throw her out for that. Still, the school had its limitations. Teena was involved in the theater, for example, and although she had the freedom to put on skits and talk baby talk and make people laugh about "poopie" diapers in acting class, when it came to putting on an actual play, school officials would not allow a performance of *Grease*—too many sexual overtones. The Pius kids had to settle for shows like *Brigadoon*.

Of course, that didn't bother people like Teena or her friends—they were the ones who did things to deliberately stand out. Her friend Bryn Gallager dyed her hair purple, and Teena and Sara would skip chapel whenever possible, singing church songs as they cruised in the car, making fun of the lyrics, and spicing up the gloomy tunes with their own words. They were goofy kids out for a good time. It wasn't that they didn't like church—they did They just wanted to have fun.

Teena would go over to Sara's and purposely make a big deal of getting down on her knees in front of the altar in the living room. Sara's mom, Mary, would watch and just turn the other way. Teena thought it was hilarious.

"Three-fourths of our jokes were about my mom," Sara later said. "We'd make fun of the woman and her Catholic channels and Catholic books and pictures of saints. We'd call my mom Sybil, you know, the one with multiple personalities. We'd call her Sybil or crazy bitch from hell, and we'd just sit there and roll all night long."

9

DURING HER SOPHOMORE YEAR AT PIUS, TEENA WORKED at McDonald's over on 27th and Vine—she didn't like it very much. but she put her best foot forward. She made her spending money that way and eventually was able to save enough to move out of JoAnn's and in with her buddy Traci Beels. By that time, late 1989, JoAnn was living with her boyfriend Mike, tangled in a unhealthy love-hate relationship, so she understood why her daughter didn't want to hang around. Meanwhile, Tammy was on the other side of town, involved with some dude who was beating on her. Teena couldn't stand it. Still, she had no power to help either her mother or sister. All she could do was run, and Traci's mom provided her a place to go.

Traci was a year ahead of Teena at Pius. She was a large framed girl with long, thick brown hair who apparently led Teena around by the nose—at least that was Sara's and Bryn's perception. According to Sara, Traci kept Teena all to herself—she was possessive; she was a dominator who would kick Teena's ass when Teena didn't follow her rules. But clearly, Teena had feelings for Traci. They became close enough that she pasted a scrapbook of their times together, calling herself Teena Brandon-Beets.

The two young women shared larger-than-life experiences, going places like Mount Rushmore and Crazy Horse, traveling the back country of the Badlands and the Black Hills, seeing as much of the seven wonders of South Dakota and Nebraska as possible, letting themselves run wild. Teena put a half-dozen pictures of the two of them in that scrapbook, most of them happy and carefree outdoor shots, although there's one of Teena rubbing Traci's foot, where Teena has a strange look on her face, kind of despondent and confused.

Teena was changing. She had this cute girl giving her attention, and she liked it, yet she liked guys too. For years, Teena had a crush on Brian Van Slyke, the tall, blond, popular guy at school. But really they were just good friends more than anything else. She wasn't sure what she wanted.

Teena knew she wasn't like other girls. When she'd look at women, she couldn't picture herself acting like them when she grew up. There was no one on television, no female movie star, that she could relate to or that she hoped to emulate. Somehow she was different Something was missing in her that often made her wish she'd never been born.

When her breasts grew, Teena hated how they hurt. When someone stared at her chest, it would make her feel sick. She liked her body before puberty and *despised* it when it started to develop. She wasn't feminine, she wasn't graceful, and she didn't want to be.

Her inner feelings made her think she had something wrong with her, but she couldn't change herself. She never stopped feeling guilty, believing that her friends and family would be ashamed of her if they knew. She wasn't clear about what was going to happen in her life, about who or what she would become.

She had no dream of ever marrying, of putting on a white gown and raising kids like everyone else. She told Tammy she wanted to play quarterback on the Pius football team. She liked the idea of carrying the weight of the equipment and wearing the uniform tight across her shoulders. She was serious about it, and this time, unlike the days when she spoke of becoming a priest, Tammy didn't laugh.

"There's no saying a girl can't play football with a bunch of guys. Go for it!" Tammy told her.

She always knew Teena to be the tough type, to be the one who would pick herself up without ever shedding a tear.

In fact, Teena rarely showed emotion. Tammy actually thought her sister could make the team, but Teena didn't try out. It was all just talk.

* * *

When Traci started *doing things* to her, that just added to Teena's confusion. Traci would hold Teena down on the ground and give her hickeys, and it became a regular habit after a while. Teena never complained, although sometimes Traci got rough with her in these little wrestling matches.

Never the best judge of character, Teena kept her mouth shut, even when things became more involved and Traci allegedly started batting Teena around.

"What the fuck is that on your neck? Where'd you get that?" Sara remembers asking her one day.

"Oh, Traci did it," Teena told her.

"What do you mean, Traci did it?"

"Oh, she held me down and kept doing this to me, sucking on my neck. I don't know why. We were just kidding around."

But Sara didn't think it was very funny. As the months passed, Teena would show Sara the hand prints on her upper arms, on her wrists, and it made Sara really nervous. She didn't know or care whether there was a sexual component to their relationship, but she felt like reporting what she considered to be domestic violence.

When Teena had first moved in with Traci, everything seemed peachy. Sara could see they were having fun—they were all hanging out together and Sara used to visit a lot because she had a friend who lived right around the block. Sara thought Teena was happy, that it was great she had found a home. But then all this shit started happening.

"It went from Traci slapping her to Traci pushing her to Traci holding her down and hitting her," Sara recalls. "Teena would do something and Traci would get mad and hit her, then she'd apologize and Teena would forgive her.

"One day I was with Teena and Bryn over at McDonald's, and Traci walked in and saw us. Well, Teena was supposed to be at home, waiting for Traci. So Traci just walked up to Teen, took her outside, slapped her across the face so hard that when she came back in, she had a welt of a hand print on her face. Bryn and I jumped up, went outside to chase this bitch. and she was gone by then. That's when we said 'You are moving the fuck out of there.'"

But Teena didn't want to hear it. When Traci would hit her, Teena would try to rectify her "wrongs" by complying with Traci's whims. All Teena wanted was to win Traci's love again.

"She was attracted to men, but at the same time she had these confused feelings inside. She didn't know if she actually wanted to be with a guy. It was kinda like a back-and-forth type thing," Sara explained. "Teena hung out with Brian Van Slyke so long they basically got in a buddy-buddy relationship, and he didn't know that she liked him. By the time he found that out, it was too much of a friend relationship that he didn't want to destroy."

All through her senior year, Teena and Brian had a blast racing cars—each trying to outdo the other on the highways in Lincoln. Teena was pretty good at it, and she scared a lot of people when she got behind the wheel, but there was a price for that fun. Like many crazy kid drivers, she paid stiff traffic fines and at one point had her driver's license suspended.

More than anything, Teena wanted Brian to ask her to the prom. She had even discussed it with JoAnn. By then it was the winter of 1990, and she was through with Traci and living back home again. Of course, Teena didn't want to wear a prom dress. She envisioned them going as a matching pair in black tuxedos, and JoAnn thought that could work, no problem. But then Brian never asked her; be took another girl instead and broke Teena's heart.

Before moving back in with her mom, Teena had stayed with Tammy for a while, but it didn't last long. Something seemed strange about Teena, and all of a sudden Tammy was seeing a totally different person. Always a decent student, Teena now had no desire to go to school. Tammy would drive her sister to Pius to make sure she wouldn't skip, but it didn't do any good. Teena was out of control. Pretty soon things started coming up missing at Tammy's, which caused some big fights. Money was gone, socks were gone, things seemed odd and strained. As the sisters' relationship deteriorated, Teena retreated to the comfort of her mom's place. There, she knew she could get away with practically anything. JoAnn didn't question her much and besides, she didn't pick up on things the way Tammy did. Teena had managed to finance an old clunker of a car, so she was mobile, which was the most important thing. And JoAnn was busy working in a shopping mall, so she wasn't home much. On top of that, Mike had moved out of the trailer, and JoAnn was going back and forth to his place, so it was a perfect setup for Teena.

"I thought she was a happy camper when she moved back in here with me in October and we had Christmas and everything seemed so cool," JoAnn remembered.

"She would come out to T.J. Maxx all the time. She would take me there when my car wasn't running. I had a little Chevette, and whenever it didn't work, she would drop me off and go on to school. She'd always come in there. She'd come in and leave flowers and teddy bears for me. I'd come back from lunch break and find them. Teena always did that for me."

But Teena wasn't really Teena anymore. Secretly, she stomped around the house in briefs, examining herself in the mirror. With two pairs of socks down her pants, she could easily pass for a boy. It gave her a thrill just thinking about it.

10

TEENA BRANDON PLANNED TO ENLIST IN THE ARMY TO take part in Operation Desert Storm in the fall of 1990. She had talked to a recruiter at Pius, and she was sure that she was cut out for it. This was the one place in the world where she could fit in. She was parading around her mother's trailer in fatigues the day she got the call that she didn't pass the written entrance exams.

"She was really upset," JoAnn vividly remembers. "And other things started happening. She started to change."

Teena had just turned eighteen in December. She was nearing graduation and had no idea what she wanted to do with herself. Her moods swung. She was depressed one minute, laughing the next. She kept her hair short, started lifting weights, and told people she was going to become an artist. No one seemed to be able to read her, not even her best friend Sara. Not a soul noticed she was binding her breasts with an Ace bandage every day, doing whatever it took to hide her femininity.

Tammy was almost completely out of the picture by then, not really someone Teena could confide in. Having gotten herself pregnant that year, Tammy was in the process of giving her baby up for adoption to a pair of gay women in San Francisco and was all caught up in her mixed emotions about that ordeal. Tammy had never even met anyone who was a lesbian before, and now she was concerned about the welfare of her unborn child. As an expectant mama, she had little time to notice that her sister was broken up about the adoption, that Teena wanted to be an aunt in the worst way. Teena very much wanted to be a part of that baby's life, but it wasn't meant to be.

Teena had to settle for working with Sara at Bishop's Buffet, an all-you-can-eat place that they affectionately renamed Bishop's Barf-fay. There they refilled food, cleared off tables, rolled silverware, and did kitchen prep. When they both got fired after one of their food fights, things became more difficult all the way around because Sara had just found out she was pregnant and the child's father was refusing to help. Teena offered to move in with Sara and financially support her, but Sara didn't think that would be right "You're not thinking about abortion are you?" Teena blurted out one night.

"Of course not, no way."

"If it was legal, you and me could be the parents to this baby. I'd like to be the parent," Teena pressed. "If anything, I'll take the baby if you decide you want to give it away."

Teena loved kids; she wanted to raise kids—yet she never wanted to have kids of her own. She could never picture herself giving birth. For one thing, she said she hated sex, so that made it impossible right there.

"I wanna be a virgin till the day I die. I don't wanna have sex, it's gross," Teena often told Sara.

"But just try it, Teena. It only hurts the first time, then it's great," Sara would say.

"I don't care. I don't want to have to do that."

"But it could be a nice experience for you if you find somebody that you really care about," Sara cajoled.

Throughout Sara's pregnancy, Teena hung around making sure her friend was taken care of. The two of them eventually moved into a trailer together, Teena cooking meals seeing that Sara got enough sleep, driving her to school in the morning, doing everything a husband or boyfriend should have done.

At about that time, before Sara was showing at all, Drew Lyon came into Sara's life and for both of them, it seemed to be love at first sight, although it took a while for things to actually materialize.

Drew was a high school dropout with a real aggressive nature, who couldn't stand authority. He was a rebel without a clue, who would later describe himself as a problem kid growing up in a problem family. He was already tired of society, already in trouble with the law at the ages of fifteen and sixteen.

"I've got a quick temper. You don't want to piss me off," he habitually bragged.

His older sister Kris pressed charges against him for assault with attempt to maim after Drew swung at the back of her head one night, knocking her out cold.

Drew complained about feeling alienated in his household, being the only boy with three ill-tempered sisters to contend with. The four of them fought heavily with each other, and Drew felt they were constantly ganging up on him.

"It wasn't normal fights. We'd punch each other, we pulled out knives. I broke a crutch over Drew's head once," Kris admitted. "I mean, our parents tried different things to make us not fight, but we went through family counseling, and it was a joke."

Drew described his mother as a "wacko" who had very little to do with his upbringing. Apparently his dad was equally detached, hiding in his bedroom, reading books most of the time, rarely involved with his children's activities.

"When he was younger, my mom was able to get him off his fat lazy ass, and he'd come outside and play softball with us," Drew remembered, stretching to think of any fun times he actually shared with the man.

Allegedly, there was a child abuse charge brought against the Lyons, but nothing ever came of it. According to Drew, the charge was a result of his younger sister blowing her ear out while playing with a Q-Tip. Drew says his sister Kris tried to blame it on their dad, that she called the police under false pretenses.

Still, he bitterly remembered occasions when his dad locked him and one of his sisters in their bedroom overnight.

"They used to lock Cheryl and me in our room, and the problem was, there was no bathroom in there."

So much anger was building up in Drew Lyon that by the time he met Sara, although he thought he loved her, he wasn't able to handle it. All he had known was abusive hands. By Drew's account, even one of the babysitter's sexually molested three out of the four Lyon kids, including him. Drew said his parents never believed them when they tried to report the girl, admitting that all four kids spent time back and forth in foster homes, which he felt was a safer environment for them growing up.

Throughout his youth, Drew went through group homes, psychologists, ink blot tests, you name it, and none of it did any good. His anger was still there. With Drew, the law stepped in, and a case worker from social services recommended he attend Whitehall, a special needs school in Lincoln that provided counseling for kids in trouble. At Whitehall, with a total population of only twenty-five students, someone finally got through to Drew and he became a more responsible person. Realizing he was a young stud with a world of women after him, Drew decided to join Job Corps and get his act together. He would soon be off to learn a trade, ready to take his place in the world.

Drew and Sara had originally met on Halloween night 1990, enjoying a wild sex session on her front lawn the very next day. Of course Sara was love struck, and immediately she brought Teena around to meet her new guy. Drew was working under a car at the time, a little too busy to pay exact attention.

"Who's the dude?" Drew stuck his head out and asked.

"That's a girl," Sara whispered.

"Oops. Sorry," he snickered.

Teena heard them and got so incensed she went out to Sara's car and pouted, waiting for Sara to hurry up and finish her flirting.

"That was about a month before the call from Liz Delano," Sara recalled. "Up until Liz Delano, if you had called her a guy, Teena would be offended. She didn't want to be recognized as a guy. She didn't feel like a guy. People kept saying she dressed like a guy. She didn't.

"She dressed in clothes that she felt comfortable in. She didn't go to the guy's section to buy those clothes. Those were women's clothes she was wearing. She just liked baggy clothes. She wore short hair. Does that make her a guy?"

11

TEENA AND SARA WERE REALLY JUST BUDDIES; THERE was nothing else between them. They were open with each other and felt so close that Sara could walk around the house naked and Teena would think nothing of it.

"She would come up to me, grab my tit, and run away, and I wouldn't care cause I knew it was a joke," Sara insisted. "I wouldn't think, *Oh, she's hitting on me.* I didn't take it like that."

The most Teena ever did with Sara was shower her with compliments. Teena loved to love people, to make people feel good, especially Sara, whose mom had hurled insult after insult at her. Incredibly, Sara grew up thinking she was ugly. It wasn't until Teena came along that she realized she was an attractive young woman.

Sara tried to reciprocate Teena's positive reinforcement by encouraging her friend to look hot, to dress sexy, but it never worked.

Sara will never forget the day when Teena got decked out in a black biker's dress, skintight to the hips, three inches below her butt. She thought Teena looked like such a babe in her fishnet hose, push-up bra, and high heels.

"I dressed her up in this dress, I did her hair, and she's sitting there, walking around the house, posing and shit," Sara fondly recalled. "I mean, this girl had a body on her. She was just afraid to show it."

Truth was, Teena's body didn't have an ounce of fat on it. Her stomach was super flat, her hips narrow, her breasts lean and tight. She had the figure of a young supermodel, and if she wanted to, she could have had lots of guys. Drew tried to set her up with his friend Craig, who was all for it, but Teena backed out at the last minute because she was afraid—she had never been on a date before.

After Sara's son Erik was born, Sara and Teena split as roommates. Sara moved in to what she called "a shithole one-bedroom" apartment; Teena temporarily went back home to JoAnn. The two still considered themselves best friends and saw each other as much as possible. As time passed, however, Teena was mostly hanging around a girl named Heather Kuhfahl, a cute young redhead who knew Teena only as *Billy*.

The Billy identity started when Teena had gotten a call in late December 1990 from Liz Delano, a girl who happened to dial the wrong number. Liz thought Teena was a guy and started flirting with him and carrying on. As soon as they hung up, the phone rang again.

"Hello, Billy?"

"Yeah," Teena mustered in a deep voice.

"This is Liz again. I was just wondering, what's your last name?"

"Brinson."

"How old are you?"

"Eighteen."

"You think you wanna meet me sometime?"

"Sure, baby," Teena told the caller, busting out laughing as she hung up the phone.

Secretly, Teena was thrilled she was able to pull it off. She could hardly hide her excitement at the idea of passing as a male. She had thought about it for so long, but she never believed she'd actually go through with it. From then on, Liz kept calling "Billy," and finally the two of them agreed to go out on New Year's Eve.

Teena pretended it was a prank, getting Sara and Drew to tag along for the ride that night. Billy wore Dockers with a T-shirt under a button-down. and he made a great impression on Liz, holding hands with her on the roller rink as Sara curiously watched from the sidelines.

Sara thought it was a scream, and soon she started going over to Liz's with Teena on a regular basis. Sara loved the idea of Teena play-acting this *man* thing. At first, she felt there was no real harm in it. The girl, Liz, was so young, just thirteen, and of course, there was nothing sexual going on. It was just funny.

By the time Drew came back from Job Corps, in mid-1991, Teena was living with Liz's friend Heather, and the joke had become a reality: Teena was now Billy Brinson.

All the while, JoAnn was furious, trying to call Heather to warn her about what she had gotten herself into, but Heather was refusing JoAnn's calls. Billy told Heather his mother hated all his girlfriends, that his mother was a crazy drunk who made up stories just to cause trouble.

Meanwhile, Drew was having a hard time getting back together with Sara—she wanted nothing to do with him because she heard reports that he was seen kissing another girl at the Village Inn, their local hangout. When she confronted him about it, Drew stupidly admitted that the girl gave him oral sex, and when she heard that, as far as Sara was concerned, she was out of there for good.

Desperate to win her hand, Drew called JoAnn looking for Teena, thinking Teena could be of some use, but Teena didn't live there anymore. Although she barely knew him, it didn't take JoAnn long to give Drew the lowdown on Teena. She was just dying to confide in someone who might be able to get through to her daughter.

Teena was passing herself off as a man, JoAnn told him. What's more, just days before, on June 21, 1991, she had been confronted by a policeman at her doorstep, and she had been served with a criminal complaint for disturbing the peace. JoAnn had never been in trouble with the law in her life. She couldn't believe her own daughter would instigate such a thing—she couldn't believe the nerve of Teena, Heather, and Heather's mom, Ruth Laudenschlager.

The complaint was made after Teena and Heather saved the answering machine tape of JoAnn's harassing messages and had brought it to the police. On the tape, Joann was heard calling them lesbians; she was threatening them. She had an incredulous look on her face as she confided to Drew that she had been cut off from seeing her own child, that because Teena was legally an adult, there was nothing she could do about it.

Five days later, the complaint was dropped, but Joann was still on the warpath about the game Teena was playing, and she hoped Drew Lyon might help her somehow. Apparently, Drew knew these people well enough that, shortly after his talk with Joann, he managed to move in with Teena, Heather, and Ruth. Unfortunately, he didn't prove to be a very good spy for Joann; he was only there because it was a cheap and convenient route to Sara.

Still determined to put an end to this Billy thing, Joann would drive by and try to catch Teena's car, sometimes knock on the door, begging Teena to come home. She knew her daughter had no business living with a girl who was only fourteen or fifteen years old—if they were having sex she could easily be brought in for statutory rape.

12

BILLY WAS HEATHER'S FIRST KISS. SHE WAS IN NINTH grade at a Lincoln junior high school when they met, and she was definitely after him. Heather thought he was gorgeous, just right for her. He was about her height, five feet four inches, and something about him was masculine yet dainty at the same time, which she loved. She was bowled over by his sleek crew cut and Kennedy jaw-line. She couldn't stop talking about him; she was always fantasizing about him. He would be hers, she assured her friends.

On Valentine's Day 1991, she had sent him roses. They arrived at Pius X with a card labeled Billy Brinson. Luckily for Teena, the flowers were received without notice—she knew they would be, because she was working in the main office at the time. The few people who watched her accept the delivery basically kept it to themselves, the standard hush-hush at Pius.

As things got more serious, Heather called Billy at JoAnn's home constantly. Usually he was there for her calls.

He was obviously falling in love with her; they'd stay on for hours. But sometimes, Billy's mom would answer, and that always presented a problem. Billy told Heather not to pay her any attention, but it was kind of hard to do when she had this lady hanging up in her face all the time.

"Hi, can I speak to Billy?" she'd ask JoAnn in her sweet voice.

"I'm sorry, there's no one named Billy here."

"Are you sure?"

"I don't know anybody named Billy that lives here. Do you have the right number?"

"Yeah, this is the number he gave me."

"I have a brother named Bill, but I doubt very much that you want to talk to *him*," JoAnn finally told her.

When she had about all she could take of the calls, JoAnn confronted Teena, and of course, her daughter denied everything. The calls never stopped, so she'd bring the subject up every now and then, and Teena would just flat out lie.

"You know, someone keeps calling here and asking for Billy. You have any friend who calls you that?"

"No, Mom, I have no idea who it could be."

"Well, for some reason they keep calling here."
"I don't know who would do that, Mom. It's not anyone I know."
"It sounds like some little girl, very young."
"Really? I wonder who it is. It's got to be phony phone calls."

* * *

In the time that Drew lived with Billy, Heather, and Ruth, he paid his rent by doing odd jobs around the house. He'd fix their cars, mow the lawn, things like that. He shared part of the basement with Billy and Heather; they had rooms separated by a curtain.

Of course, he knew Billy was really a girl, but Drew didn't want to betray his friend. He didn't know if he should tell Heather, if that would piss her off or what. He figured that since Billy and Heather had gone to the trouble of reporting JoAnn to the police, Heather had to know what sex Billy really was.

It was easier not to discuss it.

Whenever JoAnn would come around looking for her daughter, Billy would get in the car with her and take off for a while, always returning with a smile and a gift or card for Heather. Billy couldn't do enough for his girl, he always thought of her, and it seemed to Drew that Heather and Billy had a good thing. Drew wasn't sure what they did in their private lives, and he didn't really care.

"It was none of my damn business. Every time I was around and those two were doing that which they decided to do, it was when I was sleeping, before I got up," Drew maintains. "When I saw them, they were running around, joking, laughing, wrestling, having a ball. Sure, I've seen boyfriend-girlfriend do that shit, but I didn't care to notice, I didn't pay attention. I don't have the vaguest idea if those two kissed, rubbed, nubbed, fucked, whatever. If they did it, they did it behind closed doors, or, in this case, curtains."

13

"HE WAS LIKE EVERYBODY'S DREAM GUY. HE KNEW HOW a woman wanted to be treated," Heather affectionately remembered. "He was romantic. He took you out to dinner, bought flowers, roses, just everything. He liked to spend quality time, and he got along really well with my family." Heather was just fourteen when they met, at a time in her life when she didn't know a lot about sex, when she didn't want to be coerced. Soon after she asked Billy to move in with her, he changed his name to Brandon. He preferred it that way, and Heather went along with it, happy to have him by her side at any cost. Brandon cushioned her from her mother's messy divorce from her step-dad; Brandon distracted her.

"It was weird because he didn't pressure you into anything. He was always there for you, no matter what you did to him or what happened," Heather happily said. "He was there if you needed a shoulder to cry on, or somebody to talk to. I went to him about school or if I was having problems with my mom. He would help me with just anything. He helped me deal with the fact that my father wasn't around."

As they came to discover, the two of them had a great deal in common in terms of family background. Both were raised by a single parent Both knew the struggle of the lower middle class, sometimes going without enough food, without enough clothes. Moreover, both had been victims of sexual molestation by a family member.

For a while, Brandon and Heather were more like brother and sister, more like best buddies than anything else. Brandon was somebody easy to get along with, and Heather never questioned his sexuality. As far as she was concerned, he was a guy through and through. When they weren't together, Brandon had a pack of guy friends he would hang around, playing basketball or football or drinking beers.

Most of the time, he and Heather would go out cruising, blasting the radio, eating at drive-ins, and just goofing off.

She felt she could be herself around him, that he would understand just about anything she told him, and she needed that Brandon could make her laugh, even when she was in the worst mood. He always had a funny comment or a compliment to throw out.

"When he first met me, he told me he didn't see how somebody so beautiful and so perfect would want somebody like him," the willowy redhead recalled. "He was always full of compliments."

Heather had taken Brandon away from Liz, which was easy enough to do since he and Liz were only casually dating. The major turn-on for Heather was the fact that Brandon didn't act macho—he was totally different from most guys. He didn't care if you saw him cry. He wasn't afraid to show his emotions.

"The first time I saw him cry was two days after we started going out, my mom had left for bowling and I was on the phone with Liz, his girlfriend," Heather reminisced. "At the time, me and Brandon were seeing each other, and he came in and I told him, 'You can't have both of us.' I said he couldn't be kissing on her and then coming over here and kissing on me. It didn't work that way. Well, he started crying, and I was just devastated. I had never seen a man cry. The guys in my family have to be macho. They cry behind closed doors."

Three months after they started going out, Brandon bought Heather a promise ring, sort of a pre-engagement ring. He promised to give her his love forever. She promised to do the same in return.

"He treated me like I was somebody. Like I was important. He let you know in so many ways that he cared, without pressuring you for sex. The subject of sex came up maybe every once in a while," she explained. "All my friends thought that we were having sex, and I was like, 'No, we haven't.' They thought we were lying because we shared a bed together. I was like, 'Yes, that's all we do, we close our eyes and we sleep, we cuddle, that's it.' But nobody believed us."

They talked about marriage. They talked about kids. Brandon made it clear that if any of his girlfriends ever got pregnant, he didn't believe in abortions. He would want her to have the child. Heather agreed. She would only consider abortion under extreme circumstances—it would have to be something drastic, like if she ever got raped again.

The subject of Heather's rape had come up one night when the two of them were watching Jodie Foster in *The Accused*. Shortly after the film ended, they both fell asleep, and the next thing Brandon knew, his girlfriend woke up screaming.

"What's wrong, baby? What's wrong? It's OK, you can tell me; I won't tell anyone," he promised.

"I just had the most awful dream, but yet it was so real, and I starting having flashbacks of what happened when I was young."

"What happened? Will you at least tell me?"

"Well, I was only like five or six, I was really little when they did it."

"Did what? Did they hurt you?"

For the next hour, Heather told Brandon about the sexual provocation that went on, about the abusive relatives she had and their evil ways.

"One of them would wear short shorts that were cutoffs and wouldn't wear any underwear, and he would sit on the couch with his legs spread so that his genitals would hang out," Heather confided.

"They were just really abusive. One night they tied me down to a mattress and put a gag in my mouth."

Brandon confessed that rape was one of his biggest fears.

He went on to explain that he was a hermaphrodite, born with both sexes, that he was raised as a female. He told her that when he was younger, as a female, he had been molested too.

"You mean, you were once *female*?"

"Yeah, but I'm not anymore," he assured.

"What do you mean?"

"Well, I'm not female now. I had an operation."

"I was confused about the whole thing; I just didn't understand," Heather would later insist. "He didn't go into details about the molestation; he just said that it was nonconsensual sexual foreplay. It bothered him so much that he just got up and walked out of the room."

14

HERMAPHRODITE. HEATHER RAN TO THE LIBRARY TO look it up. She didn't do a computer search; she did nothing but browse through an encyclopedia, which gave her no substantive knowledge to speak of. For her purposes, discovering that there actually was such a thing as a person or animal with the sexual organs of both the male and the female was validation enough. She wanted to believe Brandon so badly, and she decided she had no reason to doubt his word. The two possible sex change operations—*phalloplasty*, the creation of a penis, or *genitoplasty*, which maximizes the prominence of the clitoris—she never even dreamed of, much less thought about researching.

In reality, Brandon didn't have the money for sex re-assignment surgery of any kind. In addition to the organ he needed, he also would have required a bilateral mastectomy and transplantation of the nipples to become a full-fledged male.

No matter. Heather was satisfied that he was a man, strictly by the way he carried himself. He had all the mannerisms of a man and most of the outward appearances of one. If he was missing anything, Heather seemed not to notice. She stayed with him for almost two years, allowing him to pleasure *her*, without technically consummating the relationship.

When the day came that Brandon asked Heather to marry him, she automatically said yes. He was the most romantic guy she ever met, the kind of guy she dreamed of spending the rest of her life with. He would brush her hair, greet her at the door with kisses, and feed her chocolate ice cream spoonful by spoonful. What most guys think is stupid, gushy nonsense, Brandon put to use.

The two of them contemplated going on an exotic cruise for their honeymoon. Heather wanted to set the date, and she was ready to be with him, fully, to finally go all the way.

"I want to wait until the time is right," he told her as they lay in bed together, making plans.

"I totally understand that, but, I mean, if we're getting married, then it's OK, I think."

"I don't want to pressure you into anything because of what has happened in the past. I want it to be good for you. I want us to be as one."

"But I feel that way now."

"If we can, I want to wait until our wedding night."

Heather didn't argue with him. She figured he was just trying to do the right thing.

In the meantime, she went on the Pill just in case. Besides, it was a way to regulate her menstrual cycle. Of course, her friends all concluded she was having sex with Brandon for sure, but she'd deny it, telling them she was in love but was waiting for the right moment. To a few people, she confided that Brandon made her feel sexy and vulnerable in bed. His whole goal was not just to please her sexually, but to make her feel loved, to feel like a woman—that's all she wanted. He was into sensuous kissing, affection, talking, and taking breaks; coming wasn't the most important part.

"We did go just a little bit further than kissing a couple of times, but he would always stop and he would say, 'This isn't right.' Most of the time it would be like when we were drunk after a party or something," Heather explained. "He would do stuff to me, and he would get all this pleasure in doing it. It was foreplay, and that was the furthest it went"

In her mind, Heather didn't even need the foreplay. She cared more about the non-sexual caresses, the verbal reassurances of love and commitment. She just wanted to hug someone, to be held.

"I had no problem with waiting, because I knew no guy would ever hold me or kiss me or be as intimate as he was. Guys these days aren't like that. They just want to get their satisfaction out of it and that's it. They don't care about your pleasure or if you're getting off or not. They're just like, 'I am going to get mine and I'm out of here.'"

All the more reason to wait until marriage, she figured. She didn't think

Brandon had any motive other than his Catholic upbringing. If she secretly wondered whether he truly had a man's body with all the working parts, she was thrown off by the pair of rolled up socks he kept stuffed down his pants. There was no way for her to tell for sure without fondling him, something she claims she never did.

Heather didn't want to face any gory details. She just wanted *him*.

"The whole time I never knew, because I never went into the bathroom when he was taking a shower. I never saw him naked," she insisted. "He would put a towel around his neck and drape it over his chest so I couldn't see his chest. When we'd go swimming, we would go to the lake, and he would wear two shirts and go in the water. I mean, sometimes he would moon me, pull down his pants and show me his butt or something, but that was it."

15

TAMMY AND JOANN DISCUSSED TEENA'S PROBLEM BACK and forth. Tammy kept saying she had socks coming up missing. They both noticed the bulge in Teena's pants, but neither had the nerve to say anything to her about it. JoAnn felt shut out of her child's life, and she just wanted the truth to be told. She had been completely in the dark about Traci Beels. Now, with Heather Kuhfahl, she knew something was up. She was sure her daughter was gay.

Heather very seldom came into her house. When she did, JoAnn would refer to her daughter as Teena, and Heather wouldn't bristle.

"You know she's female?" JoAnn asked her one day.

"Yes, I understand that," Heather said blankly.

"It would all go back to the hermaphrodite thing," Heather would later explain. "He had a legitimate answer for everything. He'd tell me his mother couldn't accept the fact that he was male, that she wanted two little girls, that she was just playing a joke."

JoAnn was dumbfounded. She didn't know what exactly was going on, why they stayed together if they were just friends. She was told Teena slept alone in the downstairs bedroom of Heather's house, but she never believed it.

"I knew that Heather's mom was never really home," JoAnn said. "I knew that all of a sudden there were beer parties going on and I have an eighteen-year-old daughter over there that's not supposed to be drinking or doing anything."

JoAnn would call over to David Drive and get Ruth on the phone. This started back in the Billy days, back when they bad reported her to the cops. For years, Ruth would be nothing but rude to her.

"Her name's not Billy, it's Teena. She's a female," JoAnn would insist.

But Ruth never listened. Here JoAnn had this stranger telling her what sex Teena was, arguing that Teena was a male. It was really crazy.

"Why would another mother tell somebody that their child is not really who it is?" JoAnn wondered. "I just couldn't fathom that. It bothered me that she was with this young girl. It bothered me that the mother of this girl would not listen."

"That's when I started hearing stories from other people that Teena was saying she was a hermaphrodite. Heather's mom would even say this to me, and well, I gave birth to her; I know what sex she is. There were no other attachments anywhere that had to be removed."

"Are you a lesbian?" JoAnn finally asked her daughter.

"No," Teena said emphatically.

"I don't care if you are, Teena. You can be whatever you want to be, just be honest with me."

"I'm not, Mom."

"Look, if you are, that is your choice. All I care about is your welfare. I don't want you walking around, lying to everybody, and I need to know what is going on with you."

"I'm not a lesbian, Mom. I have no desire to be."

"Teena, your hair is awfully short. It almost makes you look like a guy." Teena had no response.

JoAnn decided to let it rest, to get off Teena's back. She had done all she could do, had even sent some gay women coworkers from T. J. Maxx over to Ruth's with Molly, but no one could get through to her. Molly had been armed with a picture of Teena as a little girl and a copy of Teena's birth certificate, but Ruth refused to look at the stuff.

"I remember the night they went over to talk with Heather's mom. Teena came over here. She sat down and was mortified that they showed up, that they were doing this," JoAnn explained.

"Well, honey, if there's a problem, we need to talk. I need to help you. I need to find out what's going on," JoAnn prodded.

"Well, I'm not a lesbian, Mom. I'm just not!"

"Well, I'm not saying you *are*. I'm just saying, I'm here, and if you want to go to counseling and we need to talk, I'll do that with you."

At that time, Teena was so adamant about it, horrified by the very suggestion that she might be homosexual, JoAnn just felt lost. Teena had gone through most of JoAnn's photo albums, tearing up every picture of herself as a female she could find. She was *willing* herself into existence. She started shaving her face and was using the men's room in public.

Her voice had become lower and more scruffy. She was now altogether

Brandon, a lean, muscular, popular guy.

"I didn't know what to think," JoAnn admitted. "I didn't understand. I haven't been around a whole lot of gay people. Teena just sat there and hugged me and cried and that was about the extent of that."

In the meantime, Brandon was busy taking Heather on shopping sprees all over Lincoln. He spoiled her terribly, and Sara felt like Heather was taking advantage of the situation. When Sara first met her, Heather was dressed in rags from bargain stores. Now Sara would go over to Heather's and find new clothes in her closet every week.

Heather seemed to be raking in a small fortune, and Sara started to wonder where it was all coming from. Brandon had gotten himself a fake picture I.D. over at Fast Bucks, a check-cashing place, and he used it to hold down jobs in gas stations like Costal Mart and U-Stop, but still, he didn't make that much money. For a while, he worked as a pizza delivery boy at Fat Pat's, but his pay was so bad that, in his off time, he resorted to begging truckers for money.

Sara knew all about it; she knew Brandon thought it was funny. The truckers would give him money because he'd claim to have a broken-down car and no way to make it home from the highway. He'd collect five or ten bucks from each one and leave after a few hours with a quick fifty, sometimes more.

"He showered me with gifts all the time, and I would totally not expect it," Heather professed. "I'd be just browsing through a shop, and then I'd go to the ladies' room or something, and he'd be like, 'I'll be right back.' Then he'd show up with a coat or a ring for me, whatever I had pointed to."

But if Brandon was good in the gift-giving department, he sometimes spoiled it by being a big flirt. More than once, when he was drinking at the house, he'd start kissing one of Heather's friends, and later she'd hear a report. He always rented porno movies and would talk about having two girls in his bed. Then Heather thought he was sick—she had no intention of sharing him with anyone else. When he'd watch porno, he stared blatantly at the women, and Heather would get really annoyed.

"I would get grossed out when there'd be two girls on going down on each other, and he would just sit there in awe," Heather recalled.

"I would have to put a drool bucket under him. He was loving every minute of it.

"If you knew the Brandon that I knew, you could just get pissed off as hell at him, you could have your fist doubled up and everything, but you would just give him a little love pat," Heather confided. "You could not hurt this person. He would get this weird goofy-ass look on his face and make you forget you were ever pissed off. I could be so mad I wanted to kill him sometimes, and he'd just sit there and laugh. Then I'd start cracking up."

Still, she didn't like that Brandon teased every girl he ran across, including her best friend, Monica. He was so sure of himself that he gave Monica a neckful of hickeys one time, just because. Heather happened to catch him in the act, and she was furious. He assured her that he was doing it because Monica was ticklish, and since Heather knew Monica wasn't his type, she let it go at that. The three of them were spending a lot of time together, and they were close.

By then, early 1992, Sara and Drew had reunited and were living together in a small house not far from Heather's.

Because they were both so involved in Teena's life, they found themselves in a strange predicament. They felt indebted to her—she had been responsible for them getting back together, she had been the middle man, and they had her to thank for that.

Now they found they were defending Teena, keeping her secret, calling her Brandon around other people, going along with Brandon's story that he had been through a sex change operation in Omaha. To everyone around them, they insisted that Brandon was a *he*.

Of course, there were certain people who refused to believe it, particularly male acquaintances of Drew's who would often make demeaning comments behind Brandon's back, calling her a dyke, butch, every name in the book.

There were times when some of them would get drunk and talk about beating Brandon up.

Some of Drew's buddies didn't like Brandon's charade. They felt they were being made fools. "If she wants to be a man, she better well *fight* like one," one of them threatened.

"If all she wants is a dick, she could ask me," another teased. "I'll give her some."

16

TEENA BRANDON HAD PEOPLE TALKING, AND IT WAS about more than just tongue kissing Heather Kuhfahl. Teena was stealing, and everybody was starting to find out.

The first time it happened, Teena took some guy's checkbook and went and wrote all these checks as a joke. According to Sara, Teena forged the man's signature and brought a bunch of crap she didn't need—music tapes, shoes that didn't fit, T-shirts. It was a teeny-bopper heist.

"Heather and Teena both got caught, but Heather said she wasn't involved. At first I thought it was casual, you know, ten dollars here, fifteen dollars there," Sara remembered.

But Teena Brandon got a big charge out of it and started writing out checks for two million dollars, just in jest.

Apparently, though, jesting wasn't enough. Soon she got hold of Ruth's checkbook and ATM card, and she went after the cash.

"Ruth told me you've been taking money out of her ATM. Have you?" Sara called and asked the minute she heard the news.

"Yeah," Teena admitted.

"Well, what have you been buying?"

"Gas for her car, food for her house, food for her daughter, clothes for her daughter."

"There's no food in her house?"

"Hardly, unless I bring it in."

"Well, I think you're going about this the wrong way, Teena."

"I'm taking money out of Ruth's account to take care of her daughter. What would you like me to do? Let her starve? Go without clothes?"

"OK, so you did it for a justifiable reason. I'm not going to judge you. You're going to do whatever you want anyway, no matter what I say. I mean, fine, if that's how you want to handle it, I won't tell anyone. But let me ask you something. Are you taking big chunks of money?"

"Not really, just a couple of dollars to make ends meet."

"That's not what I heard."

"Really? Who've you been talking to? Ruth?"

"Heather told me Ruth's going to the cops."

"Well, she can't do that. First of all, I've signed the bank slip with Heather there, so I don't think they'll come back to me. If anything, they'll go to her, and then what can Ruth do? Put her own kid in jail? I really don't think so."

"Well, I hope you know what you're doing."

But evidently, Teena didn't. When all of Ruth Laudenschlager's checks started bouncing, the woman reported it to Lancaster County authorities.

On October 17, 1991, Teena Brandon was tracked down at Luigi's Restaurant in Lincoln and handed citations for two counts of second-degree forgery. The count involving Laudenschlager was eventually dropped, but count 2, stemming from a $154.38 check written on the account of Brad J. Tullis, was bound over to district court, and this time, it looked like Teena Brandon was actually going to have her day in court.

Teena had already had a brush with the law twice that year-in March 1991 she had been charged with possession of stolen property and had to pay a five-hundred dollar fine. She satisfied part of the judgment by spending three days in the county jail. She eventually changed her plea to no contest and agreed to pay the balance of the fine by making time payments.

Then in July, she had been charged with second-degree forgery for an amount under seventy-five dollars. That charge was still pending. Of course, Teena had convinced herself that the charge would be dismissed, and lucky for her, it was.

Now, however, in late '91 with this new second-degree forgery charge hanging over her head, things were getting more frightening. Her case was assigned to Scott Helvey, an attorney at the Lancaster County public defender's office, and suddenly, JoAnn was asking questions. Teena got quizzed because JoAnn caught a piece of mail with the public defender's address.

"At first Teena told me that Ruth had OK'd these checks, then when I found out that she was wanted for forgery, I just about died. I thought, *No way, this child's never been in trouble for anything*. But the law came here looking for her. They always came here even though she wasn't living here anymore," JoAnn explained.

"She'd never give you a definite answer. I went to all her court sessions with her, but she'd just plead not guilty, and she just kept putting it off. Even when all the proof was there, she wouldn't tell me anything. She just said nothing."

With everything else that had been going on, JoAnn felt she had no right to interfere in Teena's life, so she just let the matter drop. For one thing, Teena had been having a lot of psychological problems, and she didn't want to pressure her. For another, JoAnn's mom, Frances, had just died a horrible death. A victim of cancer, Frances had been on high doses of morphine and had preoccupied JoAnn for months. In the shadow of grief, everything else became pretty much forgotten.

It would take a while to resolve, to get through all the red tape in the court system, but on March 4, 1992, there was finally restitution: Teena R. Brandon was found guilty of the second-degree forgery charge.

On April 15 of that year, the Honorable Paul D. Merritt sentenced her to an eighteen-month term of probation, the conditions as follows: Brandon would have to report in writing and in person to a probation officer; Brandon could not consume or have in possession any alcoholic beverage; Brandon would complete a GED within one year; Brandon would satisfactorily attend and continue counseling at the Community Mental Health Center of Lancaster County until no longer required.

By the time Brandon was sentenced, the relationship with Heather had almost completely crumbled. Brandon did everything possible to salvage it, but it's destruction had been a long time coming. In early January 1992, Brandon had moved out of Ruth's house. Brandon told his mother he was staying in a trailer with a couple of guys, buddies of his.

By the middle of that month, Heather started getting letters from Brandon about how sorry be was for all the things he had put her through, about how they needed to stick up for each other, to stay together. "I'm still the same person you were in love with, but there's one big difference, and that will all change," Brandon promised.

17

"ALL I WANT IS TO HAVE MY DAUGHTER BACK," JOANN demanded in her calmest voice. "I know that. I want her back too," Sara agreed.

"Well, why don't you do something?" "Like what?"

"You could go over there and talk to Heather, because you know I've tried and she hates me for it. I'm not getting anywhere with her, and Teena just tunes me out."

"Well, I'm starting to get scared for Teena. I think she's making herself sick." "That's why I'm saying just drop by Heather's, OK?"

As far as they could tell, the pastime of being Brandon had gone too far, and everything with Teena was coming to a head.

Teena wasn't Teena anymore; she wasn't acting right about anything. Sara and JoAnn were becoming concerned for her safety and well-being. The guys she was living with might discover her secret and beat her up; anything could happen. Teena needed to sort out her life, to face the reality of her existence, whatever *that* was, and they were determined to bring her somewhere for help even if they had to drag her, kicking and screaming.

They were both convinced that Heather was a closet lesbian, that since she had seen Teena's real driver's license, she in fact knew Teena was a she. Teena had supposedly told Heather her name was Ten-a, an odd Irish name, but they never thought she believed that. They persuaded each other that somehow Heather had influenced Teena, had encouraged Teena to put on this masculine charade as a way to bide her gayness. Still, they couldn't be sure. What if Heather was just *naive?*

"Heather was basically in denial," Sara insisted. "On the one hand, I thought Heather had figured it out for herself, that she wanted to be in that situation, that she knew what she was doing. On the other hand, I think she believed Teena was going to go through a sex change. She had all these feelings for Brandon, and she wanted to believe it."

It was early in 1992, a year into the transformation, that Sara really started getting nervous about Teena's behavior. By then, Teena was hardly eating at all—maybe one bag of potato chips in a given day. She was dwindling away down to 100 pounds. She also now had this weird compulsion to take showers. as many as six or seven times a day. She was always changing her clothes. As Brandon, Teena went through more outfit changes than a Calvin Klein model Sara just didn't get it.

This shit has got to stop, Sara thought to herself. *I don't want to ruin Teena's relationship, but at the same time, what if Heather really doesn't know? What will it do to her when she gets older? The girl's going to go completely psycho because some girl portrayed herself as her boyfriend.*

"Sara, I think I'm gay. I mean, I don't feel like I'm gay, but I want to be with other women," Teena tearfully confessed after a big fight with Heather.

"It's OK if you are. I don't care," Sara assured her.

"But I mean, to me, I'm not gay. I feel like a man inside. I don't know what I'm supposed to do. Do you hate me?"

"It doesn't matter to me what you are, Teena. You should know that."

"You still wanna be friends?"

"Teena, we'll always be friends."

"Do you think any less of me?"

"No, I mean, if you think what you're doing is right, then fine. I told you I'd go along with you months ago, and I have, right? But just make sure that you're not hurting a bunch of innocent girls in the process."

"When she finally told me that her and Heather were more than friends, I just kinda played it off like I didn't know," Sara remembers. "She was afraid to tell me, 'cause she didn't want me to look down on her."

Sara talked to her about having a sex change operation, but Teena wasn't very sure about it. In fact, she didn't have much to say at all; she just gave Sara a confused look. But Sara inspired her, told her at least to check into it.

"I'm not sure," Teena said at first. "I'm still thinking."

"I understand that, but it doesn't hurt to just find out."

"Well, what if I'm wrong? What if I have the operation, and then decide this isn't what I want?"

Sara's reaction was comforting. She said she would be there to help. Teena had a dilemma, Sara told her, but in the meantime, she promised to keep her friend's secret, calling her Brandon when they were out in public, dodging people's questions whenever the issue of Brandon's sexuality came up. By then, Brandon had a new roommate, Kendell Hawthorne, a friend of Drew's. Now Drew found himself in the middle again, and it presented a problem. Kendell wanted to see Brandon's I.D. or he was going to kick Brandon out. Brandon had nowhere to go, and Drew and Sara knew that.

"Kendell didn't know what to think. He kept asking me," Drew recalls. "I told him, 'Decide for yourself.' I told him to ask Brandon. If he had found out that Brandon was actually a girl, I think he would have cracked a shitload of jokes. I figure he was discriminatory."

Then came the day that everything hit the fan.

It was late in the afternoon, toward the end of January, when Sara finally tracked Heather down to have a heart-to-heart about Brandon. They ran into each other at McDonald's, and Heather agreed to let Sara follow her back to her house.

"You better sit down, Heather," Sara said, mustering her most solemn voice the minute they stepped through the door.

"No. I've been sitting down at school all day, and I have a lot of energy. What do you have to say?" Heather wanted to know.

"For what I have to tell you, I think you had better sit down."

"Just say it."

"Brandon is not Brandon," Sara blurted.

"What are you talking about?" "Brandon is *Teena*."

"I know."

"No. I mean Brandon is Teena like you are Heather and I am Sara. She has a *period* like you do, she has boobs like you do." Heather just let her mouth drop to the floor.

A few moments later, they beard the front door slam. It was Brandon, just stopping by.

Sara told Heather not to leak a word. The two of them said they were going out to get something to eat at Arby's, which was right by JoAnn's, and they promised to return with a hot ham and cheese sandwich for him. "We went to his mother's, and she showed me pictures of when he was a little kid, of the birth certificate, just everything." Heather explained. "She showed me pictures of family vacations with Brandon and Tammy, and Brandon had long hair and was dressed in tittle girls' clothes. This one picture I saw, it had something to do with Catholic schools. She was in a little white lace dress with a bow in her hair. I was just aggravated because I felt like I was betrayed. I was freaking out, and Sara was, like, trying to be there for me."

On the way home, the two of them skipped Arby's, barely muttering a word. Heather's face was pale. Nothing really registered with Heather until she walked in the living room. When she saw Brandon, she went into hysterical tears. Brandon threw herself at Heather's feet, desperate to explain. "I never meant for it to go this far, but I fell in love with you, and I couldn't find a way to tell you," Brandon bawled as she choked out the words. "I tried to tell you, but you just wouldn't listen." When her "boyfriend" wouldn't get out of the house, Heather called the cops. She had enough. The screaming and tears were never-ending. By the time police arrived, however, Heather had calmed down a bit. She told them everything was OK, that everything was under control.

A few hours later, JoAnn got an emergency call from Sara: Teena had swallowed a bottle of antibiotics, and Sara and Heather were outside Kendell's place, scared Teena was going to die.

Someone needed to bring her to a hospital right away.

18

ON JANUARY 29, 1992, THE LANCASTER COUNTY CRISIS center admitted a nineteen-year-old Caucasian woman who had repeatedly threatened to kill herself. Friends told crisis center workers that just a week prior, Teena Brandon had overdosed on antibiotics, was treated at Saint Elizabeth's Hospital, and released.

Teena had been brought to the crisis center without knowing why. Sara and Heather had taken her; they tricked her, making her think Sara's mom was an outpatient there. Once in the building, Heather pulled Teena aside into a tiny private waiting room.

"I don't care what you are, I'll always be in love with Billy, but you need to get help. You're too depressed," Heather told her.

"What do you mean? I'm only depressed because I hurt you. I love you and I never meant to do that. I can make everything work out for us. I'll do anything you ask, anything at all to get us back again," Teena insisted.

Heather was confused and angry. She loved Brandon, but now she had her own crisis to deal with. She had never faced the idea that she herself might be gay. At the same time Brandon was begging her to take him back, she was considering the ramifications. She wished things could be more simple.

"I just started crying, and I walked over and gave him a big hug and tried to kiss him," Heather remembers. "To me, it hadn't sunk in. It wasn't real to me; it was just a dream. He pushed me away and asked if I was sure this is what I wanted, and he started crying. We just sat there and talked about what was going on and how it made me feel. It hurt him to see me cry."

In the waiting room, Heather confessed that she couldn't eat, couldn't sleep, that she spent every waking moment thinking about their love. She said that without him, her world just fell apart. She too wanted things the way they used to be, even though everybody was telling her that was impossible.

Much as Teena didn't like the idea, she agreed to be an inpatient at Lancaster Crisis. Immediately, she was placed on suicide alert, and her family was called in. JoAnn would later tell crisis center workers that for years Teena had been refusing to visit doctors because she objected to being examined, to wearing a hospital robe. She also admitted that she had a difficult time understanding her daughter, that Teena would never be honest with her. Instead of showing emotions, Teena would make jokes, JoAnn told them, asserting she was shocked to learn that her daughter preferred having sexual relationships with females.

"I feel like she hates me because her father's not around," JoAnn said in a moment of exasperation. "I feel I have been made a victim."

"When we got there, Teena was very, very angry. She didn't want help; she felt she didn't need it," JoAnn recalled.

"The psychiatrist Teena talked to said she needed long-term extensive treatment, that she was becoming a pathological liar, that she was losing her identity."

In her initial statement to crisis center workers, Teena admitted to having a sexual relationship with Heather, explaining to Dr. Klaus Hartman that she had been introducing herself to younger girls as Billy Brandon, that she wanted to be a man.

Teena also reported having twelve forgery charges pending against her (an exaggeration) and possibly a sexual assault charge on a minor. She denied being suicidal.

In terms of recent history, Teena told the attending physician that she was finishing up two courses at Bryan Learning Center in order to complete her GED. She said she intended to move to Denver, where she planned to enroll in an art school.

She confided that she had been raped in October 1990 but would not give details except to say that she received no subsequent treatment. She denied having any need for therapy, denied having any family problems, and mentioned that her father died at the age of eighteen in a car accident, a result of drunken driving.

Dr. Hartman viewed Teena as pleasant and cooperative. A slender girl of small stature, she seemed to have no unusual mannerisms. She did not appear to be depressed, nor did she appear to be functioning at the psychotic level. In his estimation, hers was a mild case of identity disorder.

"Her judgment seems somewhat impaired as it concerns her personal relationships," Dr. Hartman wrote in his initial report. "She has some appreciation that her sexual needs are different from those of the majority of the population."

After a few days of counseling at the crisis center, Teena finally sat down with JoAnn and had the nerve to open up about her sexuality. When she told her mom that a therapist had suggested a sex *change*, JoAnn thought Teena was joking. JoAnn figured the talk of a sex change was bogus. Teena always talked big. She knew it had to involve a lot more than just a few days' counseling. Teena made it sound like this would be happening overnight, and JoAnn just couldn't believe her ears.

"She said that she felt more like a man inside than a woman, and I didn't know what to say," JoAnn said. "You have to realize how devastated I was. I raised this child for eighteen years and never had a clue there was anything different going on in her life."

The only thing JoAnn knew about sex changes was what she picked up from talk shows. Still, she tried to play the role of the authority, telling her daughter that a sex change operation would require a lot of psychologic analysis. She said that, as far as she knew, most people who had a gender identity crisis usually knew it by puberty. She was concerned that Teena was confusing the issue.

"She sat there and talked to me like it was nothing. She was just giving me enough to think about, to back off for a while," JoAnn later reflected. "But she was telling me, '*This is what I want. This is what I want done.*' I knew she was serious."

"You know it's going to cost a lot of money, it's going to take a long time," JoAnn cautioned. "I know that, Mom."

To mental health care workers, Teena would later deny that she ever told her mother about wanting a sex change.

Teena spent seven days at the center, hardly participating in group activities and just minimally responding to counseling. Her chief concern was that she be allowed to call Heather, which she did as often as possible, even abusing phone privileges to the point of being reprimanded twice.

She couldn't call Sara anymore. Sara's mother informed the crisis center that police would serve Teena a citation if she dialed the Gapp home number.

By early February, 1992, Teena was responding well to a book, *The Courage to Heal.* She told mental health workers that she identified with certain problems listed and began to keep a daily journal. For a while, she seemed somewhat cheered up—playing cards, watching TV, and going outside to play football in the afternoons. Still, she was displaying great difficulty "feeling" her emotions. As much as she was encouraged to get in touch with what she was feeling inside, she couldn't. Teena also had trouble accepting any positive feedback about herself. When workers would tell her she was a worthwhile person, Teena had no response to that.

At one point, Teena was confronted and asked why young girls were calling the center asking for Billy Brandon. Teena would give no direct answer. Even though she had admitted being Billy to Dr. Hartman, Teena told staff members that her friends were mad at her, that they were trying to get her in trouble.

During a one-on-one counseling session with Deb Brodtke, a mental health clinician who would later see Teena as an outpatient, she talked about feeling unloved by JoAnn, about her family dysfunction. She described hours of sexual abuse in her childhood and adolescence, saying that she felt intimidated by certain men, that she always felt sexually oriented toward women.

Teena told Brodtke that she wanted to be a male to not have to deal with the negative connotations of being a lesbian and because she felt less intimidated by men when she presented herself as a male.

She eventually admitted that she swallowed the handful of antibiotics "to get a point across." Her therapist observed that Teena seemed immature at times, that she seemed not to show emotions other than joy. Teena was encouraged to live as a man in preparation for possible sex change surgery, a concept that pleased her immensely. However, Brodtke observed that Teena did not feel she had any problems, that Teena had no goals to continue therapy. Someone would have to persuade her.

While in the crisis center, Teena contacted the Lancaster County attorney to attempt to place a hold on her second degree forgery case. She told the county attorney's office that she had agreed to commit herself voluntarily and promised to appear at the county jail upon her release.

On February 6, Teena Brandon was discharged from the crisis center after the Mental Health Board met and decided she should go into outpatient treatment. Her discharge diagnosis: axis I, transsexualism; axis II, personality disorder.

Brandon was placed on home visit and initially taken to jail, where she spent a few days until her grandmother Doris bailed her out.

There was one item listed in the discharge summary evaluation that JoAnn Brandon would later deny: "Mother does report patient was born hermaphroditic. At birth, mother requested patient be female."

19

ONE OF THE FIRST THINGS BRANDON MUST HAVE DONE when he got out of jail was go out and buy a plastic penis as a psychological boost. His new girl, Reanna Allen, happened to see it one day, hidden in a pair of socks. It was the soft kind, somewhat real looking, and when Reanna came across it, she didn't know what to think. For a while, she just let him stay at her trailer and carried on as "boyfriend and girlfriend" in public, although nothing was really that way at home.

Before he moved in with Reanna, Brandon had tried to will back Heather's love with dozens of letters and cards, but Heather had her mind made up, she was not meant for Brandon—now—or ever. Brandon had put her through hell—he tried to make her believe they would be a family, that they would still be able to have children through adoption; he tried to make everything sound *reasonable*, but she just couldn't do it anymore. He apologized for being an asshole, for being so jealous, for loving her too much, but none of it mattered. The gig was up.

"Now that we are done and over with and I finally accept that I have lost you, all I can do is wish I had never fucked up," Brandon wrote in the end. "I'm a failure in your past that you fear... but I just want you to believe in me." He took back the promise ring, at the same time begging her to help him, to at least *spend time* with him, and Heather said she would. No one else could ever fill his heart as she did. He needed her around.

He guaranteed that he would not lean on her too much. Although Heather felt like slitting her wrists because she was so tired of his crap, she was convinced that they could still be "best friends." He still wanted her to call him Brandon, and Heather went along with that. It came naturally to her. If Heather didn't like the idea of facing her friends, of telling them about Brandon's sexuality, luckily she didn't have to worry about it. She could leave that to Sara. Sara was only too happy to explain things to people, to stand behind Brandon at every turn.

Even though Heather didn't want him anymore, when she first found out about Reanna, she was incredibly jealous and mad as hell. By the time Heather met Reanna, she was barely able to keep up the pretense, but she did it, because she realized that for Brandon, there was no other way. When she finally accepted that it was OK for other girls to want Brandon, she began turning her eyes elsewhere.

Actually, there were a number of people making adjustments in the period following Teena Brandon's crisis, especially JoAnn and Tammy. Granted, JoAnn started making jokes that she had two daughters and a *son*, but deep down she knew she had a serious problem on her hands, one that she could not afford financially and did not know how to cope with emotionally. And obviously, the whole thing was weird for Tammy. As her sister, she tried to go along with the name Brandon in front of others, but she would slip, so their time spent together could often become an awkward embarrassment.

Moreover, JoAnn and Tammy had a tough time dealing with the rest of the family, certain that none of them could accept the possibility of Teena's maleness. Of course, not everybody in the family knew about Teena's crisis. The ones who were around her had their own opinions about why she dressed like a man, but no one really knew a thing about XY hermaphrodites, hormonal puberty, ambiguous genitalia, or what, if any, genetic factors might be involved. It just didn't occur to them.

The only thing her family could be sure of was that being around Teena, or *Brandon*, as she now called herself, had become a bit too confusing and way too much trouble. It was like living a talk show; seeing it on television was one thing, but none of it was honestly supposed to happen to you.

As Brandon, Teena started going to regular counseling sessions with Deb Bodtke and she seemed to be making progress in accepting herself as a he. Brandon was being encouraged to explore the past, to accept the present, and the positive reinforcement really seemed to help. At least JoAnn thought so.

Two weeks into the sessions, JoAnn was invited to attend, and she went, expecting a lesson in transsexuals. Instead, the very first time the three of them sat down together, Teena brought up the business of being molested, and JoAnn was flabbergasted. She had no idea anything like that had happened; no one had ever told her a thing about it. Now she found herself watching Teena weep, crying like a baby about being violated many years before, and JoAnn was left speechless.

"When I found out about it in therapy, I got on my knees, I kind of crawled over to her," JoAnn remembers, "and said, '*God, I'm so sorry about this.*' I felt like shit. I felt like I allowed it."

She wanted to confront the man right away, but Teena asked her not to. Teena just wanted the matter dropped. Of course, JoAnn couldn't do that, especially when she discovered that he had molested both her girls. She was horrified, and because she couldn't get any detailed information out of

Teena, she went to Tammy as soon as she left Bodtke's office.

When Tammy confirmed everything, JoAnn wanted to press charges. She couldn't believe that her girls had hidden something like this from her, and she wanted to see her slimy relative put away in jail. She felt sure he destroyed Teena, and that was why Teena wasn't interested in men. She hated him for that and vowed she would make him pay for his wrongs.

20

BRANDON HAD BROUGHT PAPERS OVER TO HEATHER from the crisis center to prove he wasn't gay, to rule out lesbian transsexuality. He wanted her to know that he was trapped in the wrong body.

But with Reanna Allen, it was different. She was fifteen, he was nineteen, and she had been falling in love with him from a distance even before he and Heather split. With her, he didn't need to explain anything, and he liked it better that way.

"He was so cute, he was gorgeous," Reanna reminisced. "Anyone who laid eyes on him, they're like, 'That's what I want, that's Mr. Right.'"

Even though he could hardly hold down a job, Brandon was good at making young girls think that he had all kinds of money. There was a whole group at Reanna's junior high school who were after him, who would whistle when he'd walk by, do whatever to catch his attention, to impress him. They all thought he was a great dresser, that he had a lot of class. He was a definite catch.

Reanna was not too bad herself. With long light brown hair, hazel eyes, creamy skin, and a perfect smile, she was absolutely stunning, a kind of fantasy girl-next-door. Brandon carried around a picture of her wearing a navy blue button-down shirt and men's necktie. She was trying to look butch, but no matter what she did, she was still girlish. He just adored her.

Reanna had dreams about Brandon being her lover, but by her account, it didn't seem to work out. She says all they ever did was kiss.

"He basically told anybody anything they wanted to hear. He knew what a girl wanted," Reanna explained. "I was a virgin at the time and Brandon wasn't the kind of person who pressured people into things. He sat me down and asked me if I was going to lose my virginity with him. He sat and told me he wanted to be with me the rest of my life."

Bringing Brandon over to the house was a lot easier than bringing around the other guys she used to date because Reanna's mother, Brenda, accepted him more readily. Brenda didn't like the huskier guys, the guys with muscles and mustaches who seemed too old for her daughter; she was concerned they would try to force Reanna into something. But Brandon was such a gentleman, she knew she didn't have to worry. Brenda liked him right away. He became one of the family, instantaneously making himself useful around the house.

"He would come up to my door all the time, come in with roses and pizza," Reanna happily remembered. "Brandon was so energetic: he could go to sleep at five, wake up at seven, and he would be up steam cleaning our carpets. He would wash the dishes, scrub the bathroom, he was more or less kissing my mom's butt."

As soon as JoAnn found out where her child was living, she called over there to speak to the girl's mother. JoAnn told Brenda that she couldn't really explain things on the phone, that they needed to talk in person. Somehow she convinced Brenda that it was urgent, that she and her daughter should come over right away. Because they lived just a few blocks from each other, Brenda decided to jump in the car and take a quick ride.

The minute they walked up to the door, Brenda recognized JoAnn: they had gone to high school together and had grown up in the same neighborhood. As Reanna listened in disbelief, the two women marveled at what a small world it was—Brenda even remembered when she helped change Teena's diapers.

"Teena does this all the time. She's trying to talk me into calling her Brandon in front of her friends, and I won't do it," JoAnn finally confided.

"I thought he didn't look quite right," Brenda told her. "I even asked to see a driver's license and some kind of I.D."

JoAnn asked Brenda to send her daughter home. She explained that Teena was in therapy, that she had been missing her sessions lately and needed someone to watch over her.

Brenda agreed, not really asking too many questions about Teena's identity crisis. She was busy focusing on her daughter, who, in essence, was hysterical at the time.

"I didn't want to believe it even when JoAnn sat there and flashed the birth certificate," Reanna recalled. "I read the word female, and I started bawling. Then I got out of there, and I was thinking maybe JoAnn's lying, because when Brandon was telling me the hermaphrodite story, he said his mom makes up stories all the time."

"She tells people that I'm a girl because I've got a little bit of breasts. She thinks she can get away with it because she wants me all to herself," Brandon told Reanna when she confronted him later that day.

She so much wanted to believe Brandon that when he denied everything, she begged her mom to let him stay.

Even though Reanna had walked into Brandon's room, had looked around at the artifacts of a little girl's childhood, she found a way to ignore the concrete proof. Her heart was racing when she saw the baby pictures, the fake I.D. cards, all the evidence JoAnn had out on display, yet she was able to make believe Brandon was never a female, that somehow JoAnn had doctored Tammy's pictures to make it look like it was Brandon.

Of course, Reanna had all kinds of questions, and as soon as she could, she tracked down Heather, hoping for some answers there, but all she got was a brick wall.

"JoAnn's a liar. She's just saying that because she wanted two daughters," Heather insisted.

"Oh, come on, Heather. You've got to know what Brandon is. She's a girl. Why don't you just admit it?" Reanna pressed.

"I'm not a whore. I'm not like you think. I didn't sleep with him. I don't know what he has down there."

"You're so full of it, Heather."

"Well, if you think he's a female, why are you still with him?" Heather taunted.

The two girls acted like they hated each other. They called each other names; they accused each other. In the end, Reanna and Heather spent a hour going back and forth, neither of them really owning up to anything.

"Brandon was still going to deny it no matter what; he was still going to make me believe he was a guy somehow. He manipulated people, and he could fool everybody, even the smartest people," Reanna would later say. "I didn't sleep with Brandon or feel Brandon. I used to rub his back all the time, but he would have his arms next to his chest so you couldn't see anything."

Regardless of what anatomical parts he had, Reanna and Brandon remained the closest of friends, the two of them happy to pal around together. For a while, they both got on a country music kick, they took line-dancing lessons, and Brandon started to wear a big black cowboy hat and a big old pair of cowboy boots a few sizes too big for his feet. Brandon looked extremely handsome in the western gear, and Reanna loved the idea that people thought he was her boyfriend. Eventually, he convinced her that his grandmother had a ton of money, that she was sending him to France to have sex change surgery. He even asked her if she'd come along with him to Europe, and Reanna was ready.

But their special friendship, whatever it was, wasn't destined to last very long. It couldn't last, because Reanna and Brandon were constantly fighting, and she was always in tears. One day, Reanna's cousin got hold of her and forced her to realize that Brandon wasn't right for her, that she needed to break up with him, to move on while she had the chance. Her cousin pointed out that even if Brandon did get a sex change, it wouldn't matter, because he was too jealous, too stressful, not the kind of person anyone would want to marry.

"All I could think of was, *What if I let him go, and he really is a guy*? I was just so madly in love with him," Reanna confessed. "After we broke up, I missed him so much. I missed being around him. I missed everything, but I knew I was just wasting my time, getting hurt and fucking my life up."

When the moment came that he moved out, Reanna took all of the pictures of her and Brandon and cut and burned them. Even though it killed her, she stopped taking his phone calls. Whenever she felt weak, those moments when she felt like picking up the phone and calling him, she'd remind herself of what JoAnn had told her. Teena bad gotten the hermaphrodite story from an episode of the *Donahue* show. The whole thing just made her feel sick.

Sometimes Reanna would come home from school and find a rose and a card waiting for her at the front door. It was Brandon at his best, using all his juicy love poetry to pull at her heart strings.

Months later, after Brandon had turned twenty and had already found the love of his life, the girl who he planned to marry, be ran into Reanna and her half-brother, Allen Killburn. They were hanging out down at "the loop," the area surrounding what they affectionately called "the penis of the plains," Lincoln's 400-foot-tall state capitol, a phallic-shaped building.

By then, Reanna had pretty much forgotten all the trouble Brandon had caused her. She only remembered the good times, how much he used to make her laugh, bow much fun he was. The minute Brandon invited her and Allen over to his place for a beer, Reanna jumped in his Firebird, signaling for Allen to follow.

At Brandon's place, Reanna tried to get to know Gina, Brandon's new main squeeze, but without much success.

Gina seemed snotty; she had nothing to say. Of course, Allen and Brandon were engrossed in a ball game and were oblivious to what was going on with the girls.

Reanna didn't stay long. The bad vibrations from Gina were too much for her, and she made her way out of there pretty quick. She figured she'd never see Brandon again, but after a few weeks of phone calls and invitations, Reanna had become tight with Brandon again—she and her brother were hanging out with him practically every day. Reanna was worried that Brandon could convince her that he was a male somehow, that their romance could start all over, that she would fall back in love with him, but she didn't let Brandon know that.

21

BRANDON MOVED IN WITH HIS GRANDMOTHER DORIS for A while. It was the most logical place to stay, it was free, and he could come and go as he pleased, often crashing with Sara or Gina or whoever he happened to be with. His half cousin Maury, who was around his age, lived with Doris too. Doris was the type never to say no to a family member, and she was tolerant— she'd make jokes about having "two faggots" living with her, but she really didn't judge the kids. Whatever they did was OK as long as they worked and kept out of jail. Maury was flamboyantly gay, the kind of guy who drove around in his boyfriend's Lincoln Town Car just trying to show him off. Brandon was more of the shy type, very self-conscious and private about his sex life.

It was early 1993 when Maury had moved to Lincoln from northern Nebraska. He was a party guy who made Brandon familiar with the loop and with the Run, a gay bar in Omaha. Brandon needed Maury's friendship, he wanted his cousin's approval, and interestingly enough, he gave Maury the money to buy his first pair of freedom rings, multi-color rings that signify a person's sexual alternativeness. Brandon had no problem with Maury's gayness, it was female homosexuality that revolted him.

"He hated lesbians; he was totally against lesbians," Reanna would later insist. "He told me a story about how his sister got pregnant by a black guy and gave her baby up to lesbians. He just sat there and was just dogging on that forever."

By then, Brandon was intensely in love with Gina Bartu, a lovely young girl who he met through Maury. They were a hot item, Brandon and Gina, but in the beginning, Gina wasn't totally sure about the relationship. She loved him but wouldn't sleep with him for the longest time. Gina only had one other boyfriend before him, and she made the guy wait nine months to have intercourse.

When she met him, Brandon had just gotten out of jail.

He said it was for some speeding violation, and Gina never questioned it. If he had been some big burly guy, she might have thought twice, but with Brandon, he was so sweet and innocent looking, in her mind, there was no way he could be a troublemaker.

Coming from a solid middle-class background, already nineteen years old, Gina really didn't belong with a guy who had no goals, no career to speak of. She was looking for stability in a man, for someone she would be proud to spend her life with. But she just couldn't resist him. Whatever trouble Brandon had been in, however unclear his future was, all that was irrelevant. He treated her like gold.

Gina had no way of knowing that Brandon was constantly running from anything and anyone that reminded him of his former life. Even though she brought him up to her parent's suburban home, Gina didn't get to meet his family for quite a while, mostly because he started to move around a lot, staying a few days here, a few days there. He was never living at Doris' long enough to bring her over, and when he spoke of JoAnn and Tammy, he made them seem distant, more like echoes from his past.

Eventually Brandon and Gina moved in with Reanna and Allen; the four of them shared a place at Chaney Trailer Park over on 27th Street. They were a nineties kind of family—everybody vaguely connected, held together by need rather than blood, just trying to make ends meet.

Brandon and Allen got jobs selling Kirby vacuum cleaners, which seemed to bring in decent money at the time. Gina still kept her room in the dorm at the Lincoln School of Commerce—that way, when her parents called, they'd get her machine. It was easier not to tell them anything; they would never approve of her living with a guy.

Actually, when Gina first met Brandon, he was going out with Danielle, a heavy-set girl who was so in love with him that she started tracking him and Gina down, following them through the streets of Lincoln. Brandon couldn't seem to shake her, and finally, he threatened to call the police.

It wound up being Gina who made the police complaint, and that was more or less the last they saw of Danielle until one day when she showed up at Gina's dorm, pounding on the door, begging Brandon to come out, to talk to her, to take her back. The girl made so much noise that the dorm director got involved, and Brandon was almost banned from the premises. He finally had to confront Danielle and make her understand they were never going to get back together again. It was over. He loved Gina.

In their first months together, Brandon worked at Highland Lumber, and Gina would drive by and watch him in his hard hat, laboring with huge stacks of wood. She loved seeing him out there with the dirt and grime. It was sexy.

One day he had Gina come to the lumberyard for lunch. She wore a dress and heels, and the men were all eyeballing her. When they found out she was Brandon's girlfriend, none of them could believe it. Brandon was just loving it, especially when Gina told them they were in love.

Gina was impressed by how much Brandon noticed things about her. He commented about everything she did or said, always complimenting her, going on and on about how great she was. The first time they kissed, he told her there was never anybody who kissed him the way she did, that she was so sensuous, he could melt in her arms. He told her what wonderful lips she had, what wonderful eyes.

"I felt like I was a princess or a queen or something, just the way he would touch me," Gina confided. "He would stroke my face with his fingers, just the outline of my face, and play with my hair. He loved to sit there and just stare at me."

"What do you want to say?" she would ask him.

"Nothing. I'm just looking at you. I'm just admiring your beauty."

She'd never had a guy do that before. It made her heart pound. Rick, the one guy she had been involved with, wasn't romantic that way. He'd say "I love you" almost as an obligatory response in bed. He never bought Gina flowers, never really paid her attention. Rick liked to drink and would always be out partying with his friends. He would often leave Gina hanging by the telephone, waiting to find out if they had plans.

But Brandon was just the opposite. He couldn't get enough of Gina. He was always bragging about her to everybody, telling people how smart she was, proud that she was on the dean's list, a straight-A student. Rick had taken all that for granted. Gina didn't realize it was such an accomplishment until Brandon made her see it.

The first night they met, Brandon and Maury had taken her to a party. They rode in a sports car together, Gina sitting on Brandon's lap. They stayed out so late that the two guys wound up sneaking into Gina's dorm room and crashing there. Brandon and Gina slept next to each other, kissing and laughing all night. It set the pace for the closeness the two would always feel, for the love they shared without having to boil everything down to orgasm.

A few days after they met, Gina took Brandon to meet her parents. She didn't even know his last name, and when her dad asked, she felt stupid for being so negligent, but Brandon was the kind of guy that overwhelmed her. He was the kind that had her thinking, *Where've you been all my life?*

Brandon told them his last name was Brayman, an Irish name. Later he would confess to Gina that his last name was really Brandon, that he was born with the name Ten-a, which he hated. It would be the first of many changed stories that Gina would hear.

After they toured the house, Gina's mom gently pulled her aside to reprimand her. She didn't approve of her daughter's behavior—Gina seemed too familiar with this young boy, a virtual stranger.

"He looks like he's twelve years old. Are you sure you're not baby-sitting this guy?" her mom prodded.

"Mom, he's older than me. He's twenty."

"No way. Are you serious? He looks so young, like a little kid."

"Well, he's twenty."
"He's kind of all over you, don't you think, Gina?"
"What do you mean?"
"He follows you, and he has to touch you all the time."
"So what? I like it, I like every second of it."
"OK, I just think it's a bit much."
"I don't want him away from me, Mom. You're being ridiculous."
"Well; I guess he seems nice," her mom conceded.

They stayed at the Bartus' for about an hour. The visit didn't turn out to be monumental.

Gina's dad never said a word; Brandon had seemed nervous around him.

Afterward, they cruised around Crete, her hometown, and Brandon told Gina what great parents she had, how much he liked her home. It turned out that Pius X and Crete were big rival schools, and they both wondered how it was they had never met before, certain that their paths had crossed many times without knowing it.

"You have everything I've looked for in a girl, everything," he told her. "I just hope that I am with you forever. I would give anything to stay with you."

"Well, you don't have to worry about that. You're with me now."

"I know, I know. I just don't ever want to lose you."

"You're not going to."

Although she thought Brandon was going a little overboard, Gina did have most of the same feelings. They started seeing each other every second they could.

* * *

A constant theme in Brandon's life was theft. Although he worked, he continued to steal from people he knew, forging checks on Doris' account, running up $895 on Sara's ATM card. By mid-1993, the criminal activity was completely out of hand, and at the end of that year, Brandon had been charged with eighteen crimes, mostly forgery and failure to appear in court. Of course, Brandon saw no wrong in stealing because everything he took went to the one he loved. He was the ultimate giver.

Of all the girlfriends he ever had—and there were numerous one-nighters between Heather and Reanna—it was the dark-haired, dark-eyed Gina who was the most appealing, the most like him. As far as Brandon was concerned, she was the greatest thing that walked the planet. There just couldn't be a more perfect fit. She was a real Nebraska farm girl, she held down a full-time job, and she had a killer body. She was marriage material. It was only a matter of time before he would pop the question.

22

"I COULDN'T BELIEVE THAT I COULD FIND SOMEBODY like this, someone who could make me feel just wonderful and didn't care about the sex. I didn't see that as something that needed to happen until after we were married," Gina remembered. "I mean it was OK to sleep in the same bed and whatnot, but in the beginning, I always kept my bra and underwear on and I just thought maybe he was the same way."

Gina was sure the sex would come eventually, thrilled that Brandon was being considerate in the interim. He was the guy she always dreamed of. She knew someone like him would come along, but her mother was right, he *did* look very young. Gina half-convinced herself that perhaps he was late in going through puberty, that he was one of those people who didn't mature at the usual age.

"I was thinking that at twenty, maybe he should be showing some facial hair or something. Maybe that's what I was naive about," she confessed. "I thought he was developing slowly. I wasn't feeling any parts on his body, I mean, any parts that would have clicked."

To her friends, Gina swore Brandon never touched her in a way that would have aroused her. She denied having a sexual relationship, even though people would see cards from Brandon that talked about how horny he was.

"It's just caressing, more emotional than physical," Gina would insist. "He shows me the affection I've always wanted, and sex isn't even something that I'm thinking about."

Sometimes Brandon couldn't sleep, he was so into holding and caressing Gina. He would do it all night, long after she fell asleep. Gina thought it was great; she loved being worshiped in bed. Although she had told herself that she was never going to live with a guy, from the moment she met him, he was starting to move in, leaving clothes and toiletries in her dorm.

When Brandon finally got his own place with Reanna and Allen, he was able to reel Gina in gradually, always encouraging her to leave her things there, setting up a makeup area for her in the bathroom, a hanging space in the closet, and plenty of room in his dresser drawers. He wanted her there with him every night. He told her she'd be safer there. So Gina just kind of got caught up in it. She loved being with him, she needed him so much, and because she was paying for college on her own, she eventually decided to ditch the dorm room. She didn't need to incur that expense when she could put the money toward food or something at Brandon's.

"Mom, I moved out of the dorm," Gina confessed to her mother about two weeks later.

"What are you trying to tell me?"

"I moved everything out, and I'm not going back. I'm living with Brandon."

"What do you mean? There's no way on earth we'd allow that."

"Mom, this is what I want."

"Well, it's not right. This isn't how you were raised. How could you, Gina? Are you getting married to this guy?"

"We're not sure at this point."

There was dead silence at the other end of the phone.

"Mom, I know this isn't how you perceive the way things should be, but I'm happy."

Gina's mom went into a tirade, sure that her daughter was being taken advantage of, certain that Gina was Brandon's maid, Brandon's cook. She told her daughter that people would see her as a tramp, reminded her that she wasn't raised without morals. Even though Gina told her mother the way it was, that people could live together and still respect each other, her mother wouldn't listen to reason. As far as Mrs. Barto was concerned, until Gina moved into her own place, she no longer had a daughter. The two of them had a screaming match, and in the end, Gina felt guilty as hell. Still, when she hung up the phone, she knew she was right; she had a great thing with Brandon. *He* was the one who cooked and cleaned and he was the one who paid the bills.

Not long after Gina moved into the trailer park, Sara and Drew came by to meet the person they'd been hearing so much about. Immediately, Gina thought Sara was stuck up, and she didn't like Drew; neither of them was her type. She didn't want them hanging around.

Whenever she and Brandon would go over to Sara and Drew's place, Gina would make excuses to get out of there as quickly as possible. She didn't like the part of town they lived in, their apartment complex was noisy, she always had a complaint. Drew talked about a hundred miles an hour, never letting anyone else get a word in edgewise, which was another thing she couldn't stand. Sometimes Gina would get so exasperated over there that she'd just fall asleep on them.

Brandon would wind up carrying her out in his arms, carrying her down their long flight of stairs.

What Gina wanted was Brandon all to herself. Between work and school, she didn't have a whole lot of time to be with him, and she didn't want to share any of it with others, especially Sara and Drew.

All through their relationship, Brandon was the perfect gentleman, always good to her, always taking her out to eat, opening up car doors, never letting her pay for anything. Gina found herself falling more in love every day, more emotionally attached to him, unable to get by without him.

Never mind that he was demanding and overbearing beyond belief. Gina just figured that was part of the territory. It was worth it, but Gina's friends didn't think so. They noticed a change in her. She seemed to have lost her identity, lost all outside interests. She wasn't fun anymore. She had no time for anyone else, and it all seemed unhealthy. Her friend Amy tried to tell her to take it slowly, tried to warn her that Brandon was getting too possessive, but Gina never had time to listen. She was too busy being showered with gifts. At home, he'd bring her flowers; at work, it was fancy food and all kinds of chocolate.

One day some new guy at work spotted Brandon and asked Gina who her girlfriend was, and Gina couldn't believe it. Brandon didn't look like a *girl* and she couldn't understand why anyone would think that. She was flustered.

"How can somebody say that?" Gina asked Brandon later that night. "That's just really mean."

Just like a guy, Brandon didn't have a response. He just thought it was funny.

Whenever the subject of sex came up, Brandon made it sound like he was tired of being an object, describing the way Danielle made him "do it" all the time, telling Gina how he would wake up in the morning and find Danielle's hand down his crotch, how he hated it, how fat and disgusting she was.

"He just made it sound like the only thing these other girls wanted was sex, that they wanted him for his body and not for who he was on the inside," Gina recalled. "The more I didn't want to go down his pants and want sex, the more he praised me for it."

Brandon was tired of all these girls using him for his money, he told Gina, and he made a big deal about it. She felt sorry for him; she couldn't understand how girls could treat him so badly, how they could just use him to get gifts and then toss him aside.

"If they needed money, needed food, needed anything, he would do it, he would do anything for them," Gina explained. "I told him I wasn't going out with him for the material things he could give me, that I was with him for who he was on the inside."

"I want to give you expensive jewelry. I just can't do it right now, but I will," Brandon would often tell her when they'd pass by a shop.

"That's great, honey. I'd love to have jewelry, but that's not really what I want from you. That's not going to make me stay with you," Gina would coo. "I'm not going to make you give me things. It doesn't matter to me."

But it mattered to Brandon.

Rather than allowing her to buy groceries, he forged checks, and when he got caught, it was Gina he called from the county jail.

On May 28, 1993, Gina posted $100 to bail him out, confronting the name Teena Renae Brandon for the first time.

It was a shock to her, and Brandon tried to explain his way out of it, finally confessing that he hadn't yet had the operation, vowing that he had already taken steps to start the procedure, explaining that living as a man and going through counseling sessions was a requirement first. Brandon never told her that he had given up on the counseling a long time before. He let her think he was active in sessions during the day, that he was following through with psychological treatment while she was at work.

"He told me how all his other girlfriends had treated him like crap when they found out, and it made me really angry," Gina would later relate. "I started thinking, *What does it really matter what a person is like physically?* He was a man to me, and I'd never been happier in my life. I told him to get the operation if that's what he wanted to do. I said I'd stay with him."

Brandon told her he had already scheduled the bilateral mastectomy for later June, but when that day came and went, he weaseled around the topic, saying he just didn't have the money, that he would have to reschedule it. As time passed and Gina pressed him, he ultimately admitted that he wasn't sure he could go through with the sex change.

Gina was bewildered.

"All you care about is what society thinks," he argued.

"You think I have to fit society's definition of a man instead of accepting the man that I am."

"If you aren't going to do it, then this has got to end," she told him. "It would just be too hard for me to deal with it otherwise."

But then came the proposal.

Brandon had already tattooed her name on his arm. He had proclaimed his love for her so many times. Of course, he didn't have a ring yet, but he wanted her to be his wife.

Gina was torn, but she said yes.

Brandon rented three rooms at the Harvester Hotel to celebrate. He was the last of the big spenders, charging everything he could to the room, even cigarettes and film.

They had maybe thirty people up, filled the hot tub with beer and ice, and had a slew of pizzas delivered. He even rented a tux for the occasion. Then at just the right moment, he ordered everyone to be quiet and he got down on bended knee, took Gina's hand, and made it official.

"Brandon made a speech about how he was settling down," Kendell Hawthorne recalled. "We all saw him as a ladies' man, but now he said it was time for him to stop looking. Gina was loving it."

They set the date for May 28, 1994, one year from the day she had bailed him out. They thought it was fitting. He belonged to her.

Then all of a sudden, Gina got cold feet. She realized he was saying little or nothing about the surgery, and from what she understood, there was no way anyone could create a fully functioning penis, yet here she had Brandon insisting it could be done, that it was being done every day in Europe. She couldn't imagine what her life would be like without him, but she needed to know the truth.

"Of course it bothered me," Gina would later confess. "People believe what they want to when they're in love, you know? I mean, I just couldn't understand why a girl would trick you into that if she knew you liked the opposite sex."

It was one of the stormiest summers in Lincoln's history: straight-line winds had tumbled fences, damaged roofs, and downed trees in their wake. Maybe it was the weather, the changing winds that affected her. Maybe Gina felt whipped and uprooted herself. Now she needed time to think.

In August, to her parents' delight, she got herself a one-bedroom apartment on N Street. It was the first floor of a quaint house in a good neighborhood, and she felt it was ideal. For one thing, she had her freedom again, and she could call whomever she pleased. Brandon had always been so jealous. He'd hang up the phone whenever she called a male friend, and she resented it, particularly when Brandon had all these girls calling, people like Lindsey and Daphne and other names she never heard of. The way Brandon saw it, it was OK for him, but not OK for her, and Gina hated that.

Of course, Brandon practically moved in with her from the get-go anyway. He was always around; always spending the night, and Gina let him. Every time she tried to send him on his way, he'd come across with jewelry, clothes, party supplies. He was an endless source of giving.

But it wasn't enough anymore—Gina felt stuck.

In desperation, Brandon went out and charged a diamond ring for her, popping the question a second time as she opened the black velvet box.

"What were you thinking? We're not getting married, Brandon," she reminded him.

"I always told you I'd come through with a ring. Now you have to marry me," he said, half joking, half serious.

On September 3, 1993, Gina received another call from the Lancaster County Jail. Brandon was in for forgery again.

She agreed to bail him out once more, posting $150 that she didn't really have, but it was OK, she told herself, because this time would be the last.

As the weeks in September dragged on, Gina grew more and more suspicious of him. She wanted to trust Brandon, but when she discovered he was served yet another forgery ticket for writing a $135 check on the account of Christopher Holland, that was the last straw. To the court, Teena Brandon claimed that her aunt had just died, that she had to attend a funeral, and she somehow got released on $150 bail and got a continuance on a trial. But with Gina, those lies weren't going to work; Brandon was going to have to face the music.

Gina had reason to believe that he was using one of her credit cards. It was missing from her wallet. Sure enough, she soon received a $454 bill from Montgomery Ward. She called the store at the Gateway Mall in Lincoln to have them run a check, and in late September, the day after Brandon was bailed out, Gina received an affidavit of fraudulent credit purchases.

The jewelry, the compact discs, Brandon's menswear, and the diamond ring—*all of it* was on her account.

23

EVEN THOUGH SHE FELT LIKE PRESSING CHARGES, SHE just couldn't.

She still loved him.

Long before Gina caught him for fraud, before they were on the skids, Brandon had become really close with Allen Killbum. They had a special friendship. The two of them confided in each other about their love lives, so they were a support team.

A tall, husky, good-looking young man with wide-set eyes and thick blond hair, Allen had dated a number of women in the past, but he never felt quite right about it. He needed someone to help him out of the closet, and he trusted Brandon.

The first time the subject came up, they were in the car on the way to sell a Kirby vacuum in Ceresco, a farm town about twenty miles north of Lincoln. When Brandon heard about Allen's struggle with his gayness, Brandon broke down. He told Allen he was really a female, that he had female parts, that his female body disgusted him. Allen loved being Brandon's confessor; he couldn't help thinking back to the days when Reanna got her rude awakening, and the idea of hearing it straight from Brandon's mouth was a kick.

It was weird, because as the two of them sat there and described their fears, Allen found out that he and Brandon had more in common than be realized.

In their eyes, everybody in Lincoln seemed to be friends, seemed to know each other, and for both of them, being discovered meant being subjected to gay bashing by the very kids they grew up with, the folks they lived next door to.

As it was, they already had people up in arms, anonymously calling and making rude comments over the phone, driving by their trailer in the middle of the night, sometimes yelling threats, sometimes insults. They knew mostly where it was coming from—neighborhood youths who didn't like having "alternative" people living around them.

The Beenblossom twins, two husky young women, Erin and Alysia, would drive by and harass them the most, yelling "Strap on... strap off," like the commercial, "Clap on... clap off... the clapper." They thought they were so cute.

Brandon's friends hated it. They knew Alysia had tried to beat Brandon up at least once, had thrown him against a fence when she was drunk one night.

"We'd be sitting on the front porch in lawn chairs, and they would be screaming shit when they were driving by, I 05 saying that Gina was a fucking dyke for going out with him," Allen recalls, "and I would chase them down and scream at them."

But the Beenblossoms weren't the only ones they really had to worry about. There were others. There were the people who would stand outside the Run and take cracks at gays, strangers who would pick fights for no reason. Brandon eventually resorted to hiding pepper spray around his neck because of it And in Brandon's case, there were all the people he had stolen from, his former roommates who wanted to get even. The fact that Brandon was rumored to be a girl was only fuel for the fire.

When Allen and Brandon became buddies, Reanna faded out of the scene for a while. She was involved with her new boyfriend, Hank, a young, small-framed guy who she clung to. Eventually, as they got closer, the two of them started spending more time at the trailer, hanging out with the guys.

Because he couldn't seem to get regular work, Hank would sometimes do odd jobs around the place to make himself useful. Like most of the young people in that crowd, he'd work for a few weeks, then get fired or quit, and move on to something else. It was an endless cycle for Brandon's friends, because none of them had any college education or vocational training, none of them had any allegiance or sense of purpose. Gina was the exception.

"Hang up the phone, Reanna, hang it up *now*," Hank urged one day.

"Why? What's your problem?" Reanna asked, confused. "Just get off the phone and go in the bathroom. There's something I want you to see in there before Brandon comes back inside. There's two towels in there. Just pick the top one up and tell me what you see."

When Reanna lifted it, a soft rubbery dildo rolled off the towel. Even though she was afraid to touch it, she had to pick it up off the floor and put it back. No way did she want Brandon to know she'd been there.

It shocked her—it was a more realistic version than what she had seen the first time. It sparked her curiosity.

Living together with him, Reanna had gotten used to seeing Brandon's K-Y Jelly lying around. He wasn't shy about that—in fact, he used to tease her with it, telling her all the things he could do with it, if only she'd let him. Now, suddenly, she felt very funny about seeing this rubbery mass.

All the guesswork about his sex life was gone.

"It looked like a normal-sized penis, but it wasn't the color a normal penis would be—it was a really light peach color," she remembered. "I was really freaked out I took the other towel and picked it up, and I was like, *Oh my God*, look at this. Then I saw Brandon's wallet lying there, and I picked it up and found a bunch of other people's credit cards. I saw this guy's California driver's license and this guy had a really baby face, like Brandon's, only with a mustache." While she was at it, Reanna went through Brandon's pockets, finding Gina's Montgomery Ward card cut in half.

Just then, she heard the front door swing open. Brandon peeked in and offered to clear his stuff out of the bathroom, pushing Reanna aside. Of course, Reanna shoved her way back in there, hoping to catch Brandon with the dildo in his hands. But she didn't see anything.

"I went in there, and it was gone. I was trying to figure out how his mind was working, how he did things," Reanna confided. "I knew he couldn't have come out of the bathroom without me seeing him hide it down his pants, so I hunted around the dresser in the bathroom. I looked behind this square-type mirror on the dresser, and I saw it. It was lying on the floor behind the mirror with a pair of shorts lying on top of it."

Reanna never found out exactly how Brandon packed and used a dildo: to Allen, Brandon disclosed he applied the fake cock to himself with surgical glue.

Although Allen found that very difficult to believe, he had seen some kind of strange glue lying around. At the time, Allen never said anything about it. He figured that was Brandon and Gina's business.

In the weeks following the charge card fiasco, Gina received dozens of letters and cards from him, all of them begging for her forgiveness, for her love.

"I love every secret moment we share. I love waking up in the middle of the night to hear you breathing beside me," Brandon wrote. "I love holding your hand and whispering your name."

Gina's hands shook as she clutched the card. She needed to keep hearing that. Nobody would ever love her as much as Brandon, she was sure.

Brandon did everything he could to find the right words, the right song, the right gift that would be good enough for her. He refused to let her close the door. He told her he'd never replace her, that as long as she needed him, he'd wait for her. He admitted to crying himself to sleep, asking her for just one more night to hold her, just one last time to see her and say good-bye.

He loved her more than ever, he said, and he wanted to mend the relationship. He was ready to do whatever that might take if only she would let him. He apologized for hurting her, for lying to her, for scaring her. He asked her to think of the good times, wished that he could go back and start over fresh.

"I often think of what it would have been like if I had told you the truth from the beginning. Would you have stayed with me or gone away?" he asked.

"I wanted to let you know how good I could treat you before you found out," he insisted. "I honestly never wanted to hurt you or destroy you. I just wanted to be everything to you. I tried so hard to do that."

Brandon promised to send her money orders to cover the credit card bill, told her he was planning to buy a Datsun 280ZX, and mentioned he was taking a girl to her homecoming dance. Gina was miffed. She didn't want him, yet she couldn't stand for anyone else to have him. She took refuge with her ex-boyfriend Rick, spending as much time as possible over at his place, licking her wounds.

When Gina went away to spend a weekend by herself in the country, Brandon couldn't stand it. He tracked her down via telephone to tell her his grandfather had died, that he needed her with him at the funeral. Of course, Gina came running home, only to discover it was a ploy to get her in his arms again. She was livid and felt so hounded she called the police to get him off her property. When the law offered to set up an order of protection from her boyfriend, Gina said she'd consider it.

By the end of October, after having sent Reanna and Allen over to Gina's to act as middlemen, after the constant calls and discussions and letters, Brandon realized he had to let Gina go. When she handed back the diamond ring, Brandon wanted her to know that next time, when he found the next right girl, he would tell her the truth from day one. He thanked her for helping him see his mistakes, for helping him straighten out his life.

The withdrawal process was similar to the type of deal he had gone through with Heather—the suicidal thoughts, the manipulative letters and cards were almost identical. The sorrys, the promises to change—it was the same broken record. At one point, Gina ran into Heather, and they actually compared notes. The two girls shook their heads. They felt sorry for him.

24

"TEENA, IF YOU NEED MONEY, WHY DON'T YOU GET A job?"

JoAnn would nudge. "You used to work all the time."

"I have a job at Kirby."

"But you're not really selling anything."

"People don't want expensive vacuums, Mom. It's hard. I'm doing all I can."

"Well what are you doing for money? Writing bad checks?"

"No, I told you. I'm getting blamed for something I didn't do."

"Well, if you didn't do anything, why do you have to appear in court? This is serious, Teena—I mean, because you could wind up in jail."

"I really never knew what to say to her. I was scared to say too much because I didn't want to push her away from me. I always wanted contact with her," JoAnn would later reflect. "I didn't want to lose where she was at, because she was moving all over town with Allen and them. She was starting to run with more guys, gay guys."

When JoAnn saw Teena with her new friends, she realized her daughter had shifted into high gear. Teena looked more masculine, she had taken up weight lifting, she had become a he, at least on the exterior, and that was shocking. Teena would brag about being able to lift a 200-pound guy into the air, and JoAnn thought it was unreal, even though it kind of went in one ear and out the other. If Teena wanted to be a guy, fine. If she wanted a sex change, that was OK too. It didn't matter to JoAnn either way. She just wanted Teena to stay safe.

"Back then you were hearing reports that there was a gay man in Omaha found dead or another gay guy beaten. It was always something to do with their sexual identity," JoAnn recalled. "People are cruel and mean, and if you're different, people don't want to deal with it, so I was afraid for her." For most of 1993, JoAnn and Tammy had used a system with Teena called tough love as a way to try to help. The theory was, if they turned her away, it would force Teena to get her act together. If Teena was going to be a thief, her family didn't have to encourage that conduct by bailing her out and giving her a free place to live. They both thought that by letting Teena sit there behind bars, maybe she would straighten up and fly right. But it backfired.

As it was, Teena would go to Tammy every week asking for money, and Tammy would hesitate, but she couldn't say no. She'd always fork it out, and tough love would go right out the window.

"We try this tough love, and of course it doesn't work, because we have other people interfering, like Doris bails her out of jail after we told her not to," Tammy complained. "Teena didn't need to be out writing checks to get money. She knew she had a family, that she could always count on us to be with her. We tried to do things together at home to keep her out of trouble, we'd watch , go out to eat, but she never stuck around that much."

What made matters worse was that Teena never paid anything back. She acted like she had it coming to her. A waitress in a twenty-four-hour coffeehouse, Tammy worked hard for her dollars. But still, she knew Teena needed the money, that her sister had a difficult time keeping a job because of her mixed identity. Teena had all those fake I.D.'s, but none of it could get past an employer, and she absolutely refused to work as a female. She just couldn't.

"I asked her several times why she couldn't be Teena Brandon and keep a job under that name, you know, and be whoever she wanted to be outside of work," Tammy remembers, "but Teena just said it wouldn't work."

Tammy thought her sister was using the money for basic needs like food, but she was actually using it to buy her friends gifts. Tammy hated that her tips were going to someone who didn't even appreciate it. She couldn't understand how her sister had become a virtual thief, having no regard for other people's money.

"Why are you doing this?" Tammy finally asked her. "Why are you taking people's checkbooks? You know you'll get caught again."

"I don't know why," Teena said blankly. "I'm really confused."

"Well, it's just *killing* Mom."

"I know that"

But every time the subject would come up, Teena managed to change it without giving Tammy any concrete answers or solutions.

"I told her she'd wind up in the women's penitentiary, and she was afraid of being in jail," Tammy disclosed. "I know she wanted to get out of all this trouble. I know she wanted to change the way her life was going, but I think she got stuck in this mode, you know. She thought she had nowhere to turn, nowhere to go."

It was late October when Brandon hooked up with Daphne Gugat, a tall, thin, attractive eighteen-year-old blonde who was always out for a good time. Daphne was Allen Killbum's friend, and Brandon had met her through Allen. The two of them became casual lovers. Daphne says it was never more than just kissing, but others say they spent a lot of time in the bedroom together.

Right around Halloween, Daphne said she needed a roommate, and Allen decided to move into her place over at 32nd and Adams. For Brandon, it was a familiar location, right across from JoAnn's. He spent many a night over there, eating pizzas, getting drunk, taking the whole bunch with him over to the Run. Rumor had it he was half in love with Daphne, and she seemed to be crazy about him, but later she would deny that, claiming she only thought of Brandon as a friend, nothing more.

"I thought he was a little kid. I seriously didn't think he was old enough to be driving a car," Daphne insisted. "The first time I met him, when Allen and Brandon left to go get cigarettes, I asked Reanna what the story was, but she didn't tell me the whole truth. I thought Brandon looked like a pretty boy."

The fact was, Brandon was still so madly in love with Gina, he would use anyone to make her jealous, and Daphne was just one of a number of girls in the mix.

"We tried dating for a while, but that didn't work because we were just too much alike—he wanted to be the boss and so did I," Daphne admitted. "I guess I was just somebody to fall back on because Brandon and Gina were breaking up."

Whenever he had the chance, Brandon would sneak off to Gina's work, sending up a rose or T-shirt with Reanna or a card with Allen. There was definitely still love there on both sides—she still drove around with a Gina and Brandon bumper sticker on the back of her car, and he still spent as much time kissing up to her as possible.

"When Gina would throw him out, that's when Brandon would go over to Daphne's," Reanna remembers.

Daphne was fun—she threw wild parties, had people over all the time—but she was a user. According to Allen, when he moved in, the first thing he did was go out and buy $200 worth of groceries with her, and although Daphne promised to get to an ATM machine to pay for part of it, she never did.

It turned out that Allen couldn't handle the living arrangements for very long. He says he was paying for everything—the food, the cleaning supplies. Daphne sponged off him for a month or so, then he finally couldn't stand it anymore.

"I never trusted Daphne. The only reason she stayed with Brandon is because he gave her anything she wanted," Allen complained. "I was just getting sick of this whole trailer park scene. There was always fights in the trailer park. Everybody knew everybody, and if something happened, people would stick together and then fight. It was just trash, and I was above that."

Daphne didn't need Allen anyway. She had a number of roommates, including her best friend, Lindsay Classen, to support her. She and Lindsay were inseparable, closer than most sisters. They had everything in common.

The two young women spent a lot of time talking about Brandon. They thought he was just so adorable, so perfect. They loved getting all that attention from him even after they figured out that he was a girl, or a hermaphrodite, as they came to understand. Of course that didn't matter. They loved Brandon. They were always *Can you do this for me? Can you do that for me?* and Brandon was only too happy to comply.

When Gina found out about them, about who Brandon was hanging out with, it sickened her. It would anger her to hear how he allowed himself to be used that way. Gina warned him, told him to get rid of these babes, but Brandon insisted that they were like little sisters. They needed him.

"They would go to his place, sleep in his bed, and he would have to sleep on the couch. They would want any money he had so they could buy food and cigarettes," Gina recalled. "Daphne would ask for money for her rent, and he would give it to her. He would go way out of his way for people. He was too nice, way too nice."

Brandon's spending habits particularly enraged Gina because he still hadn't paid her back for bailing him out. He told her he was selling a vacuum a day, that he was making a $250 profit from each sale, yet he never had any money for her.

At one point, Gina went on vacation and got strapped for cash, so she called Brandon. He promised to wire her money, but she checked in at Western Union for three days and wound up having to call him again. Finally, Brandon withdrew money from some guy's ATM account so he could get it to her. When Gina found out about it, that was the last straw.

"Brandon, I told you, never do that," she scolded.

"Well, I needed to give you the money," he argued.

"You knew what you were doing was wrong."

"Yeah."

"I'm sure there are other things you can do to get money. other jobs."

"Yeah."

But his words didn't mean as much anymore. Gina was fed up.

Brandon still cared, but now that he had Daphne to focus on, he threw himself into her scene. Daphne was going through a life crisis; he was helping her get over her ex-boyfriend. When Brandon would hear rumors that Daphne was bragging about him as being a great lover, he loved it.

He needed people to think they were having all kinds of sex. That way people would believe he was a guy.

At one point, Daphne took it so far as to claim Brandon got her pregnant, and of course, Brandon played the role to the hilt, swearing he used protection, that it couldn't be his kid.

"Brandon's the only one I've had sex with, so it's got to be his," Daphne announced in front of everyone one afternoon.

"So Brandon's going to be a daddy?" Reanna asked.

"Yeah. I took a pregnancy test today, and it's for real."

25

"HE WAS A BIG PART OF MY LIFE" DAPHNE WOULD LATER say. "We were together all the time; we did a lot together. He was somebody that I could rely on, and I didn't want anything happening to Brandon. I didn't want him getting beat up because people might decide he was a freak."

Of course, her friends never really believed for a minute that Daphne was pregnant. Still, it ticked people off the way Daphne wrapped Brandon around her finger. Reanna especially didn't like it, and she went over there one night, hoping to set things straight. As it happened, she brought Heather and one of the Beenblossom twins with her. They stayed outside while Reanna went to talk with Brandon.

"You know I love you to death, Brandon, but I just want you to know something," Reanna blurted out.

"What?"

"I know what you are."

"What are you talking about?"

"What your *mom* talked to me about."

But Brandon played dumb, and Reanna was forced to change the subject.

When Reanna got back outside, Daphne had just pulled up with Carrie Gross, her buddy from Humbolt.

"Daphne, you're just a fucking lesbian, so why don't you stop playing these little games, because we all know it," Reanna taunted.

"That's right, I stick my nose in fucking crotches," Daphne sneered. "How nice of you to let me know that."

"You're just one big smart-ass, and I should kick your ass right here because you're such a liar," Heather threatened.

"Really? Well, what I'd like to know is like, how dare you guys find me out without even coming out of the closet yourselves?" Daphne snapped.

And the screaming match began.

Instantly, everybody was cursing and ready to fight.

"They were all starting shit with Brandon," Daphne later claimed. "They said they were going to beat the crap out of him. All of them had turned on him because, supposedly, Brandon had stolen money from Allen. But

Brandon never took any money from them because he was too busy stealing money from Lindsay's dad, so that's a fucking lie."

Whatever the case, whether the fighting was about Brandon's sexuality, Brandon's thievery, or both, before it was all over, someone had pulled a knife—and Daphne wound up with a superficial cut.

Although Reanna swears she didn't do it, she was arrested and put into a juvenile detention center for a few days.

When she got out, Daphne had a protection order to keep Reanna 100 feet away, but Brandon didn't think that was necessary. He did everything in his power to get the two of them back on speaking terms, coaxing them to put their differences behind them. And it worked, at least for the moment.

"Reanna has seen every single fight I've gotten into," Daphne later confided, "I used to be a little rebel. I'm not really proud of that."

"That's just how Brandon was; he hated to have enemies," Reanna would recall. "He wanted everybody to like everybody."

Even so, during his last few weeks in Lincoln, everyone around Brandon seemed to do nothing but cause trouble. little by little, all of them were getting known by local law enforcement. At one point, Daphne even wound up in jail for a week in mid-November.

On the day Brandon picked her up from the detention center, the two of them came up with a game plan: Daphne and Brandon would go hide out with Carrie Gross until things blew over. Daphne and Carrie were new friends, and already she had Carrie eating out of her hand. Daphne was sure she could get Carrie to do just about anything.

As far as Daphne was concerned, Carrie was an outsider, a country bumpkin, totally out of her element in Lincoln. Daphne had told her that Brandon was her half-brother, and Carrie actually believed her—Carrie was so gullible.

Daphne figured that staying with her in Humbolt would be a piece of cake.

26

THE NIGHT BEFORE HE LEFT FOR HUMBOLT, BRANDON sat with Reanna over at Lindsay and Daphne's place. They had a pepperoni and cream cheese pizza and guzzled Dr. Pepper, watching *Pure Country* with George Straight. Reanna had no idea why he and Daphne were up and leaving. Even though they had had their differences, she wanted him to stick around.

"I made him promise me that he was going to write to me and call me when he was up there," Reanna remembered. "But he didn't. He didn't write me at all. He called me once and it was like hi and bye."

Humbolt is way down in Richardson County at the southeast tip of the state, where Nebraska comes down like the edge of a skirt. It feels like somewhere back in time, almost like the Wild West—you can just imagine Jesse James riding through, and some say he did.

Beyond that, Humbolt is a spot on the map—far from civilization—140 miles from Kansas City, 80 from Lincoln, 85 from Omaha. It's a hog feeding and farming town, and outside of a few agricultural industries and some small retail businesses, there's not a whole lot going on there.

For the 1,003 inhabitants, there's a VFW Club and Mike's Tavern, but if you want any real action, you have to go to Falls City or Rulo, where the restaurants, bars, and gambling are.

When Brandon and Daphne arrived, they didn't even see Humbolt. It was one of the coldest autumns in Nebraska on record, so they saw nothing but bleak winter farmland. Carrie brought them directly to Lisa Lambert's farmhouse, a tiny gray one-story shack with three small bedrooms just two miles south of town.

Lisa rented the place for $125 a month, so she could afford to be gracious, and she let friends stay there for little or no charge. Carrie Gross and her boyfriend Mike Lang were already living there off and on, so hosting Carrie's friends wasn't a big deal. Daphne seemed sweet and Lisa liked Brandon. She thought he was so cute; she loved his slicked-back hair.

A beautiful young woman with long sandy blond hair and striking turquoise eyes, Lisa really had just come into her own. She had just turned twenty-four, and she finally felt like a woman. She thought Brandon might be a little too young for her, but then, something about him seemed so right. He was the perfect size: small framed, not too muscular, and lean. Then there was the added bonus of his personality: the way he acted around Tanner, her seven-month-old son; it was obvious that Brandon automatically took to the child. Being a single parent, Lisa couldn't have been more pleased. It was a great starting point for the two of them.

At the time, Lisa was still half in love with Carrie's good-looking brother Shane; she always would be. But whatever they had once was over. Shane had sort of used her, Lisa knew, but she couldn't stop herself from caring about him.

When she finally found another guy, Troy Newburn, he wound up getting her pregnant and running out on her, so Lisa had just about given up her faith in men by the time she met Brandon. She had decided she was better off without them.

But Brandon was different.

Not long after Brandon appeared, Lisa started having health problems. She only weighed ninety-five pounds, and she was getting sick a lot. She told people there just wasn't enough of her to fight off the flu. As a nursing assistant at the Colonial Acres Nursing Home in Humbolt, Lisa was a trusted and valued employee, but her co-workers were getting concerned about her. Her friend at work, Tammy Dush, a petite young woman herself, finally confronted Lisa about it, but Lisa acted like everything was fine.

"Woman, you need to eat and gain some weight, you're gonna blow away," Tammy scolded.

"I do eat; I eat a lot. You've seen me," Lisa insisted. But that wasn't always true.

"She was just tiny; she'd always been that way. All the people at work were, like, 'She can't lift anyone; she's going to break her back,'" Tammy recalled. "She was getting the flu a lot. I know she ended up in the hospital, and at one point, she told me she weighted eighty-six pounds. There was nothing left on her bones."

Tammy Dush was not merely an acquaintance, she had known Lisa for almost three years.

Herself a single mother, a year younger than Lisa, the two of them were very close.

They confided in each other, especially when they were on the night shift at work, while the old folks were sleeping.

"I wouldn't say she had problems dating guys, I'd say she was probably like the rest of us, always looking for the perfect match," Tammy reflected. "When I first met her, when she was with Shane, she wasn't into getting married, having a family, that kind of thing. But, you know, over the time that I knew her, she was getting into it, getting ready to settle down."

No doubt Lisa wanted someone to act as a parent figure for Tanner. Her father, John Lambert, long divorced from her mom, had found a new woman and had moved to another town, so she didn't see all that much of him. Her mother, Anna Mae, always seemed to give Lisa a hard time, and this was particularly true when it came to Tanner. According to a close friend of the Lamberts, Anna Mae didn't like the idea that her daughter was giving birth to an "illegitimate child."

"She was always down on Lisa. I guess she wanted Lisa to be better than what she was," Lisa's friend reflected.

"Anna Mae's really different. She really screwed up with her daughter. One time she would be for the pregnancy, and the next time she wasn't. She was always rough on Lisa. I don't know if it was because Lisa was an only child or what."

"Her mother expected too much," another pal of Lisa's said. "I'm sure Anna Mae loved Lisa dearly, but I think she was partially ashamed because Lisa wasn't married, and the baby was the result of a one-night or two-night thing."

Whatever the case, Anna Mae must have put her disapproval aside, because when it came time to be a grandma, she adored Tanner. She was present in the delivery room, and from the moment of his birth, she made a big fuss over the child. After Lisa came home with him, her mom helped throw a belated baby shower. She beamed as she watched Lisa open the gifts—newborn toys, baby clothes, all the trappings her beautiful grandson deserved.

That didn't mean, however, that Lisa was off the hook. More than ever, say her friends, Lisa was subjected to Anna Mae's hounding. Anna Mae didn't live in Humbolt. She was still in Pawnee City, about twenty minutes away, so much of her complaining took place by telephone. And Anna Mae could rile Lisa up—often she would call Lisa an unfit mother. When it came to living up to her mom's standards, Lisa just couldn't seem to do anything right.

Maybe that's why Lisa was so drawn to Brandon—he gave her so much positive feedback, made her feel worthwhile.

Brandon saw Lisa as the perfect mother; he was always complimenting her innate abilities, her displays of unconditional love. Naturally, Lisa bragged about Brandon too—he was so wonderful with Tanner, he was so good to her. She loved it best when they just spent time at home relaxing, watching a movie or talking late into the night. She appreciated him being there.

Before she had Tanner, Lisa had been on the run constantly. She had even moved to Phoenix for a few months when she was first pregnant, looking for a more exciting life. But now she didn't need all that. She was happy to be back, just miles away from her hometown. In Humbolt, she knew everybody, and the pace was slow and easy. She didn't care to go out all the time anymore. She didn't think it was a good idea to drag Tanner places. When Brandon told her that he wanted to adopt Tanner, Lisa thought she had found the ideal person.

Tanner was a sick baby. He had been born two months premature, weighing just over four pounds, and he had been in an incubator in a neonatal nursery for a week. At home, he suffered from allergy and respiratory problems, so it was rough going for a while. Lisa had her hands full with Tanner.

She had to take him up to Lincoln once a month to be checked by a specialist. Luckily, Tanner ate a lot and gained weight quickly, and slowly he was building up strength.

Still, under the circumstances, it wasn't easy to be around the baby on a constant basis. He was cranky a lot of the time and that strained the household. Of course, Brandon would never admit he was getting weary, but Lisa could sense it. At first, she didn't question his nights out with the guys—that was to be expected—but then his outings became more frequent.

Shane Keaton hung around Lisa's place a lot. After all, his sister Carrie was there, and he was still big buddies with Lisa, so he had every reason to feel at home. At the time Brandon appeared, Shane was dating a young girl in Falls City, Michelle Travis, so he spent a lot of hours commuting, and it wasn't long before Brandon and his "sister" Daphne were joining him, checking out the possible prospects Falls City might offer.

Not that Brandon didn't want Lisa—he did—but he always had his eyes open. That's just how he was.

Sometimes Shane and Brandon would go down by themselves and would hit the Kwik Shop, a gas station hangout on Harlan Street, probably the best place in town to see and be seen, especially if you're a teenager. After a few weeks, by early December, Brandon connected with Michelle's friend, Kelli Rue, a cute sandy-haired high school girl who flipped over him right away. She couldn't believe that he was twenty; he looked more like a kid. He told her his name was Tenor Ray Brandon, that he went by the name Brandon because it was easier.

The day after they met, Brandon took Kelli roller skating over in St. Jo, Missouri, about a forty-five-minute drive away. They really had a blast and Kelli thought they might fall in love, but then she discovered that Brandon was officially seeing Lisa and instantly pulled away.

As it happened, Kelli and Lisa were good friends—they had known each other for years— and Kelli didn't want to do anything that would hurt her. Still, Kelli didn't stop seeing him completely—Brandon and Lisa were suddenly always fighting, and more often than not, he'd wind up staying at

Michelle Travis's place, partying with the Falls City crowd.

"He just loved to go out and meet people. It seemed like everywhere he went, he met somebody. Lisa would get mad because he'd come to Falls City, and three-fourths of the time he had her car, and he'd be late getting back," Kelli remembered.

Daphne would only occasionally join him. She had become comfortable with Lisa and her friends. There were always good-looking guys hanging around Lisa—just friends—so Daphne had struck gold, and she was happy to stay home. However, as the arguments between Brandon and Lisa intensified, as he pushed harder for a relationship with Kelli, gradually moving more of his stuff to Michelle's in Falls City, Daphne started getting antsy.

In early December, Brandon and Kelli drove her old Thunderbird up to Lincoln so they could be alone together.

Brandon needed Kelli more than ever. At that point he and Lisa were basically through. Lisa had cut him off from using her car because Brandon had gotten into a wreck a few weeks prior. Caught with open alcohol, he was written up for a minor in possession charge.

At the time, Brandon had handed his cousin's driver's license to the officer, presenting himself as Charles Brayman, and lucky for him, it worked. His Richardson County court appearance was scheduled for December 15, but he didn't sweat about it. He figured he'd easily get it reduced to a traffic violation. Days after his appearance, Brandon got stopped for doing seventy-two miles per hour in a fifty-five mile-per-hour zone. Again, he posed as Charles Brayman—none of it fazed him. But when Lisa finally heard about it, she decided she was tired of having *her* car wrapped up in his problems, so now he needed a new set of wheels.

While Brandon and Kelli were up in Lincoln, he never even stopped to see JoAnn or Tammy; instead, he called them from a pay phone at a check-cashing place. As soon as he finished his checking business, he drove Kelli around the city, pointing out the hot spots he planned to take her to, and along the way, he made a special effort to ride by his so-called grandfather's house. It was a mini-mansion in the swankiest neighborhood in town, and Kelli was thoroughly impressed.

Before the ride back, he went into a grocery store and bought three red roses—for Kelli, Carrie, and Lisa. Then Brandon stopped at Lindsay and Daphne's place. He said he just needed to pick up some asthma medication from a friend, and he was in and out of there in five minutes.

When he handed Kelli the rose and said he wanted to get into a relationship with her, that he really cared about her, Kelli hemmed and hawed. On the way home, she admitted that she was still a virgin—she was saving herself for that special someone. Brandon understood that. He totally agreed she should.

27

"BRANDON, I DON'T KNOW WHAT IS RUNNING THROUGH your mind, but it bothers me," Lisa wrote in a lengthy letter. She went on to tell him how much she loved him, insisting that she didn't care what other people thought. All she wanted was not to lose him, Lisa insisted, because he was so important to her and Tanner.

"I thought things were settled between us so that we could go on with our relationship," Lisa said, asking him to give her another chance. She blamed their separation on other people, telling Brandon not to listen, not to let others break them up.

Lisa was obviously upset. She wanted to sit down with Brandon and get everything out in the open. She wanted to make things work out. She hoped he did, too. She apologized for being jealous about his spending so much time in Falls City. Apparently, Lisa felt her romance with Brandon was being threatened by his new alliances there and as far as she was concerned, she wished Brandon had never discovered the place. Whenever she accompanied him down to Falls City, Lisa usually got the feeling she was intruding on his good time.

"Would you please tell me what I am doing wrong?" Lisa wanted to know. She asked him about the upcoming weekend and the plans for his birthday celebration. She told him she'd make sure it was his best birthday ever, that she was willing to go anywhere he wanted. She also mentioned the "problems" they were having in the Humbolt house, saying that everyone in the farmhouse was angry with him because he hurt her so much. Lisa promised, however, that she had smoothed things over with her housemates.

"I have such a sick feeling in my stomach and have not been able to eat because of my nerves," Lisa wrote, begging Brandon to take her back. She felt certain that the two of them could get through anything together. She pleaded for Brandon to call her. She needed to hear his voice so she could feel better.

But Brandon didn't call or write Lisa right away. He was playing games with Lisa's heart and Carrie, for one, didn't like it. Carrie had also written him a compelling letter, telling him to stop the bullshit, insisting that he show some caring and respect. She chided him for staying in Falls City when Tanner was sick and questioned his whole pitch to adopt the baby.

Then there was the issue of the ring. Apparently, Brandon was trying to give away Gina's engagement ring, and Carrie didn't approve. She told Brandon to get Lisa a promise ring if he wanted, to leave Gina's diamond out of it.

They all knew who Gina was. They knew how much Brandon had loved her—he made sure of that by carrying around their "wedding album" in his luggage. It was a book full of pictures from their engagement party, showing Brandon in his tux with Gina glowing beside him. Brandon talked incessantly about his former fiancée, about what went wrong, about the mistakes he made, but Lisa didn't mind that. She thought it was good for him to get it out of his system.

After he read Lisa's letter, Brandon felt guilty, and he did see her that week. The two of them made plans to go to Falls City for his birthday that weekend. Lisa decided to throw him a surprise party and had invited friends from Auburn, Humbolt, and Falls City for a beer bash.

As it turned out, Michelle Travis had a party for him earlier that afternoon, on his big day, December 12. Lisa was there, and she watched Brandon get birthday kisses from every female in the house. Even though Brandon carried things a bit far, picking girls up and slobbering all over them, Lisa was good-hearted about it. After all, you only turn twenty-one once.

"He'd be saying, '*Oh, baby, let's go in the back room.*' He would tease with everybody. He was a great guy," one of the girls at the party remembered. "He was a pervert, just a regular guy, always making jokes, but you know, everybody knew he was with Lisa." Brandon was having such a great time that when people said they were going up to Humbolt, he didn't want to leave with everyone else. Even though there were two car-loads of people from Falls City headed over there, instead of going back with Lisa, he asked her to drop him off at Lana Tisdel's instead. She was a girl he had met at the Oasis the week before his birthday. He promised he'd catch a ride home real soon, but he never made it back. Lisa was just livid about it. She had all these people waiting to yell surprise, and Brandon was a no-show.

In desperation, she called the pay phone at the Falls City Kwik Shop, and got Lana on the phone. Lisa got nasty with her, told her that Brandon was just using her, and Lana hung up on the girl. When she reported the comment to Brandon, Lana was very upset, on the verge of tears, so Brandon picked up the telephone and called Lisa, telling her to stay out of his and Lana's affairs. Lisa denied having called the Kwik Shop. Both of them were yelling, then Lisa got so irate, she threw the phone against the wall. No one at her house could believe it; that was so out of character for her.

"I don't know what happened, but after she threw the phone, we called and talked to him and he said he wasn't coming up," Kelli recalls, "That's when Daphne got mad. She went out to the car and got a folder that was underneath Lisa's seat. She brought it in, took it to the kitchen, and showed Lisa. And then we all found out. There was like tickets in there and a whole bunch of papers saying it was Teena Brandon, Teena R Brandon, tickets that said 'female' on them."

Brandon had popped into the local bar to have a beer in the mirrored dance room, to watch the people on the karaoke stage. When he spotted Lana singing "The Bluest Eyes in Texas," his heart was pounding. Of all the girls he'd known before, Lana had the most sex appeal. He could see it in the way she licked her lips; he could see it in her eyes. He loved her high cheek bones, the squareness of her jaw, her flowing strawberry blond hair, her rail-thin figure. He just wanted to touch her. He had to meet her.

Right after her song, Lana and her entourage got up and left, and Brandon followed them outside. He drove around, undetected, waiting to see where they were headed, and eventually they stopped at the Kwik Shop. Brandon watched as an older woman got out with two other girls. Just his luck, Lana had stayed in the car. There was someone else in there with her, it was Rhonda McKenzie, John Lotter's girlfriend, but that was OK. Brandon pounced on Lana without missing a beat.

"I've been looking for you all over. I wanted to find you," Brandon told her as he leaned into the car window.

"Why?" she asked, jolted by his brazen attitude.

"I don't know. I just wanted to find you and talk to you. What's your name?"

"Lana."

"Will you come out and talk with me a minute?"

"I don't know," Lana said, rolling down the window a little bit more.

"I've been looking for you for about a month. I've been watching you sing karaoke at the Oasis and you've never even known it."

"Really? I've never seen you there before."

"Well, I've seen you. You're so beautiful, honey. You're such a babe. I'm sure all the guys tell you that."

"They don't."

"Why? You're the most beautiful girl in this whole town. I want you to go out with me."

"What was your name again?"

"Brandon."

"How old are you?"

"Twenty."

"Well, let me think about it."

"I want you to think about it now, baby. What are you doing tonight?"

When Lana first saw him, she thought Brandon might be a girl, but then when he talked, he sounded like a man. She was attracted to him, not only because of his baby face and sparkling blue eyes, but because he was well dressed and really polite. The guys Lana knew in Falls City weren't like that. They weren't like that at all.

Lana thought he was a sweetheart, and after a few minutes, she agreed to have him over that night. When her mom, Linda, had finally come out with a bag of ice, she and the girls were ready to party.

At the Tisdel house, just a few blocks away on 21st Street, Lana served Brandon beer and chips. She couldn't do enough for him. Actually, she was up and down all night, busy playing hostess to the whole bunch. Lana loved to have people at the house, and Brandon seemed to get along with everybody, which was great. Tom Nissen was there with Missy, Linda's half-sister, and John Lotter and his sister Michelle were around, as usual—the Lotters were like family to Lana.

Leslie and Linda took an immediate liking to Brandon. He was first class, they told him, and he was welcome to stay with them anytime. They wanted him there. He was the kind of guy Lana belonged with.

So even though Lisa was still in the picture, even though Kelli was still in the background, Lana and Brandon had hit the ground running. On their second night together, they were already doing some heavy kissing, and Brandon was thinking of ways to get out of Lisa's clutches for good.

At nineteen, Lana was more sexually experienced than anyone Brandon had been with before. When the two of them started sleeping together, it was like heaven. She was the best there was in bed, and Brandon couldn't stop fantasizing about her.

28

AT 9:00 A.M. ON DECEMBER 14, TWO DAYS AFTER HER twenty-first birthday, Teena R. Brandon failed to appear in the Lancaster County Court for a preliminary hearing regarding her 1992 forgery conviction. When she had pleaded guilty on April 15 the year before, the judge had sentenced her to a lengthy probation, and Brandon had intentionally violated the conditions set forth.

Back in August 1993, Daniel Jarzynka, the district court probation officer in Lancaster County, had submitted the following report to the county attorney, delineating Teena Brandon's reckless regard for the law:

DATE OF PROBATION: From 4-15-92 to 10-15-93
CONVICTED CHARGE: Second-degree forgery (class IV felony)
ALLEGED CONDITIONS VIOLATED: #3, #13, #14, and #17

Condition 3: Must report in writing and/or in person. Since being placed under probation with this office on April 15, 1992, Ms. Brandon had failed to appear for seven (7) scheduled appointments.

Condition 13: Shall not use or have in her possession any alcoholic beverages.

On March 25, 1993, during a scheduled office appointment, I did question Ms. Brandon if she had consumed or used any alcoholic beverages since our last scheduled appointment, and she acknowledged that she had consumed alcohol, being beer, the previous weekend.

Condition 14: Shall complete her GED within one year.

To this date, Ms. Brandon has still not obtained her GED. In speaking with Greg Sandstrom, the principal at the Bryan Extension Center, he indicated that Teena still has approximately five (5) credits to complete before obtaining her diploma. He went on to add that Ms. Brandon could obtain these five (5) credits in a matter of a few weeks if she applied herself.

Condition 17: Shall satisfactorily attend counseling at the Community Mental Health Center of Lancaster County.

Once again Ms. Brandon has been terminated from attending treatment at the Community Mental Health Center due to her inability to keep appointments with that facility. This is the second alleged probation violation submitted on Ms. Brandon regarding her attendance at the Community Mental Health Center, the first being submitted on January 26, 1993.

Attached to Jarzynka's report was this letter from mental health clinician Dr. Peter Frazier-Koontz:

Dear Mr. Jarzynka,
I first saw Teena Brandon on March 24, 1993, after she had been transferred to me by her previous therapist Deb Bodtke, CMSW. Ms. Bodtke had previously terminated Ms. Brandon on December 28, 1992, for failure to comply with her treatment plan.

My last contact with Ms. Brandon was on June 14, 1993, at which time she admitted to me that she was in counseling only because the court ordered her to be.

She telephoned the Community Mental Health Center at 8:05 on June 21, 1993, to cancel an 8:00 appointment She had previously been a no-show on June 2, 1993.

Because of Ms. Brandon's inability to keep appointments, her statement that she was in treatment only because the court ordered her to be, and her apparent lack of goals, I see no reason to continue her open file.

I am therefore terminating her from treatment. If you have any questions or need additional information, please let me know.

Sincerely yours,
Peter J. Frazier-Koontz, Ph.D.

Also attached was a December 1992 letter Deb Bodtke had sent to Jarzynka, reporting that she had not heard from Teena in over six weeks.

"Teena is responsible for rescheduling appointments if she misses one. She has not followed through on this," Bodtke wrote. "Her motivation during treatment tended to be poor. She told so many different versions of things it was hard to know what to believe. Until her motivation and outlook changes, further therapy is unlikely to be of help."

Bodtke had included some progress reports, noting that Teena Brandon only did what was necessary "to get by."

Bodtke saw no changes in regard to Teena taking responsibility in her personal growth.

She stated that "Teena only goes into things superficially."

In August 1993 Teena Brandon had been ordered to appear in the City-County Building to be arraigned on a motion for revocation of probation but failed to appear. The arraignment was rescheduled for August 18, and on that date, a bench warrant was issued for her.

On September 3, 1993, Teena Brandon was arrested in Lincoln and brought before the Lancaster County Court. A preliminary hearing was set for September 10. It was then continued to October 14 and again continued to December 14, Brandon having written letters of excuse to the court, asking for extensions that had been granted.

On December 14, 1993, when Brandon failed to write, call, or appear in court, a bench warrant was directed to all sheriffs, constables, and peace officers in the state of Nebraska: Teena Brandon was a wanted felon.

Meanwhile, at 2:00 PM on December 15, Teena Brandon appeared before Judge Curtis Maschman in the Richardson County Court for the minor in possession charge. When the court went through the roll call, Brandon acknowledged himself as being Charles W. Brayman. The court advised him of his constitutional rights and proceedings were had, during which Mr. Brayman went on record to plead not guilty. He told the court that he planned to hire an attorney, that he was financially able to afford counsel, and prosecutor Douglas Merz set a pretrial conference date of January 5, 1994. Mr. Brayman was released on his own recognizance with the understanding that Brayman promised to appear.

On December 16, Teena Brandon's gig was up. A few days earlier, when Lisa and Carrie had sifted through Brandon's criminal folder, while they were still trying to get over the shock, Carrie Gross discovered that there was a forged check drawn on her account for $121.35, and she was sure Brandon had done it. Carrie, then pregnant and in need of every penny, went straight to the authorities for help.

It was only a matter of hours before Teena Ray Brandon was tracked down, hauled in on a second-degree forgery charge, and thrown in jail.

"He called me at home and wanted me and Lisa to get him out," Kelli remembered. "We still didn't believe he was a girl, but when they put it in the paper, it said Teena Renee Brandon, and that's when it really started hitting me. She was listed in the woman's jail cell up there, and that's when it started to hit."

Brandon called Kelli a few times, hoping she would help. Brandon never bothered to call Tammy or JoAnn, assuming they'd let him sit there to learn a lesson. While Brandon was in jail (he was there for seven days) Kelli and Lisa were on the phone a lot, incessantly talking about how it could be possible that this person was female. Neither of them could get over it.

"When it all started unraveling, Lisa had said that she found tampon wrappers in the heating vents and stuff like that," Kelli said. "She was wondering where those came from because Carrie was pregnant, Lisa didn't put them in there, and no one else was around."

In the middle of one of their conversations, Brandon broke through on call waiting, and Kelli took the call and told him that she and Lisa had decided to bail him out. But they hadn't. They were still furious with Brandon. They had no desire to see him ever again.

Lisa felt especially foolish because she had intercourse with him—just once, she claimed—yet she never noticed there was anything different or strange. One day after work, she and Tammy Dush went out to a bar and talked about it Lisa seemed embarrassed, yet puzzled. "The only thing I can remember is that we were really, I was really drunk," Lisa told her. "That was the only time anything happened between us."

"Well, I think I'd realize if something was amiss," Tammy said flatly.

"I was just completely loaded. I don't even remember it really happening; all I know is that it did."

Tammy was flabbergasted. She didn't know what else to say.

At 2:00 PM on December 20, Teena Brandon made a felony first appearance before Richardson County Judge Steven Tunm. After the forgery charge was read against her. the court explained the penalty: imprisonment of not more than five years or a fine of not more than $10,000, or both.

Before Teena was sworn in, she requested that counsel be appointed for her at public expense. Prosecutor Doug Merz, counsel for the state of Nebraska, asked Ms. Brandon a number of questions, beginning with her place of employment, which Ms. Brandon claimed was at Peru State College.

She said her earnings were $4.25 an hour, that she took home about $233 a week every two weeks. When asked if she was liable for the support of anyone other than herself, Ms. Brandon told Merz she had an eight month-old baby girl named Jessica, who was staying with her roommate in Humbolt. She said she paid seventy-five dollars a month for rent; she did not give a discernible response when asked what her expenses were for clothing and food and claimed that in the event that she would be released from jail she still had a job waiting for her at Peru State College.

Ms. Brandon then explained to Judge Timm that she had just transferred down to Peru State College two months prior, having lived in Lincoln all her life. When the judge asked if she had ever been convicted of anything other than traffic violations, Ms. Brandon said yes, that she had gotten in trouble through school for forgery on a computer, stating that she got one year's probation and a fine.

Mr. Merz told the court that it was his understanding, after having talked to the local deputy, that the defendant was still on probation and that Lincoln authorities were looking for her. However, Merz had no report of an outstanding warrant, so Judge Timm set a bond of $2,500; $250 would have to be posted in order for Ms. Brandon to get out.

Lana was the one who figured out how to come up with the money, having gotten a signed blank check from her father by telling him it was for a hair perm. She was able to cash it at the Hinky Dinky supermarket right across from the courthouse, but because Lana was underage, it was Tom Nissen who wound up posting Brandon's bond. Tom was doing Lana a favor.

PART THREE

ANATOMY OF RAGE

29

TOM NISSEN WAS BORN MARVIN THOMAS NISSEN AND HE used the name Marvin growing up, but he never liked it very much. He didn't like Falls City for that matter either. He left at age two and didn't return until he was fourteen—at that stage when nothing ever seems good enough.

His mother, Sharon, was from the area. She grew up in Rulo, the ghost of a town nine miles from Falls City. When she was a girl, she thought it was the last place on earth she wanted to live. She never dreamed Rulo would become infamous, *but it did.*

In 1985 on a peaceful August morning, grim-faced FBI agents raided an eighty-acre Rulo farm occupied by a group of religious survivalists led by the self-proclaimed "prophet" Mike Ryan.

When FBI agents uncovered two shallow, unmarked graves, the story of the gruesome cult murders by Ryan and his group of neo-Nazis became national news. Ryan was sentenced to die in the electric chair; currently, he sits on death row. Of course, things have gone back to normal in Rulo since then; people have pretty much erased the monstrous blemish. Others in Nebraska might associate Rulo with cult murder, but the townsfolk put it behind them long ago.

These days, Rulo is a friendly farm town with just two bars, Camp Rulo and the Old Tyme Bar. Both places serve food, and "Camp" has Keno and live music, so people come in from miles around just to hang out and party. Outside of those two places, all the town has is a public library and an auditorium. Locals do their grocery shopping in Falls City or across the Missouri River in Saint Joseph, where the drive is worth it because the prices are more reasonable and there's a better selection.

When she was just fourteen, Sharon got pregnant with her first son, Scott. Originally she was going to let someone adopt her baby, but she couldn't part with the boy. Then a year later, she met Ed Nissen at the Old Time. He was nineteen, four years older and a lot wiser, and even though Sharon wasn't in love, she saw him as her ticket out of there Ed fell head over heels for her. Sharon was everything he wanted: a perfect size 3—she still is—with long blond hair and bewitching sapphire eyes.

They only knew each other a week and a half before they headed to the justice of the peace in Auburn, so there was no time to plan a wedding. Sharon wore a cream-colored dress with cream shoes and went without flowers and veil. Both their moms were there to sign the documents. The women thought Sharon looked about twelve years old—she was so tiny and young at the time—but the kids were determined to be together, and their mothers didn't want to stand in their way.

The day after, Ed took Sharon and Scott to Seattle to live with him and his brother Marvin, and although Ed's brother was sweet to her, Sharon didn't like it there. It rained all the time, and she was homesick.

Ed was a good mechanic, and he made a decent living at it; he soon rented a nice home for the three of them. Sharon was a homemaker. They lived in a two-bedroom house, but she wasn't much of a cleaner or a cook.

Sharon eventually got pregnant. When she gave birth to an eleven-ounce stillborn baby, she was devastated. Ed decided to adopt Scott as a way to pacify her, but it didn't help. Sharon still wanted a little girl, she wanted a baby, but Ed couldn't have cared less. Sharon spent most of her time brooding; she harped on the fact that she was lonely and bored. She felt empty. She hated that Ed was gone a lot, and after a year, Sharon finally forced the issue, and they moved back to Nebraska, renting a two-story house in Falls City right across from the home of her parents, Byron and Fern Miller.

In 1970, Sharon gave birth to a daughter, Susan, which thrilled Ed at the time, until he found out that Sharon wanted another child right away. Ed wasn't too keen on supporting more mouths; besides, when Sharon was pregnant, she had gotten big, and she was sick all the time. She was no fun to be around, and she couldn't fit into those tight jeans anymore; he wanted her figure back the way it was. He told her Susan and Scott were all the kids they needed. Ed was busy in his new job as a cabinet salesman.

He was on the road a lot, so he didn't have much time to spend with her and the kids as it was.

As it happened, on October 22, 1972, the day Sharon went into labor with her third child Marvin Thomas, she drove herself to the hospital because Ed didn't want to interrupt his dinner. She said he didn't believe she was in real labor because it was too soon for her to be giving birth.

When Sharon called him from the hospital to let him know he had a son, she was so mad at him for his indifference, she didn't care if he bothered to show up to see Marvin Thomas or not.

In Falls City, the Nissens lived in a cheery house on Abbot Street with a great big yard, flowers planted out front, a wraparound front porch with a swing, and a huge kitchen done American Colonial style. Susan was always a quiet child. Very obedient, she never had to be spanked or even reprimanded; she was a pleasure.

But the boys were a different story, Sharon said. Scott was always getting hit with the belt for something. Sharon didn't agree with Ed on that, but there was nothing she could do. Ed wanted immediate action, and that was his way to get it. If Scott didn't do a chore, he got hit.

Marvin wasn't as disobedient as he was slow. His father couldn't understand how his boy could get so sidetracked, and Ed would whack Marvin for any little thing and then feel bad about it because the boy was so tiny. As a kid, Marvin was so small framed, he always looked a year younger than his age. Still, Ed couldn't tolerate the boy's idiosyncracies; his son did things that drove him crazy.

"Marvin was slow to eat. He'd still be sitting at the table after everyone was done; after the dishes were done, he'd still be sitting there," Sharon remembers. "He wouldn't eat meat, and I asked the doctor about it. He got a lot of spankings because his dad thought he had to eat meat. You could make him put it in his mouth, and he'd just chew it and chew it, and he would want to gag. I'd wait till his dad left the room, and I'd let him spit it out."

But it wasn't his eating habits that concerned Sharon. It was a lot of other things. Marvin played like a normal child, he rode his tricycle, had his favorite toys. Still, there was just something that was *different*—Sharon never could explain it.

"Like potty training—he'd get up in the morning, I knew he'd have to go because he wouldn't be wet, and he'd sit there for like an hour," Sharon recalls, "He'd have a little ring around his butt. Then the minute I'd tell him, 'All right, you can get up,' he'd stand up and pee on the floor. You'd just want to beat him and sit him back down."

Sharon would later realize it wasn't any one thing that was strange about Marvin; it was almost everything. Just little things, like when Marvin went in to take a bath, he'd sit in there forever, long after the water got ice cold. Sharon would go in and ask him why he was still in there, and Marvin would just shrug his shoulders. At the age of two, he would refuse to get out. Then there was the fact that Marvin hardly ever cried, not even when he got a spanking—that struck her as odd.

In 1974, when Ed announced he was moving the family to Memphis, Sharon had no say on the matter, and within a few weeks, their belongings were packed. They lived in an apartment complex in a Memphis suburb, but Sharon hated it, she had very few friends, she was alone with the kids all the time, and she and Ed seemed to have nothing in common anymore. Ed spent all his time with his work associates. She began to wonder if he was cheating on her.

In 1975, after their unsuccessful move to Memphis and then their return to Falls City once more, Ed and Sharon's marriage was over. According to Sharon, she came home one day to find all of her kids' toys and clothes removed from the house. When she tried to track Ed down, she had no luck.

She was convinced his parents were covering for him, and she was at a loss about what to do.

"I couldn't call the authorities because they were his kids too. I didn't know we were getting a divorce at the time, and he just took 'em," Sharon explained. "He could take his kids and go anywhere because he had as much right to them as I did. There was nothing I could do."

In hope of finding him, Sharon moved back to Memphis, staying with the one good friend she had there, Linda.

Sharon called the schools, she called Ed's job, but she ran into brick walls. It was like her husband dropped off the face of the earth. She took a job as a waitress and just believed he would turn up, then three months later, a policeman appeared at her door serving her divorce papers. Of all things, Ed Nissen had relocated to Eugene, Oregon, and he wanted full custody of the children.

"I had two days to get to Oregon to fight for my kids, and there was no way I could be there. I had no money," Sharon said.

But even after the divorce was final, Ed Nissen wasn't quite through with Sharon. He still had some unfinished business with her, because he started calling Memphis in the middle of the night, harassing her to no end.

"Susan's sick. She needs you," Ed would say. "What's wrong with her?"

"She had a nightmare. She's been up crying all night." "Well, what can I do about it from here?"

"The kids are cryin' for you, Sharon. They wanna know where you're at, why you don't come home."

"He'd call and say, 'I'm going to tell the kids you died,' and then he'd hang up," Sharon confided. "He just drove me out of my mind, so finally I just said, 'I don't give a fuck what you do. You can tell them anything you want. I don't care. They're yours.'"

Sharon considered having the phone changed, but it was in her girlfriend's name, so she really couldn't. Besides, as much as she hated his calls, she wanted him to have her number in case there was a real emergency. Then one morning, she got a call from him saying that he was in West Memphis, that he was on his way to Florida and he wanted to drop the kids off. Ed told her that be didn't want them anymore; he wanted to sign custody over to her.

"He brings them over and we talk, and he's gonna leave them. My friend Linda had three bedrooms, so there was no problem," Sharon remembers. "He was going to leave to get gas and a hamburger, then he came back around seven that night, and he wanted to take them. There was a big fight. He stepped through Linda's door, and he comes out with a gun and sticks it to his head. She thought he was going to shoot it, but then be took the kids and left."

According to Sharon, Ed called again a half hour later. He was somewhere in West Memphis, and he was going to throw the kids over a bridge. That way they wouldn't have to fight about them anymore, that way they wouldn't have to worry about what they'd grow up to be. In a panic, Sharon called the police, but of course, when they got to the location she described, Ed and the kids were nowhere to be found.

"It got to be an obsession with him, that they were his kids, and I started to think that he would hurt them if I kept butting in, so there were years I didn't see them," Sharon admitted.

She stayed in Memphis for a few more months, long enough to decide she liked it better back in Falls City. When Sharon got home, she fell madly in love with a younger man, Bob Popejoy. She married him, not once, but twice. He was a big drinker and had had some trouble with the law, so Sharon had her hands full with Bob. There wasn't much time to think about anything else.

In the summer of 1978, she finally hooked up with her kids in California. She was out there on holiday, and Ed brought them down from Oregon so they could all go to Disneyland Marvin still has the picture of him and his mom sitting in a giant red and white teacup, surrounded by colorful banners and perfectly trimmed green hedges. Sharon looks very young in her navy halter top and shag haircut, like a teenager, and Marvin's an adorable five-year-old, with light blond hair and an angelic face.

While they were there, the family got their pictures made into satin jackets. Marvin kept his until it got old and fuzzy and wore it until it fell apart.

In the scuffle over the children, in all the fights back and forth in those early years, usually when Ed would breeze through Falls City to see his folks, he hardly let Sharon get a glimpse of the kids. Apart from that Disney trip, it seemed like she hardly spent any time with them.

It would be years before Sharon was able to sit down and have a heart-to—heart talk with any of her children. The first one she was able to get through to was Scott. At that time Scott was thirteen, and she felt he was old enough to know that Ed wasn't his real dad.

When Scott checked it out with his grandparents, he was bewildered. He felt sure his dad had fed him a bunch of lies about Sharon, that his mother wasn't the witch Ed made her out to be.

Scott wanted to stay in Falls City with his mom, but Ed was furious at the very idea; he wouldn't even consider it. Scott was not going to live with a "no-good whore" as long as Ed had any say in the matter. Ed had a home for Scott in Crowder, Mississippi, and as far as he was concerned, that's where Scott belonged. He too had remarried. He had a fine young wife, Pam, who tried hard to be a good stepmother to his three kids.

In Crowder, Ed was doing all right for himself. He had a good cabinet-making business, he made enough money for Pam to be able to stay home, and he was earning a respectable name in the community. He couldn't understand what Scott could be looking for with Sharon. He had given the boy everything a kid could want.

But Pam and Ed Nissen ran a strict household. The kids were required to do homework every night, to go to church two nights a week, and Scott was tired of all that. He wanted to run free and loose with his mom. She seemed cool. She seemed more like a friend than a parent.

In the months following his talk with Sharon, Scott made such a stink about going back to Falls City, Ed finally put him on a plane to Nebraska. Scott was getting too obstinate, becoming too much of a pain.

On the other hand, despite normal kid-brother complaints and demands, Marvin was forced to remain in Crowder, compelled to obey the rules in the Nissen house; after all, he was still a little boy. Of course, Marvin never totally accepted Pam as his mother the way Susan did, but that was just too bad. Marv was lucky to have a roof over his head and family to sit down with at the dinner table each night.

30

"I NEVER THOUGHT HE WAS ODD," HIS SISTER SUSAN would insist. "I took care of him after we moved to Washington, and he never seemed strange to me."

But even though Susan may not have realized it, Marvin began a self-destructive cycle at a very young age. Whenever Marvin got hurt, whenever he fell down or cut himself, Marvin would get some little toy or an ice cream cone, some type of token pacifier from his father. Susan didn't dream that Marvin was hurting himself intentionally—that wouldn't have made any sense. All Susan saw was a sweet little boy she loved very dearly. Her brother was mechanically inclined, he was useful around the house, and he was fun to be with.

"Marvin loved to work with his hands. Like, Dad gave him a washing machine and just told him to take it apart, so he did," Susan would recall. "Well, he took it apart and then put it back together again piece by piece. That just fascinated him."

In 1981, after moving his kids to Oklahoma and then Tennessee, Ed Nissen wound up settling down in Memphis, where he met and married his new wife. Coming into the Nissen clan with a son from a previous marriage, Pam felt quite natural in the role of mother. She was a lovely young woman who did whatever she could to be a good stepmother to Ed's children even though they gave her a pretty hard time.

Eventually, Susan came around, accepting Pam as the mother she always wanted, but Marvin was a different story.

Marvin couldn't understand why he had to tolerate Pam, especially when his brother, Scott, had been allowed to move to Falls City to be with Sharon and the rest of the family. Of course, the only reason Scott wound up there was because from the time he found out that Ed wasn't his biological father, he started to run away from home. Scott had landed himself in Falls City a couple of times, and finally, Ed was just tired of dragging the kid back. It wasn't worth the trouble.

But Marvin never looked at it that way. All he knew was that when Scott was fifteen, their father decided to put him on a plane to Nebraska, and he didn't get to see his brother for a long time after that.

In Memphis, Ed seemed to be doing all right for himself, working for a large cabinet factory as plant manager. Other than having been through an accident where a piece of plywood kicked back into his stomach and he had to be hospitalized for a few weeks, Ed's life seemed to be running smoothly.

Marvin didn't know why he was forced to remain in the South, compelled to obey the rules in the Nissen house; he hated that he was still a little boy, unable to make his own choices. At the age of nine, Marvin was so miserable that he walked outside in a torrential storm and stayed out there for hours, hoping to catch pneumonia.

Of course, part of the problem was that Marvin never totally accepted Pam as his mother the way Susan did. But in Ed's eyes, that was just too bad. Marvin would just have to learn to deal with things.

"Pam stepped into the picture and that was a big adjustment," Susan admitted. "To me, she was there for me, she was good to me. She made a difference to me because I had someone to fix my hair and show me what goes with what."

But Marvin didn't see Pam as a good thing—not at all.

With Pam as part of the family, Marvin no longer had Susan and Ed all to himself, and that was a major problem for him. What's more, he felt that Pam was trying to take the place of his mom. That made him really angry.

"Pam and I never got along. I felt as though my father betrayed me. I felt like he didn't love me as much as he did before he remarried," Marvin reflected. "I knew I had a mom. Some family members say Mom tried to see me and Susan, but Dad wouldn't let her see us. Other family members say Mom never tried to see us. I don't know who to believe."

In Memphis, Marvin showed his anger in many ways. He began to have fights with other kids in the neighborhood, and he fought constantly with both Pam and her son, Sean, bitterly hating them both for taking his dad away. According to him, the fighting never stopped, and he became more and more upset each day. He would hide in his room, secretly escaping into the world of rock music, wishing he could be happy just once.

By the time he turned ten, all Marvin could think of was having a family of his own. He despised the rules Ed and Pam enforced. He didn't agree with anything they said or did. He was sure he could manage things much better himself, and he wanted to be a grown-up.

"My father had quit drinking by now, and he had turned his life over to Jesus," Marvin later said "He would no longer let us watch , listen to rock or country music, or go to school dances. We had to go to church even if we didn't want to."

Sometime in 1982, Marvin stole $100 from a friend of his dad's who was visiting them. Even though Marvin returned the money, Ed beat the living daylights out of him. The beating came at a bad time because Ed and Pam had just had their first son that year; Little Ed was born in July 1982.

Marvin wanted someone to love him no matter what he did, but his parents didn't seem to get it. In retaliation, Marvin started to spend more time by himself, to withdraw completely from everyone and everything.

"The fighting was getting worse," he admitted. "Pam would get mad because I was always causing her some kind of trouble. I didn't like her, and I wasn't about to be nice to her."

Marvin's behavior caused arguments between Pam and Ed, something the boy seemed to relish. In those days, it seemed like that was the only way Marvin got any attention, since his dad worked until 9:00 or 10:00 every night and Pam was consumed by the baby. Marvin hated that he never spent any time with Ed, who never went to his baseball games, PTA meetings, or anything like that.

In 1984, the family moved just outside Jackson, Mississippi, to a place called Ridgeland, and all the upheaval caused Marvin's grades to drop. He still got passing grades, but he loathed being in school, and he resented being switched from one school to another. By then, Marvin and Pam were fighting so much, the two of them could hardly be left in the same room alone together. Pam tried her hardest to get Marvin to cooperate, to listen to her, but there was just no winning with him. Marvin was impossible.

When Pam was nine months pregnant with her third child, Timothy, she and Marvin got into a wrestling match after she found out that he said the word damn at a birthday party. Pam cursed him for his insensitivity. The fight could have caused her to lose her baby.

That same day, Marvin ran away from home. He was picked up by police while trying to hitchhike, brought to a juvenile detention center, and eventually released to the custody of his father. On the ride home, Ed had nothing to say; he had reached his boiling point. But getting the silent treatment just made Marvin feel guilty. He didn't want to hurt his dad all the time, and it seemed like that's all he ever did.

At the age of twelve, Marvin drank Southern Comfort for the first time. It was the beginning of his colossal drug and alcohol career. Marvin found he liked the way the whiskey made him feel. He felt better, older, more in control.

He needed that feeling because all of a sudden, Susan was dating and caught up in her world at school, and Marvin felt abandoned. Turning to alcohol and marijuana seemed a logical solution.

Susan was the person he viewed as his mother, his sister, his best friend, and now, if Susan wasn't busy dating, she was spending all her time with Pam. Marvin felt they had teamed up against him. He thought there was no one in the world he could really trust.

31

"HE WAS NEVER IN ANY BIG TROUBLE UNTIL WE MOVED to Jackson, and then he started running away from home, stealing cars. Without a warning he would leave," Susan reflected. "Like one night, we could sit up, talking and watching , then we'd go to bed. The next morning, you get up, and he's gone. People say it was because he wanted his mama. When they got a divorce, he cried a lot for his mama, and there was nothing I could do about it. I mean, I missed her too. But we all just kind of dealt with that."

In 1985, little Marvin set fire to the woods behind the Nissen house. Susan remembers seeing a patch of grass on fire, but at the time, she didn't think it was any big deal.

She figured he was playing with matches, and they "just got away from him.." That same year, he got kicked out of school for drugs.

Marvin said that when Ed found out about it, he beat Marvin so hard with a sugar cane pole, that it broke in Ed's hands. As part of Marvin's drug cleanup program, his father required him to make regular appearances at their church, Agape Fellowship. When Marvin refused to clap and sing along, he said Ed took him into the back office and whipped him so intensely, he missed gym class for two weeks.

Marvin ran away and resurfaced again in early 1986, and this time Pam and Ed called their prayer group and had some people come over to the house in a desperate attempt to save him.

"They would put their hands on me and try to cast demons out of me," Marvin confided. "I just went along with it, but things at home were not getting any better. All I was doing was causing problems and trouble for my family. I just wanted to go away. I was even thinking about suicide. The loneliness and hurt in my heart were killing me. I would jump at any chance to get drunk or stoned."

In June of that year, Marvin and a buddy of his ended up stealing an eighteen-wheeler rig, but they never made it very far out of Memphis. When he was brought before the court, he was given two years' probation, and then just days after he cut the deal, he ran away from Memphis for good.

He stole a Lincoln Town Car that was sitting in a gas station with the keys in it, drove the thing to Charleston, Mississippi, and was arrested almost as soon as he got there. In Charleston, the court gave Marvin Thomas Nissen a choice: go to jail or leave the state of Mississippi for two years.

Marvin decided it was time for him to head to Nebraska. On July 9, 1986, when he packed up and went to live with Sharon and Scott, he was only fourteen years old and ready to begin a whole new life. For starters, people in Nebraska all called him Tom, which he preferred. It made him feel cool. Tom was happy to be moving up there with a clean slate, happy to be among family. But then, from the minute he arrived, Tom and his stepfather, Bob, didn't get along so great, and life in Falls City wasn't anything like he'd hoped it might be.

"Bob drank a lot; that was OK with me cause that meant I got to drink more too, but that didn't work out very well," Tom remembers. "By October, me, Mom, and Bob were fighting all the time. I was scared of Bob, and Mom was always upset with me."

Despite Tom's devilish behavior—he was always in some kind of trouble with kids in the neighborhood, with his teachers at school—Bob Popejoy did his best to make Tom feel wanted, to make him feel like a part of things, but the kid didn't want to try to make things work out.

Tom quickly learned the Popejoy family was notorious in Richardson County. Their criminal files were so extensive they actually had their own separate file area in the county clerk's office. Through the grapevine, Tom was continually reminded of the Popejoys' share of criminal complaints and convictions, and he began to lose respect for his stepfather. Although his ex-wife had filed papers accusing him of spousal abuse, Bob Popejoy never went to jail for that. Instead, he was caught and lodged for things like car theft and burglary. He also spent six months in jail for driving with a suspended license, an offense stemming from his numerous DWI charges. In those days, Bob was no angel, so Tom had reason to be afraid of him.

Sharon also had a criminal file building—charges for writing bad checks, DWI, resisting arrest, all of it misdemeanors, and she was never convicted of any of it. Tom hated that Sharon never reported any of the domestic violence that went on. She was beaten unmercifully by Bob, but she always took him back after he sobered up and apologized.

According to other family members, Bob beat Sharon so ferociously that she'd be in bed for days, unable to move.

Tom recalled a time when Bob hit Sharon with some kind of cement brick. He remembers seeing his mother's face black and blue and half purple.

By the time Tom arrived in 1986, his brother, Scott, had also built himself a criminal reputation, something that Tom was secretly enthralled by. In fact, Scott had just pulled off one of his most memorable stunts that year. On March 8 he was charged with burning down the trailer owned by James Havercamp and Lynn Theile on the paramilitary encampment in Rulo, which belonged to the religious cult led by , Mike Ryan. At that time, the FBI hadn't raided the Rulo camp yet, so Scott was allegedly able to pull off the dirty deed while the tortures and cult activities were still going on. The slow killing of a five-year-old boy and the rape and slaying of a twenty-six-year-old man were yet to be discovered.

By now, Scott Nissen was a recognized troublemaker; he had been from the time he landed in Falls City. Before the arson incident, he had served time for various criminal activities. At the age of seventeen, he was caught breaking into Falls City High School. At eighteen, he and Tyrone Popejoy were charged with criminal mischief for breaking the streetlights in Rulo. In 1985, he served a few days here and there for things like writing bad checks, and also in that year, he spent two days in jail for running over a deer.

Of course, all of that somehow impressed Tom—he thought of Scott as a stormy outlaw who was getting even with the world.

Almost from the day Tom got to Nebraska, he tried to figure a way to get out of there. It wasn't long before he stole Bob's truck and took it to Pueblo, Colorado, a place where he didn't know a soul. He called home because he had run out of money and gas, and the next day, Bob and Scott had to drive all the way down there to rescue him. Bob beat the hell out of Tom when they got home.

Tom despised Bob for that. But most of all, he couldn't stand the way Bob treated Sharon.

He just wanted Bob to disappear.

"I hated him," Tom later admitted. "I was gonna kill him."

Then Sharon came home one day and smelled gas. She knew something wasn't right, so she immediately called Bob and had him come home from work. As soon as he got there, Bob followed the trail of gas that had been poured around their home; it led to a rag doused with gasoline that was hidden under the trailer porch. Although Tom denied having done anything at first, insisting he would never go under the porch because he was afraid of spiders, he eventually confessed.

"I asked him why he poured the gas, and he said he wanted to set the house on fire and then save us by putting the fire out," Sharon confided. "He thought we'd be proud of him for doing something good."

That night, Tom overheard Bob and Sharon come in late; they had been out drinking. Bob's deep voice was telling Sharon to go in and give Tom a hug, to put her arms around the boy and say I love you as a way to calm the waters, but Sharon refused to do it.

"They thought I was asleep, but I wasn't," Tom recalled. "In the end, Mom did come into my room. I acted like I was asleep. Mom woke me up, put her arms around me, and said she loved me. I cried. It hurt so bad to know Bob had to tell my own mom to say she loved me. It crushed my heart."

As soon as Sharon left the room, Tom pulled out a knife and cut a vein in his right ankle. He watched himself bleed, never telling anyone what he'd done. A few days later, he tried to overdose on a combination of Valium and other pills.

Tom had just turned sixteen. He was stealing money from Sharon's purse, stealing other items from the house, and Bob and Sharon had reached the end of their rope. They decided they just couldn't handle him anymore.

When they turned Tom over to the Department of Social Services in Falls City, the state of Nebraska took official custody, and he went into a group home in Lincoln called Freeway Center. In August 1986, a little over a month after he arrived in the state, Marvin Thomas Nissen was placed with a foster family in Nebraska. They were salt-of-the-earth people who owned a dairy farm out in the country. Tom worked on the land every day and went to school regularly, but he couldn't stop his drug and alcohol habits.

In September, his foster parents put him into the Saint Joseph Center for Mental Health in Omaha because of his suicidal tendencies. He stayed there for a month but then was right back to drugs and self-mutilating behavior when he got home. While he was in therapy, Tom told mental health workers that he cut himself not necessarily to commit suicide, but "to see the blood."

A few weeks after his treatment at Saint Joseph's, Tom ran away from his foster parents and moved into a homeless shelter in Everett, Washington, having hitched a ride on a box car train in the middle of the night.

"By that time, I was drunk all the time, smoking dope, doing coke, anything to make me feel better. I had also sliced my stomach open. I didn't deserve to live. All I did was cause problems for people. My anger was getting the best of me."

32

TOM HAD NO REAL PLANS WHEN HE RAN AWAY.

He would just become angry, and then it was automatic—he'd hit the road. Sometimes he would feel like his memory or vision was fogged. He would black out and have no idea how he wound up somewhere.

It was always the same pattern: Tom would stay in some strange place for a while, then call either Ed or Sharon and beg to come home, and one of them would invariably say yes. He wished his family members would he more involved with him, and he tried to get them to change their ways. He wished someone in his family could be more dependable—he felt as if he was the only one who tried to solve problems.

Ultimately, for whatever reason, he felt rejected and alone, hiding his feelings from everyone.

Tom's biggest problem was that he didn't like himself very much. He didn't think he was worth anything.

In September 1989, he ran away from his new foster home in Falls City, and this time the police were called. Because he talked about suicide, the officer referred Nissen to the Saint Joseph's Center, where he was admitted for psychological evaluation and he began to get involved in an alcohol treatment group. Tom knew it was time to get help because, for one thing, his weight had gone from 160 down to 128, which was incredibly thin for his five-foot nine-inch frame. Still, when he was asked why he was there, Tom told health workers, "I was skipping school, then all of a sudden I'm in a place like this. I don't know."

Tom eventually opened up and claimed he wanted to try to stop using drugs and alcohol, saying that he was tired of being in fights and being in trouble. He confided that he began to feel that people were watching him, that no one believed anything he said anymore.

When Tom gave a rundown on his family history, he said his mother was a cook, married and divorced three times, who "suffers from a lot of headaches." He said he had no relationship with her at all.

"My mom's is the worst place to live. My dad's is the second-worst place to live. My uncle's is the third-worst place to live," Tom told a health worker.

He denied that there were any family secrets or any history of family members being in psychiatric hospitals. When he talked about certain family members being alcoholics, he made it seem like that was a thing of the past.

Tom gave vague details about his enjoyment of sports like football and skiing; said he believed in a supreme being, which he called God; and denied having ever been involved with any satanic cults, though he admitted to being active in the White American Group for White America. He said he did not talk about his feelings because no one would understand and recognized that he felt anxious and nervous for no reason.

In terms of being sexually active, Tom claimed to have had sex for the first time at age thirteen, and said he had not used any form of birth control. When asked if anyone ever tried to touch him in a sexual manner against his will, he confessed, "One time a guy tried to touch me, but I beat him up."

In speaking about his future goals, Tom said he'd like to have a wife and two kids and be a policeman. He said he'd like to have a boy and then adopt a girl, explaining that his strengths were "working with little kids, doing things with my hands, and helping other people with their problems."

Dr. Robert Kraft, the certified clinical psychologist who saw Tom, dictated a report on September 20, 1989, which concluded that Nissen suffered from a conduct disorder and possibly a depressive disorder. Kraft observed no signs of Nissen being psychotic; instead, he described Nissen as having an eccentric view of the world. He noted that Nissen was relaxed for the first half of the testing, but toward the second half, he would lean forward and look at the questions before they were asked, then become guarded and give conflicting answers.

"There are numerous signs of him seeing the world as being a dangerous place, and he sees himself as lacking in power," Kraft reported. "Masculine figures are seen as powerful but as dangerous or assaultive as well. The feminine figures are seen as not being there for him— he may see maternal figures as being highly emotional and as having difficulty maintaining control of their emotions and impulses."

Nissen was diagnosed as a person with a rigid view of the world who would likely be hostile and manipulative in his efforts to act out his emotions. Testing of Nissen against the multiphase personality criteria showed a young man who might act in an impulsive fashion or tend to overreact. Kraft's projective material showed Nissen had difficulty perceiving reality as others do.

Even though he was seventeen, achievement testing showed Nissen to be performing at an early junior high level. His reading score placed him at the seventh grade level, his math, at eighth grade. Intelligence measures showed him to be of low average intelligence, his estimated full-scale IQ being 82.

In October, Nissen had three conferences with Ms. Beverly Ritchie from the Department of Social Services. On those occasions he was angry because there was no immediate plan for his discharge from Saint Joseph's, and Tom wanted out of there in the worst way. He was cooped up, and it made his skin crawl.

When Ritchie reviewed his previous history, the problems he had with his parents in foster homes, Tom admitted to having bad thoughts revolving around plans to shoot his stepfather. When asked about other homicidal ideations, Tom stated that he did not really have other homicidal thoughts. He denied having suicidal ideations or ever attempting to take his own life.

A recommendation was made for further inpatient treatment and eventual placement in a structural setting such as Boys Town or the Omaha Home for Boys. Unfortunately, there was never any follow-through on that placement goal.

On November 6, 1989, Tom Nissen walked out of the treatment plan at Saint Joseph's, scheduled to return to foster care, return to Falls City High School, and follow up with his attending physician, Dr. David Abrisror. In his discharge summary, Dr. Abrisror observed that Nissen had "prominent sociopathic traits." His diagnostic impression was that Nissen suffered from a conduct disorder and an antisocial personality.

As soon as Tom was able, he went back to drugs and alcohol; and now, with the holidays approaching, he was making up for lost time. By New Year's, Tom was partying so hard he was regularly experiencing nausea, vomiting, muscle weakness, headaches, dizziness, sleeping problems, and blackouts.

It finally reached a point where Tom couldn't manage things at all. He was feeling sick all the time, and he had been thrown out of his foster home. He called his dad for help.

Back in Mississippi, Ed and Pam had moved their residence to Crowder, a tiny farm town with about three stop lights, two gas stations, and one cafe. Tom thought of it as a place where everybody was related to everybody, as a busybody town where the closest hint of civilization was a twenty-minute drive away, where there was really nothing to do other than stare at crop fields.

As soon as Tom arrived there, he and Pam picked up where they left off, constantly fighting, so Tom took all his stuff and moved to Ed's office at Nissen's Cabinet Company. Along the way, Tom found himself a girlfriend, Angie Houston, and he fell in love for the first time in his life. With Angie around, things seemed pretty good, and Tom eventually moved into a trailer. He worked for his dad, which was a decent arrangement, and Tom seemed to be getting on with his life.

But then Pam's mother died. Tom considered her "granny," and he was deeply affected by her death. Tom was a pallbearer at Granny's funeral, and as soon as he left the cemetery, he started drinking around the clock.

By May 1990, Tom was so unhappy about things, he put a pistol to his heart and pulled the trigger. "I missed my heart, but it went through my lung and out my back," he would later reflect. "I really can't do anything right."

When Tom was found lying on the floor of his trailer, a rescue squad was called, and he was airlifted to Memphis. Less than a month after the shooting, Tom had fully recovered—he had managed to puncture a lung but nothing more—and he was admitted into Memphis House, a United Way drug rehabilitation center.

In the first four weeks at Memphis House, Tom seemed to bond with other individuals and respond to the counseling and spiritual guidance he received. He was participating in scheduled activities, and he appeared to be ready to share. He told others he planned to go back to work at Nissen's Cabinet Company, that he was going to get his GED, and that he was patching things up with his girlfriend, Angie. He was encouraged to begin praying every morning, to share honest emotions in his men's group, and to learn to identify his feelings and keep a daily log. However, in group therapy, it was noted that Nissen did not make eye contact.

Observing him as a patient there, workers thought Nissen was making some progress, but then on August 11, Tom got a pass to the bathroom and proceeded to walk in a southerly direction, right out of the facility. The clinical director was called, but by that time, Marvin Thomas Nissen was out of sight.

He never signed his Survival Plan, which called for his attendance at AA meetings, NA meetings, and Aftercare Group. He left on foot with no car, no job, and no place to live. His primary counselor, Rhonda Selph, reported that Tom "never got honest with himself or others."

On September 24, Nissen was arrested back in Falls City on a false reporting charge. Apparently, Nissen had cut himself up with a knife, then claimed he had been attacked by Clyde Bums and a group of his friends in the Hardee's parking lot. While he was being treated in the Falls City Hospital for superficial wounds to the abdomen, local law enforcement investigated Nissen's report. Before he was released, Nissen admitted that the wounds were self-inflicted.

Two months later he was fined fifty dollars and had to spend four days in the county jail.

In the interim, Byron and Sharon and the rest of the Miller clan tried to rally around the boy, but they were at a loss about what to do for him. When Byron asked his grandson why he was hurting himself, Tom had nothing to say.

33

"SHE NEVER SHOWED HIM ATTENTION. SHE NEVER seemed to want to be close with Tom. She was so busy with her own life," Wanda Miller reflected. "I don't blame Sharon for anything; it might not have been her fault. I just think she got so used to not having any kids around her that when she had the chance to be a mother, she didn't know how."

For years, Wanda and her husband Randy had tried to become substitute parents to Tom, but it was practically impossible. Yes, they were his aunt and uncle, but they were two young kids themselves, just in their early twenties when Tom first arrived in town. Besides, he was gone so much, always back and forth to Mississippi and so forth, that they really couldn't keep up with him.

Of course, Wanda made sure that Tom knew he always had someone he could talk to in Falls City. She knew he didn't like Sharon. Tom often spoke about how evil his mom was. More than once, Ed told him Sharon was into witchcraft, and Tom believed it, even if it wasn't true.

"When they arrested him for stabbing himself, they took him up to Lincoln for a psychiatric evaluation, and we thought maybe he was receiving the help he needed, but he would never talk about it," Wanda recalls. "I guess Tom came to me as a mother figure, I don't know."

Wanda insisted that Tom be a part of the family, that he come over to the house not just on holidays, but whenever he felt like it. She always had a place for him at her table, even in the rough years when she and Randy were without jobs and living on welfare. Her heart went out to Tom because he always seemed like a confused, vulnerable kid. She and Tom were only about ten years apart in age, so they could drink and let loose together. At times Tom would really open up to her, especially when it came to getting advice on how to handle Kandi Gibson, the girl he eventually wound up marrying.

"When he talked about Kandi, I just sat with my hand in front of my mouth the whole time because I couldn't believe how stupid she sounded," Wanda said. "The way he described her, she just hung all over him like a dumb blonde; she just couldn't let him out of her sight. But I think that's what he was looking for, that type of attention."

Tom met Kandi in October 1990. He had just turned eighteen, she was a couple of years younger. When he and Kandi went out on their first date, he considered her a one-night stand, but still, he jokingly asked her if she'd marry him just to see what she'd say. Of course, Kandi said yes. She had a six-month-old girl, Bobbie Faye, who needed a daddy, and Tom seemed a perfect candidate.

Tom fell in love with Bobbie the moment he laid eyes on her cute face and full head of blond hair; he thought she looked like him in a strange way. Still, he had no idea he would marry Kandi. They loved each other, but they really didn't get along very well, and he considered her a sleeparound, so he felt he never could trust her.

"Me and Kandi had our fights. Mostly it was me that started them," Tom admitted. "It scared me to fall in love so quick. I wanted to push her away."

But Kandi hung in there, determined to be with Tom no matter what. He was so good to her in every way—he combed her hair, bathed her, he did everything she ever asked him to— she felt she could never replace him. And then too, he was great in bed. Kandi never knew anyone could please her so much. She loved him for that. He was the sexiest guy she'd ever been with.

In early December, less than two months after he and Kandi met, Tom got arrested on a minor in possession charge and was sentenced to serve five days in the Richardson County Jail. Instead of doing the time, he took Kandi with him and fled the state. He figured it was the perfect opportunity for him to introduce her to his family back in Crowder.

As it turned out, Kandi got along wonderfully with Tom's sister, particularly because Susan baby-sat whenever Kandi asked her. Susan didn't have kids of her own yet, and she loved having Bobbie around, which made Kandi's life easier. Kandi liked to be out drinking and having fun with Tom.

But the drinking caused major arguments between the two of them. Even when he wasn't drunk, Tom was wildly jealous. With a little booze, he'd go crazy. Whenever Kandi just looked at someone in a bar or had a conversation with anyone of the opposite sex, Tom always accused her of fucking the guy. Finally, he had himself convinced that Kandi was a cheat. On a whim, he sent her packing.

Kandi called her dad and had him come get her in Crowder, but Tom called her a few days later, begging for her to come back. By then, she was so in love with Tom she couldn't stop herself. Tom sent her a one-way bus ticket, and Kandi used it. No sooner did she get to Crowder than Tom started in with the accusations all over again.

The second time Kandi called her dad to rescue her, Bob Gibson agreed to drive to Mississippi with the provision that she live at home and never see Nissen again. Kandi agreed, but Tom soon followed her back to Falls City and started sneaking into the Gibson house every night. After a few weeks, the two of them got caught making love on the Gibsons' living room floor. Red faced and breathing curses, Kandi's dad warned Tom never to set foot on his property again. Tom just couldn't understand why her dad hated him so much.

In March 1991, in a desperate attempt to escape everything, Tom ran off and joined the army. Before he left, he asked Kandi to marry him. They didn't set a date, but that was OK with her.

Once Tom enlisted, it was only a matter of weeks before Tom had a breakdown, and he was sent to Sheppard Air Force Base (AFB) in Texas for mental evaluation and alcohol treatment. He arrived via ambulance, clean shaven, wearing nothing but BVDs, but from just looking at him, there was no way to tell that he was suffering from a major depression. He just seemed like a drunk with a minor laceration to his right hand. Apparently, Tom had been beating on the walls in his barracks.

Tom told army health workers that he understood why he needed to be hospitalized but said he was ashamed to be there. It was something he didn't want people to know. Tom hoped the hospitalization might help him to be able to deal with things that were bothering him in a rational way.

When asked how he viewed his family, Nissen described them as "backsliding back stabbers," who played one side against the other. His mother and father had fed him so many negative things about each other, it seemed he didn't know who to believe or trust anymore. The only people he cared about now were his fiancée and "his" child, Bobbie.

The attending psychiatrist, Major Mari Jo Gingrich, placed Nissen on a standard alcohol detoxification protocol, with no pharmacotherapy planned. He was admitted to Ward 2-North and given a physical exam, which exposed numerous well—healed linear scars on his abdomen and upper arms as well as an injury to the chest that indicated a possible gunshot wound.

At the time of his hospitalization, he was still in boot camp; Marvin Thomas Nissen was an Active Duty U.S. Army PV1 with one month of service. In his clinical record at Sheppard AFB, he admitted to smoking two packs a day and drinking alcohol daily. In giving his history of involvement with illicit drugs, Nissen admitted to using cocaine, heroin, speed, unknown street drugs, Quaaludes, and marijuana. He denied taking routine medications, denied having had any childhood illnesses, including the usual ones, and denied having made any suicide attempts, although he admitted he once shot himself in the chest, saying he just "wanted the pain to go away."

Dr. Gingrich observed that Nissen tended to use "all or none" thinking, that the patient tended to externalize responsibility and often referred to others in his life as objects. He'd say things like "my fiancée" and "my baby." On the same day he was admitted to the base, while on the way to a doctor's appointment that had been scheduled after Tom complained of a respiratory problem, Nissen went AWOL.

He hitched a ride with a traveling carnival, working the kiddie rides, and made his way back across country to his uncle's place in Everett. By August of that year, he landed in Crowder, working for his dad. Throughout 1991, he went back and forth to Falls City to see Kandi, but she wasn't as interested in him anymore. He was miserable in Mississippi, and he'd constantly call just to tell her that he loved her, that he had never used her. Of course, Tom says Kandi would be all over him whenever he came around, but she had found someone else to fill in the gaps.

When he found out about it, Tom was devastated. Kandi was the girl of his dreams. "No girl ever compared to Kandi," he reminisce.

"She could walk into a room and just look at me and get me going."

34

IN APRIL 1992, TOM NISSEN MOVED BACK TO FALLS CITY for good. He felt he didn't have a choice. He had lost his job at his father's place, had quit another job, had wrecked both of his cars; his house burned down, his dog ran off, and Kandi was about to give birth to her second child, which he thought might be his. He stayed with his secret girlfriend when he first got back to town, someone he'd been seeing on the side all along.

On May 6, when Tiffany Sue was born, Kandi told Tom she was his child, but he wasn't sure. He might be the father—there had been a window of opportunity, Tom knew that. But he didn't know if she'd been with anyone else while he was away. In any case, he was Kandi's coach for the delivery, and he was happy to be there. While Kandi was in recovery, Tom kept Tiffany with him as much as the nurses would allow. The infant was his pride and joy.

Just a week after she was born, the law caught up to Tom. He was arrested on a warrant stemming from the unfinished business on the minor in possession charge. Nissen was fingerprinted, photographed, and placed in the custody of the Richardson County Sheriff's Office. On May 18, he was charged with escape for having failed to serve the five-day jail penalty, a felony charge that required a $2,500 appearance bond to be paid in cash. Nissen plead guilty to the lesser charge of obstructing government operations, and on May 20, he was sentenced to serve one year in the Nebraska Penal and Correctional Complex beginning September 11, 1992. It was a verdict that put Marvin Thomas Nissen into a complete tailspin. Now that he was finally a father, he was being ripped away from his family, all because he had some *beer* in the car a year before. It was outrageous.

ALL *HE* WANTED

On June 3, 1992, just days after his release from the county jail, Tom and Kandi were married under a great big pine tree out at Stanton Lake, a picturesque Falls City park complete with a log cabin and children's swings in the background. Sharon and Wanda were the only adults in attendance, and Sharon held Tiffany in her arms as the justice of the peace performed the service.

Kandi, a petite brunette with a coquettish smile and a button nose, looked inviting in her denim shirt and high heels, and the wedding was so sweet and easy, all done in a matter of minutes. Of course, Wanda and Sharon both had their misgivings about Kandi—they had warned Tom about her, but he just wouldn't listen. Kandi was immature and had a bad reputation around town. They thought she was using Tom, making a fool of him with this story about "his" baby. If fact, when Tom first invited Wanda to the ceremony, she was so angry about him marrying Kandi, she slapped Tom in the face.

"I finally told Tom that as long as he was happy, that was fine, but I still couldn't believe he married her because he could do better," Wanda reflected. "He had the looks, that cute boyish look, and once you get to know him, he's loving and caring. Any girl would have liked to marry him. That's why I couldn't believe he got involved with this woman. I told him I thought she would go out on him if she ever had the chance."

No doubt Tom wanted Kandi to remain faithful. Still, that didn't stop him from cheating on her. In fact, just days after they wed, Tom slept with one of Kandi's best friends. The two of them did it spoon style, Tom pressing up behind her, Tom would later boast to his friends, and he came home with hickeys all over his chest, telling Kandi he had been in a street fight.

A month later, when Kandi's friend claimed to be pregnant by Tom, he felt forced to tell his wife what really happened. He told her he wanted to take responsibility if the child was his, and Kandi became completely *unglued*. She heard the news while she was in the middle of frying him a steak, and she hurled the frying pan across the room, threatened to change the locks on the door, and told Tom to get lost. Tom threw his wedding ring at her and watched it bounce off Kandi's head, which made him snicker as he waltzed out the door.

Of course, later that day, Tom came back, and the two of them made up. He told Kandi he didn't mean it, that he was just kidding around about her friend. However, as the weeks went on, Tom's philandering became more obvious.

Kandi was horrified—they had been married less than a month—but then, she wanted to trust Tom, and whenever he was home, Tom made such good love to her, she'd forget about everything.

"I don't know why I cheated on her," Tom would later say. "I just wanted to get laid. These girls were willing, and I was ready." Tom just wanted to spread himself around.

At 1:30 in the morning of a hot June night, Bobby and Brenda Christie heard a loud knocking at their door. They were in the middle of a dead sleep, having passed out upstairs on the living room couch in front of the TV, and they didn't want to be bothered. But the pounding just kept getting louder, so Brenda finally dragged herself downstairs to see what was going on.

"Who is it?"

"It's me and it's important," the voice said, and Brenda unlocked the door. "I don't want no trouble," she whispered.

"There won't be any. Where's Bobby?"

"Upstairs."

When they got into the living room, Tom handed Bobby a beer and told him to drink.

Bobby was groggy and refused the offer, but Tom wouldn't hear of it.

"Oh, come on, have one with me," Tom insisted as he sat down next to Bobby on the couch. Bobby took the can and opened it but only took a sip. Tom was obviously wasted, and Bobby could see his face was starting to twist with anger.

"Why the fuck are you going around telling people you saw a picture of Kandi and Sammy and she was going down on him? You said she was giving him a blow job and that's a total fuckin' lie," Tom howled.

"I never said anything of the sort, Tom. I don't know what she was doing, and I can't say if it was Kandi or not. All's I know is that someone has a picture of a girl giving head if that's what you're talking about," Bobby snapped.

"I can quote you word for word, 'cause I was right there when you said it," Tom persisted. "I was in the fuckin' room when you said you saw a picture of Kandi going down on Sammy, so you're a fuckin' liar!"

"I don't remember him saying anything like that ever," Brenda told him. "If he would've said anything like that, I would've remembered it."

"I come over here tonight to slice your throat!" Tom screeched, waving an eight-inch blade he pulled from his back pocket as he pointed it toward Bobby.

"No, Tom! You're not going to do that in my house!"

The terror in Brenda's voice must have gotten to him, because Tom suddenly handed her the knife and decided to strike Bobby in the face with his fist instead. Tom hauled off and hit the guy so hard, Bobby couldn't see. He was covered in blood, and Brenda ordered Tom out of the apartment, but Tom wouldn't leave. He kept screaming and carrying on about Kandi and Sammy.

But then, as he looked over at his buddy, Tom started to feel bad about what he did. He ordered Brenda to go get a washcloth and said he was sorry, then he walked his friend into the bedroom and helped clean him up. Before he left, Tom asked Brenda if she needed a thermometer, and he pulled a large outdoor thermometer from his jacket and laid it on the bed.

"What do I need with this?" she asked.

"I don't know. I took it from Falls City Health Care," Tom told her.

The next day, Bobby and Brenda both made reports to the Falls City police. The comment about the thermometer led to a theft investigation at a Falls City nursing home, the health care center Tom had mentioned. David Simpson, a custodian on the property, told police that he had noticed items missing for about two months. First it was a green wheel barrow, then it was a shovel, then a hoe. The night before, a thermometer on the front porch came up gone.

It was June 19, 1992, that Ken Scurto, a Nebraska State fire marshal investigator out of Lincoln, had been contacted to investigate two building fires in Falls City. They involved houses that were about a block and a half apart. The deputy fire marshall who first called Scurto reported that he thought both fires were related, as there was less than one hour between them and they were both suspicions in nature.

When Scurto arrived at the first site a garage, he observed that the fire began outside the building along the east exterior wall, on or near ground level. The fire burned through the wall and engulfed the contents of the garage. Scurto took pictures of the scene. He also took pictures at the site of the second fire, and based on his observations, he felt the house fire had been intentionally started by someone.

On June 23, Nissen was hauled in for assault and theft. Investigator Keith Hayes questioned him not only about the combative incident at the Christie residence, but also about the two fires that had been reported, one of which occurred on the property where the Christies lived. A complaint had been filed by Robert Hunzeker, their landlord.

During the interview, Nissen talked to Hayes about taking a thermometer that he "found" on the street. He explained that he was intoxicated the night of June 19, that he was angry at his friend Robert Christie for showing a photograph of the back of a female's head attached to a male torso, implying this female was supposed to be Kandi performing fellatio. To Hayes, Nissen never gave a straight answer as to whether he thought the photo existed or not. He just claimed he was depressed about it and admitted he pulled a hunting knife out of a leather case and waved it at Christie. Nissen refused to produce it, claiming Kandi must have lost the knife somewhere.

While in custody, Nissen told Hayes he was thinking of suicide and asked to speak with someone from Blue Valley Mental Health Center in Falls City. A dispatcher placed some calls to Blue Valley, and Bob Kohles, the mental health worker on call, agreed to come down to the jail to talk with Tom later that night.

At that time, Nissen denied having anything to do with the fires. Hayes issued Nissen a citation for assault and larceny. He was booked and eventually released on bond, with a hearing and a trial date pending.

In the meantime, Kandi's parents. Bob and Linda Gibson, had each filed requests for temporary protection orders to keep Nissen 300 feet away from their home. Apparently, Tom had been making threats against them because they were housing Kandi. Tom was threatening to burn down their house, intimidating his in-laws.

Then on June 26, county attorney Doug Merz substantiated evidence that probable cause existed to arrest Marvin Thomas Nissen aka Tom Nissen on the charges of burglary and arson. A warrant was issued.

Around 8:45 the next night, Hayes received a phone call from Kandi Nissen. She was calling from Hinky Dinky and wanted him to come up to her apartment.

Hayes took Officer Sean Nolte with him, and together they knocked on the door of apartment 2 at 2212 Harlan Street Tom Nissen answered and was immediately placed under arrest. He told the cops he knew it was coming. He claimed that was the reason he had his wife make the call.

Once Nissen was admitted into jail, he apparently caused so many problems there, saying he was ready to explode, threatening to kill himself, that on June 29, he was sent to the Lancaster County Crisis Center in Lincoln for evaluation. The center diagnosed him with personality adjustment disorder and found evidence of an entrance and exit wound to the left chest, evidence of chest tube placement, and multiple superficial abdominal scars as well as well—healed traumatic abdominal scars. "He does not appear to be suffering from any major mental disorder, but the separation from his new family and the confinement are beginning to have an impact," Dr. Klaus Hartman wrote when Nissen was released back to custody. "At this time, it is doubtful that the patient is committable."

35

ALL ALONG, KANDI KEPT A FILTHY HOUSE, WHICH WAS a real sore sport for Tom. He would straighten and clean things, and she'd turn everything back to dirty. He was fighting a constant battle and couldn't understand how she could be so unclean, even about herself. Kandi was a puzzlement.

When Tom was sentenced to spend three years in the Nebraska Department of Correctional Services, concurrent with the one-year sentence imposed by the Richardson County Court, he knew Kandi would just let their living place go completely to hell. What little she had tried to do in the past would just get tossed aside now that she had no one to answer to, now that he had been found guilty of arson and was definitely being sent away.

Nissen was found guilty because two latent fingerprints on the scene were identified as his. He had been represented by a court-appointed attorney, a hearing was held, and arguments were submitted. On September 3, 1992, he was carted off to the state penitentiary.

With Tom away, the descriptions people gave about Kandi's indecency were so increasingly disgusting that no one could hardly believe them. Kandi would do things like leave the kitchen sink half-filled with dirty water and dishes crawling with bugs, and have soiled diapers lying around. Anyone who went into her house—Wanda, Sharon, Susan, and eventually Missy and Lana—would come away with these kinds of horror stories. They couldn't stand seeing Kandi and her kids living that way, especially knowing that Kandi could fix herself up whenever she went out to the bars.

"She just didn't have the sense. She didn't know how to take care of herself, how to take care of Bobbie," Susan reflected. "Like one time Bobbie was sick, and Kandi put wet clothes on her to wear out in the cold. But to her, there wasn't anything wrong with that."

Susan didn't think Kandi was a bad mother; she just thought the basic things in life went right over Kandi's head—the girl didn't seem to know any better. Kandi had always been that way, Susan remembered. She'd never offer to wash dishes with all the other women after a family meal; she didn't think she had to.

She was quite dense about personal living habits. She'd pick up a cookie off the floor and hand it to Bobbie, then wonder why the child refused to eat it. Or she'd give Bobbie a bowl of chicken soup and expect a toddler to feed herself.

Things like that totally frustrated Tom. He knew Kandi really didn't know how to care for their kids. He fully intended to adopt Bobbie, who was two when he'd been sent off to prison, and now his hands were tied. Kandi raising his kids alone meant they would be ruined.

"Our biggest fights were over her not keeping the house," Tom explained. "One time I fixed her dinner on a dirty plate and gave her a dirty fork to see how she'd like it, 'cause that's how she'd feed the kids, on dirty plates."

It was May 1993 when Tom got out of prison on parole. He was twenty years old, hoping to go to college, and concerned about reuniting with his family. While he was on the inside, he had stayed drug and alcohol free, that is, until the day he said Kandi confessed to him that she was sleeping with another guy, then he started to get stoned whenever possible. That began about a month before his release.

As soon as Nissen got to Falls City, he combed the town looking for his wife but ended up leaving a note on her door saying he'd be at Scott's place, waiting for her. When Kandi finally appeared late that night, she was riding in her supposed boyfriend's car with Bobbie and Tiffany in the backseat. Tom was so overwhelmed to see the girls, he hugged and kissed them even as they slept. Then, with the other guy in full view, he hugged Kandi and asked if he could come home.

Kandi said no, she told him the house was a mess and she didn't want him to see it. But Tom had her get out of the car and started his sweet talk. He promised he didn't care about the house, he swore that all he wanted to do was hold her, and after a few minutes, Kandi gave him a big smile and said, "Well, come on!" When she got back to the car, she made up some lame excuse to the guy she was with and she pulled the children from the backseat.

"She was not lying about the house," Tom remembers. "It looked and smelled like a garbage dump. I almost puked when she opened the door."

Tom and Kandi had sex on the couch that night; it was the only halfway clean thing in the house. The next day Kandi had to work—she had a job as a maid at the Heartland Inn in nearby Hiawatha, Kansas—so Tom asked her to get a baby-sitter to watch the kids while he cleaned the place up. It took him all of eight hours to tidy the one-bedroom house. When he was done, he had filled two Dumpsters with twenty-one garbage bags. But what made him the maddest wasn't the filth, it was that Kandi told him she lost her wedding rings at work—then he found them under the VCR.

"There was green stuff growing out of the carpet. There was not a clean dish in the house," Tom later said. "I had to throw away most of the dishes because they wouldn't come clean. There was bread in the kitchen with roaches crawling all over it. The bed had been pissed on so many times, I sprayed it over and over with Lysol, but it didn't really help."

While Tom was busy working, sorting trash and trying to salvage clothes for the laundry, Investigator Keith Hayes and another officer showed up at his door. They were there to follow up on a child neglect report from social services. The law had come to take the Nissen children away.

He didn't blame Kandi for it. He knew that she was never taught to clean as a kid. Still, Tom was so upset by the idea of losing his kids, he cried in front of the cops. He begged them to give him some time.

"I told the police if they laid a hand on one of my kids, I would be back in prison," Nissen recalled. "In the end, they gave me a ticket for neglect and five days to get everything in order. I couldn't believe they gave me a ticket. I had only been out of prison for two days."

By the fifth day, Nissen was able to get the place decent enough to show authorities, and he was allowed to keep his children. But things were different in the household; nothing could ever be the same with him and Kandi. The only way they had sex was by getting drunk enough so neither of them could remember the night before. Tom described one time when he woke up wearing Kandi's underwear and had absolutely no idea how it got there.

"Something inside of me changed. I didn't make love to Kandi; we just fucked," he confessed. "Sometimes at night after she fell asleep, I would put my arms around her and cry." Here Tom was trying to figure out what to do about his life—he had been home just over a month—when Kandi announced she was pregnant. She promised she hadn't slept with anyone except Tom, but he wasn't sure he believed her. Still, he moved with Kandi and the kids to a bigger house on Chase Street and hoped for the best. After the kid was born, he'd have a paternity test done, and that would help matters, Tom thought.

Nissen was no stranger to paternity questions. Not only did he have one with his daughter Tiffany, he had grown up wondering who truly belonged to his family on the Miller side because he always heard that Sharon's mother, his grandma Fern, had become pregnant by a wealthy banker from Kansas City.

In August 1993, at the time when the sound of locusts fill the shady brick lanes of Falls City and children's laughter echoes from the city swimming pool, Susan Nissen and her husband Bart came into town for Cobblestone Days, an annual homecoming event that Susan usually tried to get back for.

It's a giant summer carnival with all-American things like beauty shows, ice cream socials, fishing contests, and bake sales, and there's always a tractor pull, a big demolition derby, and a huge parade, which, of course, everyone in town attends. To most locals, it's probably the best time of year, right up there with Christmas. Everyone's in good spirits, the weather is warm, the trees are full, school's still out, and life seems magical for a few days.

Of course, right after Susan arrived, Kandi decided to walk out on Tom, and this time, she said it was for good.

Kandi stayed with her parents for about a week, during which time Tom slept with a different woman each night.

Somehow Susan became involved in their reconciliation: she coaxed Tom to ask Kandi to move back home, and she took Bobbie to live with her in Mississippi for a while to try to take the edge off things for them. Still, Tom and Kandi kept on fighting; their marriage was really over, but they just wouldn't admit it.

Then, on a whim, Tom quit his construction job at the high school—he was helping to install an elevator there on a part-time basis—and he grabbed Kandi, Tiffany, and their dog and drove to Crowder to retrieve Bobby. Tom didn't get permission from his parole officer to take the trip. He really didn't care about anything anymore, now that things with Kandi were irreparable. If he went to jail, so be it.

By the time the holidays rolled around in late November 1993, Tom and Kandi Nissen had both threatened to call lawyers about getting a divorce. Tom even went so far as to make a round of calls to check on the cost and time involved. He had set it up in his mind that they would have a no-fault divorce, and in the meantime, they were both free to be with other people and still be together when it was convenient.

"I'd sit back and I'd pray, *Please Lord, don't ever let this woman leave me*," Tom explained, "then I'd turn around and write a letter to push her into filing for divorce." By then, Tom was spending more time in other women's beds than he was at home. In late November, Tom had met Lana Tisdel, John Lotter, Missy Wisdom, and someone named Brandon. He had been invited to a party at the Tisdel house, and suddenly he was like one of the family there. Tom, Brandon, and John hung out together; they were getting really close-knit, wrestling each other on the floor, playing drinking games, and comparing notes about their techniques with women. Tom was sleeping with Missy, but he also had a thing for Lana. Once, he said, Kandi found the two of them in the bed at the house on Chase Street; they were kissing and Tom was in his underwear, but he insisted that he and Lana were nothing more than friends and Kandi had to accept that. Kandi knew that Lana fascinated Tom. She could tell he liked every little thing she did, and it made her sick to watch them. She knew Lana was dating Brandon, also that Lana had been involved with John, so it appeared Lana had plenty on her plate. Actually, John Lotter had been Lana's first love, and though he rarely admitted it, deep down, he felt they belonged together. People close to John had the impression he would always be in love with Lana, that he was totally hooked on her. Lana had a *way* with men....

Kandi and Tom fought bitterly about having Lana around, but Tom laid down the law when it came to his house, and he wanted Lana there. He'd seen her around town before, but he never dreamed that he'd actually be with her. Lana was so pretty, so incredibly sexy, she had Tom eating right out of her hand.

36

BY LATE DECEMBER, AT A TIME WHEN THE WEATHER IN Nebraska becomes violent and people across the state start wondering how they'll survive another year, Lana needed Tom's help more than ever. She couldn't allow Brandon to be thrown out on the streets.

Tom said he would provide a place for her and Brandon to hide, and she hoped to hang out at Chase Street just long enough for things to blow over. After all, her mother couldn't stay mad at Brandon forever. Sooner or later Linda would give in and let him come back to live with them.

Linda would just have to.

Slowly but surely, Lana was finding out that everything Brandon told her was a lie, but nevertheless, she had feelings for the guy and she wanted to stick by him in his time of need. It didn't matter that the car he was driving wasn't really his. She found out the Cougar belonged to Lisa Lambert, but so what. It didn't matter that Brandon was a thief. Lana had her concerns about that, sure, but it wasn't anything big enough to make her run out on him now.

"None of the money that he had was his," Lana explained. "I asked where he's getting all this money since he had no job. I thought maybe it was something his mom sent him or something like that."

Caught between Brandon's lies and his mixed-up sexual identity, Lana became pretty confused. In part, she wanted to believe he was a male. After all, she had slept with him, they had gone all the way, and she never questioned his manhood then. Still, in looking back at it, whenever they were together, Brandon had kept the lights out, he had run to the bathroom when it was over, and she didn't know why. Now, she wasn't sure she remembered an ejaculation or anything, and the more she thought about it, the funnier she felt.

"When he got out of jail, he told me he had this operation and that he does have a dick. He was explaining it really weird," Lana explained. "He said it was really, really small at first, but it's, like, a real one, and it's growing. It freaked me out."

When she had visited him in jail, Lana had seen Brandon's chest for the first time. It was when he was leaning over the visiting table, wearing an orange V-neck jail-issue shirt, that she was able to see clearly his female breasts. Lana was stunned; she couldn't believe he had managed to hide a thing like that from her. On their ride home from jail, during the discussion where he explained he was a hermaphrodite, Brandon told her he wanted the penis first, that the breast operation would come later.

That same night, the night Brandon was bailed out, December 22, Linda had just finished with her dart league, her team had won, and they were out at Sportsman's bar having a few drinks to celebrate when in walked Tom Nissen, handing her this note:

Mom,

I love you very much, and don't forget that either. You of all people should understand how I feel and what I'm going through but you don't. If I can't talk to you about this, I can't talk to nobody. If you don't understand, I know nobody will. I just wish you were in my shoes, and maybe you would be able to see things how I see them.

I'm very upset and HURT that you don't. You should accept my feelings about Brandon.

I'm all right, and being taken care of, so please stop Leslie from calling the cops on me. I am a big girl, not a baby.

I Love You—
Love Always, Lana

For over a week, Linda had noticed a big change in Lana, and it really disturbed her. With the reports about Brandon circulating around town, Lana had become increasingly withdrawn. The girl spent most of her time hibernating in the basement, refusing to talk or socialize with anyone.

Linda couldn't understand why her daughter was hooked on someone who lied to her, who made her look like a stupid idiot, yet Lana wouldn't let go. Lana was insisting that even if it turned out that he was a girl, she still loved Brandon as a friend, that they would always have each other.

"She lost respect for herself. Maybe she knew Brandon was actually a female, but she wasn't acknowledging that to anyone else," Linda remembers. "She didn't take care of herself, she didn't eat, she wasn't fixing her hair, she wasn't putting on makeup every day. I don't even think she took a shower every day like she used to."

That night at Sportsman's was the breaking point for Linda. The moment she put Lana's note away, she hightailed it out of the bar and jumped in her car. She followed Nissen over to his place and literally went in and grabbed Brandon by the neck. Twice his size in weight, Linda was an intimidating presence.

"Let's go into the bedroom," she ordered. "You just show me if you are a he or a she, and I'll drop it. One way or another I want to know which one you are."

"OK, I'll show you," be assured her.

At that point, Linda didn't really give a damn *what* sex this person was; she didn't care anymore about lesbians or heterosexuals or anything. She just wanted her daughter back. She wanted to see the old Lana, the happy teenager she loved so well, and she figured knowing the truth about Brandon would solve their problems.

But in the bedroom, Brandon hemmed and hawed. Linda got so frustrated with him, she wound up shoving the kid against a dresser and accidentally shattering the mirror, but that didn't seem to scare Brandon. When Lana heard the scuffle, she barged into the bedroom and tried to patch things.

"If it's really that important to you, Mom, I'll find out right now," Lana said, "but you can't be here. You go wait in the living room."

A few seconds later, Lana emerged and announced that Brandon was, in fact, a male, so Linda was completely at a loss for what to do. She left the house, went to a nearby pay phone to call her ex-husband, Leland Tisdel, and began to confess the whole story.

Lana was Leland's favorite—she was Daddy's girl—and hearing this kind of news didn't sit well with him at all.

When Linda told him she was sure Brandon was a female, Leland hit the roof. He asked for Nissen's address and said he was on his way.

Before he left home, he called the cops and asked them to meet him over there. Leland arrived about the same time as Officer John Caverzagie and Officer Greg Cowan, but it was too late. Just as the two policemen entered the Nissen house, Brandon had escaped out the back door.

In between all the yelling and carrying on, Leland tried to get through to his daughter. Finally, he took her out to his car and calmly asked her a few questions, but for the first time in her life, Lana was disrespectful toward him. She refused to answer. Meanwhile, Linda had gotten so loud and rowdy that, as she got into her car, Caverzagie threatened to arrest her for a DWI. Lana wound up having to drive Linda home, a welcome reprieve from having to deal with her father.

"What did you say to your dad?" Linda wanted to know.

But Lana sat silent, pressing her foot a little harder on the gas pedal. "Did you tell him you're confused? Did you say that this is a boy?"

"I don't know."

"Did you lie to him? Did you tell him the truth?" "I just don't want him mad at me, Mom."

During the confrontation that had gone on in front of the cops, the check that Lana had written on Leland's account for $250 was made known. Linda had blurted it out, and now Leland was angry. Lana had never done that kind of thing before. Still, he felt sorry for his daughter, so for the moment, he said nothing to her about it. That was the least of his worries right then.

The cops had asked if Tisdel wanted to press charges against Lana, and he refused. Although the police said they were going to pursue it regardless, he knew there was really nothing they could do. Leland had signed the check and handed it over to his daughter, so that was that. Leland didn't care what his daughter had written the amount for—really, he just wanted her to get help. He wanted to put her someplace where she could get counseling, and he and Linda briefly discussed sending her to the Methodist Hospital in Omaha for a thirty-day program, both knowing full well that Lana would probably never go for such a thing.

Then as days passed, with Leland out of the picture and Lana growing more despondent and self-destructive, Linda decided that her only recourse was to allow people like Tom Nissen and John Lotter to get involved. She didn't have anyone else to turn to. These were her daughter's closest buddies, and Linda hoped that, with their help, she could knock some sense into her daughter's nineteen-year-old head.

On the surface, John appeared calm when he learned about the whole sordid mess. He told Linda he wanted to help, that he didn't like the idea that Lana had been made a fool of. Moreover, he didn't like the fact that he had been lied to and promised he would get to the bottom of it one way or another.

Late one evening, in the days approaching Christmas, John was able to get Lana alone for a few minutes and talk to her about Brandon being a girl, reiterating some of the rumors floating around, but Lana insisted John didn't know what he was talking about. She said she loved Brandon and contended he was the best thing that ever happened to her. John was wrong about Brandon, Lana said, and besides, it was none of his business.

Exasperated, John finally told her to *go for it*. If Lana wanted a same-sex relationship, that was OK with him. John just wanted to be sure Lana understood that people knew what she was doing. She wasn't fooling anyone, he explained to her, and Lana just nodded her head.

John had never thought of Lana as being gay or bisexual. Now, he just wasn't sure.

37

"EVER SINCE LANA WAS TWELVE OR THIRTEEN, JOHN Lotter had a crush on her. When they were younger, the two of them were kind of an item," Linda revealed. "I didn't want her to marry John. I don't know, at the time he was always in trouble. It was car theft, shoplifting, bad checks, all this kind of stuff. He wasn't a very good influence for her."

Lana was close in age to John's kid sister, Michelle. The two of them were, and always have been, the best of friends.

Growing up, Lana spent more time at the Lotter house than she did her own, her parents having divorced when she was just eight year old. Even at that tender age, she and John seemed to be in love with each other. He was older and wiser, and he showed Lana the ropes.

"I told her he was going to pull her down with him," Linda later said.

"He's going to get you in trouble, and Mama ain't going to be able to get you out of it this time," Linda told Lana once she reached high-school age. She was desperate to keep her away from Lotter.

"No, he won't, Mom. John's sweet. You just don't know him like I do."

"You talk like he's the only guy who is ever going to ask you out. You're only a little girl, honey. When you get older, you'll find out you can have any boy you want."

But Linda's comments went in Lana's one ear and right out the other. Lana didn't have such a great relationship with Linda back then, so it was no wonder she didn't listen. In April 1981, when the marriage of Leland and Linda Tisdel had been dissolved, Leland wound up keeping his three lots of land in Falls City and being awarded custody and control of Leslie Faye and Lana Marie. Linda was left with little or nothing apart from "reasonable" visiting rights. She didn't get any alimony, and she hardly got to see the girls.

Although she missed her children, she was glad to be rid of Leland, a man thirteen years her senior who had been too old-fashioned for her, too much of a drinker, and too much of a gambler. In the settlement, Leland was also awarded their quaint three-bedroom house and their almost new furniture, but that was fine with her. Linda felt she had been a prisoner long enough.

"He slapped me a few times and pulled me down the street by my hair," Linda reflected, "because I guess he wanted somebody to take things out on."

In the beginning, Linda said they had a pretty good marriage. That was, until Leland became obsessed with playing poker and gambling. As time passed, she said, Leland got to the point where he'd have so much money bet on each ball game, he wouldn't let the girls sit in the living room to watch, he wouldn't let Linda watch, so they started having problems.

It didn't help matters that Linda was the housewife from hell—she was expected to handle all the domestic business, but she wasn't any good at it. She never cleaned house enough, she was new at cooking, and she was gone a lot, partying with her friends. When Leslie was just a year and a half old, Linda wasn't paying attention, and the baby immersed herself in a tub of boiling water. Leslie had second degree burns from the waist down. The trauma was so severe, the child's toenails fell off.

In 1977, Linda carried a male fetus for fifteen weeks and lost the baby. She said it was a turning point for her because Leland came to the hospital and accused her of not being "woman enough" to have a boy. Leland had a lot of problems with the way Linda ran around town, with the kind of mother she was, and he made her feel inadequate.

A year or so after the divorce, Linda moved to be with her brother in Great Bend, the place in central Kansas where the Arkansas River makes its sweeping arc. She'd see the girls every once in a while when she'd manage to visit Falls City, but they barely recognized her as their mother. Leslie, then age eleven, was convinced that Linda purposely deserted them. She'd hear horrible reports about her mother's wild behavior; from what she understood, Linda just wasn't the kind of person she would want to call Mom.

"My mom was not perfect," Leslie admitted.

To this day, she resents her bitterly.

After Leland remarried and fathered another child, Leslie ran away from home. Lana eventually wound up leaving Leland's home as well. There was too much sibling rivalry, so she moved down to Gardner, Kansas, just outside Kansas City, to be with Linda.

Lana attended junior high in Gardner, but she didn't like it there. Eventually Linda decided to move back to Falls City so that Lana could attend Falls City High, where Linda had been schooled. Linda figured it was time to move back to her roots. She had been born and raised in Falls City, it was the only place she felt safe and familiar. She was tired of being on the run in Kansas, just bouncing from place to place because of financial hardships.

All along, John Lotter was writing to Lana regularly from prison. He was serving time for escape in Buffalo County, but he kept up with Lana. He always seemed to keep track of Lana's whereabouts even though Lana and

Linda moved around a lot, living in and about the Falls City outskirts in rented farmhouses and beat-up trailers. John's letters were sometimes friendly, sometimes loving, but it seemed to Lana that he was trying to control her from afar. Lana didn't know what he wanted from her; it appeared he wanted her to wait for him to get out of prison, but every time he'd be released, he'd wind up doing something stupid and he'd be jailed again. Prison was a revolving door for him.

Lana cared for John very much, but with him behind bars most of the time, it was hard for her to make any kind of life plans. She'd always write back to him, always encourage him to think about her, to arrange to see him when he got out, but she didn't know if she meant it or not.

Leslie never moved back to Falls City. Instead, she became a drifter, someone who had no real sense of family in the traditional sense. She spent most of her time in and out of abusive relationships with men, all of them fruitless with the exception of her relationship with the love of her life, Duane, which produced a biracial child she named Jasmine. Leslie had the baby out of wedlock and wanted desperately to keep the beautiful little girl, but because she was only seventeen and was in constant trouble with the law, Linda arranged for Leslie to sign custody over to her older half-sister, Jerrylyn. With great hesitation, Leslie did, always hating Linda for it.

The only person Leslie trusted was her sister, Lana. Even though the two of them were as different as oil and water—Leslie was overweight and somewhat overbearing, Lana was the perpetual wilting flower—they shared a strong bond, almost like psychic twins. Leslie would appear in Falls City for very brief stints, popping up out of nowhere like a genie from a bottle, and the two of them would pick up right where they had left off, like no time had ever passed between them.

"Lana is my baby; she is my sweetheart. There's nothing in this world that's going to separate Lana and me," Leslie maintains, "I would *kill* anybody over my sister. She is the only person I have left."

38

LANA WILL GO TO HER GRAVE SWEARING THAT SHE never slept with John Lotter. The two of them dated on and off for years, yet she insists they didn't go beyond just petting and kissing. "We were little bitty kids when we started going out," she explained. "He'd come over to the house or I'd go to his; we'd watch or ride bikes. We were sweethearts, and I mean, I loved him, but he was more in love with me than I was with him."

By the time John was eighteen, he had become something of a stud. He was popular enough in Falls City and was having no trouble dating girls. With his thick long brown hair, compelling blue eyes, and lean physique, he had plenty of young women after him, women who didn't care about his troubles with the law, but he didn't really notice—John was considering marrying Lana.

It was 1990, and he was able to track her down in Gardner, writing to her from prison; telling her, "After all these little flings I've had, I found out that you are the only one for me" and apologizing for his mistakes in the past John asked her not to hold his indiscretions against him, but by then, Lana was already involved with someone else, and she didn't buy John's song and dance. She wrote back to inform him about her new love, an older guy, Roy, and John had no choice but to accept that.

John eventually responded and said he hoped she and Roy would be happy forever, and because it seemed so serious, he wished them all the best. He said he realized that Lana, being a girl and very mature, was looking for an experienced boyfriend, someone who could take care of her in every way. Then Lana suddenly wrote to say she was having problems with Roy, and of course, John couldn't have been more pleased. He consoled her with cards, told her he'd always be her friend, that he was someone she could count on through thick and thin.

In 1991, after he had been paroled, had made amends with Lana, and then had wound up back in prison again, John wrote to her, promising, "I'm going to do everything in my power to hold this relationship together." He asked Lana to write as much as possible, signed every letter "your boyfriend," and professed his love for her over and over.

John was almost twenty and felt he was ready to start a family with someone like Lana. She had developed into a real beauty, her strawberry blond hair reaching her midback, her body imbued with curves. On the outside of envelopes, he'd write, "I love you!" Sometimes he'd send her gushy poems, sometimes it was elaborate drawings, but always with the message, "You're the only one for me."

Of course, Lana had no desire to get married or have kids at the time. She wanted a career and was working on getting her GED and learning computers. She had no desire to get fat and be stuck in a kitchen all day. That's how she viewed motherhood, and it wasn't for her.

All along, John would keep Lana informed about what dates he'd be up for parole, about when they'd be in each other's arms again, but at the same time, he was hearing rumors that Lana was with other guys, and the more reports he received about that, the more pissed he got. He still wanted to be with her when he got free—maybe—if she wasn't the Jezebel his friends had made her out to be.

When John got back to Falls City, in mid-1992, he and Lana dated, but their relationship had begun to disintegrate permanently. Lana's biggest problem with John was that he was too jealous. Whenever he saw her talking to another guy, he'd start to call her names and make a big scene in front of people. Lana couldn't stand it. The worst of it was that John himself was the biggest cheat going, lying and sneaking around on her more than ever. One time, Lana had caught him in his living room, making out with some girl on his lap; another time it was her sister, Leslie, he was smooching with. Lana couldn't believe it. Leslie was drunk, so she had an excuse, but she could never trust John again.

Still, John was fun, so very fun, always goofing on people and pulling pranks, and Lana liked hanging around him. She needed the kind of attention he gave her, and she liked to be able to pull his strings. Even when she seriously started dating another guy, Bummy, Lana still made sure that John was in the picture. Actually, she couldn't have kept him out of it if she wanted to. When it came to Lana, John was relentless.

"One day, Leslie brought John down to Kansas, to Sabetha. She brought him down there just so he could catch me and Bummy," Lana confided. "Well, John started talking to Bummy, and I don't know what him and John said to each other, but we all left there and we cruised to my house, and John got all mad, calling me a bitch and a slut and a whore. Then I think I talked to him about a week later, and he was fine. He wasn't mad at me or anything."

The Lotter house was, and still is, a strange-looking place, but that was something Lana overlooked. In fact, Lana was like most people who know the Lotters. They tended to excuse the bizarre outward appearance of the Lotter place and, instead, talked about how much work had been done on the inside, how many walls had been taken down and replaced, how much paneling had been put up.

Most friends ignored the fact that the exterior was crawling with mold and was partially boarded up, because after all, that should have been a job for Terry, who had never really been around much to be a dad or a husband. Donna handled the inside, and working as hard as she did in three jobs—as a waitress, a grocery checkout person, and a nurse's aide—nobody ever had the heart to hold her responsible for the outward mess.

Throughout all the years they were married, Terry and Donna had a peculiar arrangement. He went out openly with other women, and when he did decide to show up at home, he slept in the master bedroom by himself. Because she worked all the time, Donna caught catnaps on the living room couch in lieu of a real nights' sleep and never socialized, much less dated.

The two of them would usually meet in passing and have little or nothing to say to each other. All the years flew by, they grew so far apart it became hard for people to believe they had five children together. There was Rodney, who eventually defected and moved to California, rarely to be heard from again, then Bill, who wound up permanently living in the Lotter house with his wife and kids, developing a reputation for being a big bully around town. There was Angie, a quiet, soft-spoken girl who moved to Tarkio, Missouri, a farm town where she could take college courses to better herself, then Michelle, a fiercely independent girl who renovated the upstairs level of the house as her apartment, drove a leased sports car, excelled in high school athletics, but never took advantage of her college scholarship. And finally, there was John, who became the family's career criminal and all-around black sheep.

Always with a smile, eyes bright, Donna had juggled three jobs most of her adult life. Determined to make up for her husband's lackadaisical attitude about earning an income, she sacrificed being at home, raising her children, without ever giving it a second thought. Terry worked, sometimes as a bartender, sometimes at other part-time jobs, but most of his money seemed to go for liquor. That's where Terry Lotter spent the majority of his time, warming bar stools at the Oasis, Subby's Southside, or Prater's Place, the three busiest hangouts in Falls City.

Anita Lundy, the Lotters' next-door neighbor for twenty years, perpetually felt sorry for Donna as did so many others. At night, she'd see Terry out partying with the single crowd, then the next day, there Donna would be at home on Wilson Street, exhausting herself on some chore or repair, knocking herself out trying to control the kids. It was endless for Donna; there was always something that needed to be done.

A widow, Anita also had her hands full raising her two boys all alone, and she'd sometimes rely on the Lotter girls to help baby-sit. Angie was only too happy to help out. Michelle was too, although she wasn't Anita's choice—

Angie was her favorite. Michelle was always a little too loud and aggressive for Anita, even as a kid.

And then there was Johnny.

He'd come over to Anita's house and wreak havoc, but most of the time, he was smart enough not to get caught. From the day he was five years old, when she first moved to Wilson Street in the mid-1970s, Anita began to think Johnny was the devil incarnate. According to her, so many bad things happened with Johnny back then, it would be impossible for her to recount them all.

"When my son Bobby was just over a year old, I was going out to get paint, and my brother was there. I had Bobby on a bouncing seat out on the porch, and I asked Johnny if he could sit and play with him for a few minutes," Anita reminisced. "I hadn't even gotten down the street when my brother came running out, telling me Johnny had hit my little boy in the eye with a hammer and cut his eye open. Bobby's still got a drooping eye today, sixteen years later."

Lundy never forgave John for that. At the time, she wanted to confront Terry Lotter about it but then decided not to. She figured it would be better just to be neighborly, to kind of let it die down. But as time rolled on, Lundy's problems with Johnny only got worse.

While she never caught him in the act, she was sure he was the one who threw house paint all over her back porch, spray-painted her truck and took a magic marker and wrote the F word all over it, threw mud all over her sister-in-law's laundry—it just went on and on. Lundy's sister-in-law called the police about the laundry incident, but they said there was nothing they could do. When Anita approached Donna about it, she had absolutely nothing to say.

"Johnny would sit and cuss you out like a trooper, you know, even at a young age," Anita remembers. "And I'd say, *'Stay over on your side. Don't come over here.'* And like, for four or five years, I wouldn't even let my younger son go out and play. I almost kept him prisoner in my house. I couldn't turn him out loose because there wasn't a time when Johnny wasn't doing something. He'd throw rocks, destroy property; he was always thinking of something devious to do."

On one occasion, while Angie was baby-sitting, Johnny tried to get into the Lundy house, but Angie was following strict orders not to allow anyone in, so Johnny decided to punch his way through the glass screen door. The boy had to be rushed to the hospital for stitches, but he seemed to derive pleasure from it.

"I know his mom sent him to foster homes. I'm not exactly sure when she started sending him, but I know she started having some serious problems with him," Lundy recalls. "We'd see each other outside, and one time, I was working out in the yard, and I asked her how Johnny was doing, and she told me that he had gotten mad in this foster place in Omaha and that basically he had taken a pencil and stabbed it all the way through a boy's arm."

With the exception of Johnny, Anita liked the Lotter kids. She treated Angie like one of her own, having the little girl over and making a fuss about brushing her hair and dolling her up. With Johnny, she felt the main problem was that he was starved for attention. Being the youngest, Johnny couldn't understand why Terry was gone more and more, why Donna worked around the clock. He was also being picked on by his brothers and sisters. According to close friends, John claimed the abuse in his household was rampant. Left to raise themselves alone, John said there were abusive acts that went on between the siblings.

"Johnny was probably eleven or twelve and I was sitting in my house when I heard screaming and fighting going on like you would not believe," Lundy remembered. "So I went outside, and Johnny had a butcher knife about ten inches long, and Michelle was lying on the ground with her feet sticking up on his chest. He and she had gotten into a fight, he had that butcher knife out, and he told he was going to kill her."

Lundy ran over, grabbed the knife from Johnny, and told Michelle to go call her mom at work. Not long after that, Johnny was sent off again, but Lundy never could keep track of where the kid was going or what trouble he was into next. Whenever she'd ask Donna about him, Donna would make a circle with her hand in the air around her ear, indicating that he was crazy, and then she'd just shake her head.

That became the standard response.

At one point, however, Donna admitted that she was afraid of Johnny, as were her daughters. When Anita heard that, she tried to get some details out of Donna about it, but that just got Donna angry. Eventually, Lundy became frightened herself, and she put No Trespassing signs out on her property. She didn't know what else to do.

"The girls, when they were younger, clear up to their early teens, were petrified of him," Lundy said. "When they'd come to my house, they'd say they were scared to death of Johnny. They told me they wished he would never come back, that they wished they'd keep him put away forever."

As a young teen, Johnny would steal money from a local gas station or rob someone's home, and he'd be sent off to a juvenile detention center for a while, but it was primarily petty stuff, so he never stayed in for long.

In 1980, John was made a ward of the state and was handed over to foster parents where he lived on and off for six years, but even with their special training, John made trouble at the foster residence. His parents, Clarence and Helen Robinson, tried to deal with his problematic behavior, but John showed an inability to establish loyalty to any person, creed or cause. They finally gave up.

By the mid-1980s, Lotter had developed such a rap sheet, it was enough to officially categorize him as a habitual criminal. As far back as 1979, he had been charged with vandalism and misdemeanor theft for taking things like bicycles and car keys. Throughout the decade, his illustrious career involved numerous assault charges, as well as joyriding, fleeing to avoid arrest, burglary, and an attempt to hang himself in jail.

In 1985, a psychological evaluation was performed on Lotter which revealed evidence of soft neurological findings: the consulting psychiatrist, Dr. James Baldwin, noted that John's head was misshapen. His ears were misshapen as well. Baldwin also noticed some facial dyssynchrony—the two sides of Lotter's face were not symmetrical.

That same year, Lotter's Child Welfare Worker in Omaha received some discouraging news—John had been turned down by Father Flanagan's Boys Town. It was the last hope for Lotter, because from then on, he lived in criminal facilities, increasingly in trouble with the law because of his attempts to escape, to return *home*. Lotter was a "very angry, hostile, violent and uncontrollable youngster," the Boys Town Director had written, and Boys Town was "not the appropriate place."

And it was true, of course, that Lotter needed to be taught respect, that he was characterized by utter defiance. Still, there was an inner core to him. He was plagued by insecurity—a cream puff inside. The year before, when John was twelve, he wrote an evaluation of himself saying, "most boys do not like me" and "most girls hate me." Because of his misshapen ears, kids called him Dumbo. John wanted to start over, to be accepted by his peers, but they taunted him.

"He was always like he hated the world," Lundy later reflected. "When he looked at me, he'd send cool shivers down my spine. I always thought he was gonna come back from a foster home and kill his family. I always thought that, looking at the glare in his eyes. He had eyes like Charlie Manson. That's who he reminded me of."

39

"SEE, IT'S LIKE THIS. LANA'S BOYFRIENDS THAT SHE would go out with, John would want to be there. John would want to know everything from the time they were born, who changed their diapers, *everything*," Leslie recalled. "Just like with Brandon. John wanted to know about Brandon."

When John and Lana broke up, he started seeing Rhonda McKenzie, a heavy-set high school girl who worshiped the ground he walked on. John cheated on her whenever he pleased, but Rhonda never quite figured that out. She wanted to believe his lies and tall tales. Rhonda's mother, Novella, warned her about Lotter time and again, but the girl had blinders on. Rhonda eventually became pregnant by him and gave birth to their little girl, Rochelle, which was one way to pin him down, she hoped.

But John still carried on with his string of girlfriends, including Lana, who he was very kissy and huggy with in front of everyone. Of course, Lana and Leslie were still very close with John and his sister Michelle. Whenever they were all in town, the four of them teamed up together, always there for each other in a pinch, more like family than friends. They pulled a lot of pranks together—stealing the signs from Pizza Hut, and turning over carts behind warehouses, which eventually Brandon participated in when he became part of their set. Brandon stole a clock from the Falls City Hospital, and he took a metal cow out of someone's yard and gave it to Lana—he was into doing those petty little crimes, the type of stuff no one could ever prove.

* * *

Of course, Leslie was always a little jealous of Lana. She had never known the kind of devotion and love that John showed Lana. Leslie was in constant search of that special someone, but she always wound up getting hurt.

In the fall of 1993, Leslie decided to get her act together for once. She figured if she made something of herself, she'd find the right guy and hopefully get married, so she enrolled herself in the Job Corps program in

Denison, Iowa—the hometown of Donna Reed—the perfect all-American setting for the ideal life she dreamed of living.

Leslie had high hopes. With the proper training in a trade, she could finally have some job prospects and might even be able to get into college one day. Her family was behind her— Linda and Lana had driven her up there and helped her get set up—so she felt good about that.

Denison is a quaint little town, about twenty miles northeast of Omaha through the Missouri Valley. You know when you approach it, because there's a big white block-letter sign on a hill, reminiscent of the giant Hollywood sign. Even though it's an industrial place, the town's slogan is It's a Wonderful Life, in honor of their beloved Donna Reed and her role in that movie.

It's a lily white town, with incredible Victorian homes lining sleepy streets, a large agricultural workforce, and two packing plants, where they slaughter cattle and hogs. On windy days, you can smell the odor of something like bacon permeating the air, but people from Denison are so used to it that they hardly seem to notice. On the cusp of middle class, the town is somewhat economically depressed, but it still has its fair share of bars and restaurants and a striptease club called Book 'Em Danos, which does a very good business. Of course, the kids from Job Corps don't go there—most of them are under the drinking age. Besides, the locals don't mix very well with outsiders. Job Corps kids basically keep to themselves.

The Job Corps sits up on a big hill just outside town, with an American flag flying proud and high. It's a place that takes in kids from around the region, gets them off the streets, gives them a free residential education, and prepares them for well-paying jobs. The facility in Denison is one of the best in the country, with a caring staff and a high-performing student body, and Phillip DeVine was one of the stars there, an exemplary kid who everyone knew and liked.

President of the Business and Professional Association, DeVine had been selected that year to represent the campus at a Job Corps conference in Washington, D.C., where he met with U.S. Senators Tom Harkin and Charles Grassley on Capitol Hill. His Job Corps family was ever so proud of him for that, and Dick Knowles, the town's newspaper editor and one of the people responsible for bringing Job Corps to Denison, encouraged DeVine to consider running for mayor.

"Phillip was a leader. He was an outstanding charismatic-type student," Job Corps Officer Ike Johnson recalled. "He was the kind of student a lot of other students would like to emulate because he had those leadership qualities. People were just drawn to him. He had the attention of adults, which is unusual for a young man. It's almost like he was destined to become so much more in his life."

Not only was Phillip a smart kid, he was a smart dresser and a good-looking guy. He had his choice of girls on campus and, having been there a while, had dated plenty. But it wasn't just the girls who liked Phillip, he was loved by those around him because he had a knack, a way of talking to people that got them on his side.

Leslie thought Job Corps was a little tike being in the military. Things were very strict on the campus, but she knew she needed that, and having grown up in girls homes and institutions, she was used to it. Leslie just wanted to learn to be more responsible, find a goal to strive for, and see the true value of life. On the day she headed up Opportunity Drive toward the campus, she felt this was her big chance.

Almost from the moment Leslie met DeVine, she couldn't help but notice him—he was one of those people who stand out in a crowd. Being just a year older than her, age twenty-two, she was already thinking of him as marriage material. He was the right age, the right size, the right color for her. Leslie had no idea what a big flirt Phillip was and hadn't ever considered that he might be jiving her a little bit when they first met. But even if he was, Phillip soon came to care for Leslie. He paid no attention to his friends when they teased him about hanging around her so much.

When Leslie eventually confided to Phillip that she had an interracial baby she wanted to regain custody of and raise, he seemed to jump at the idea. Phillip told her he'd help father the girl, and Leslie took what he said at face value. She thought her prayers had been answered.

Although overweight, Leslie still had a unique sensuality about her. Others couldn't really see it, but Phillip wanted her. He told Leslie he wanted her more than he ever wanted anyone, and before long, the two of them spent their days planning their future together. Though it seemed crazy to people who knew Phillip—they thought he was jumping into something much too quickly—Phil and Leslie had an exclusive bond, and no one could tell him he didn't really love her. Phillip thought he did.

In late November, just before Thanksgiving, Leslie was terminated from the Job Corps because of a medical problem she was having, and her mom drove up to get her. Leslie's initial motivation had disappeared. She was having pains all the time stemming from a tubular pregnancy in her past, and the Job Corps director had made the final decision: there were no more excuses that were going to keep Leslie Tisdel in a program that she wasn't really working at. Leslie seemed absolutely Crushed about it. She didn't think it was fair, and life wasn't worth living without Phillip. She made him promise to come see her as soon as the semester was over, and she hoped he would make it to Falls City before Christmas. Phil swore he would do everything in his power to get there.

Although his mother called from Fairfield, Iowa, asking him to return home to be with the family, Phillip had no intention of being with family that holiday. His sights were set on Leslie. The two of them hadn't had sex yet, and Phillip intended to make passionate love to her, not just to get laid, because he believed they had something more real.

Before she left, he took Leslie aside and told her that he planned to settle down in Colorado Springs one day, that he wanted her and her daughter to be with him. He was looking for someone to love and possibly marry, and even though Leslie was white and he had mixed emotions about that, he thought she might be the one. He said he wanted their relationship to work.

"He used to take out very nice looking girls, very nice intellectual girls, and along came this lady who was different, and everybody said, 'My God, Phil DeVine is going out with her?' They used to say it just like that," Johnson reminisced. "Somebody said she was a sloppy character. I don't remember her face. It's hard to say what her appeal was, she got connected with Phil so quickly."

40

PHILLIP WAS BORN TWO MONTHS PREMATURE INTO A life-and-death situation—his one limb hadn't formed and he had severe breathing problems. At the time, his mother, Phyllis DeVine, had been taking DES, a morning sickness pill, which they later discovered created birth defects.

"They wanted to put Phillip into an institution because they felt he would never be able to function," his mother explained. "His lungs were scarred like he had been smoking for fifty years, he had a tracheotomy, and he had a heart problem, so he was on digitalis. It was like touch and go, touch and go, and they kept trying to bring him down because they said he couldn't survive like that."

Phyllis learned how to use a suction machine to clean out the trachea, and she brought the baby home, but it was difficult, because in addition to having to give him medication and having to worry about his limbs and lungs, because of the trachea, Phillip made no real vocal sounds, so there was no way to know if he was crying, sleeping, or even *breathing*. The only noise he made was a faint whistle.

Eventually, Phillip had to have two major operations. One was on his eyes—they had to cut the muscles because his eyes were crossing—the other was on his leg. Because he didn't have a bone from the knee down, there were two toes and part of a heel sticking directly out of the upper limb, which had to be fitted for a prosthesis. Eventually, Phillip was weaned off the tracheostomy and the digitalis, but all the stress in dealing with his problems took its toll on Phyllis. She had another son, Paul III, who was five at the time of Phillip's birth in 1971, and her husband, Paul DeVine Jr., didn't help out very much with either of the boys. The burden was mostly on her.

As a way to relax, Phyllis turned to transcendental meditation. She hadn't been getting much sleep, and she figured it was worth a try, so she attended a meeting in nearby Los Angeles. The DeVines were living in Pasadena at the time, and Phyllis suddenly got heavily involved in the TM organization and started spending a lot of time away from home.

In almost no time, she became a TM teacher, was sent off to Ethiopia for a few weeks, and came back with a new name, Aisha, meaning life. By then, her marriage to Paul was rocky, and Aisha opened a little TM center in Pasadena, where she worked as a volunteer, dragging her kids along, but she and Paul still had their differences. Finally, they decided to divorce. Their split-up was messy, and it was a hard time for her.

One afternoon, when the boys were ages eight and three, Aisha went to see the Maharishi Mahesh Yogi, founder of the TM movement, who was speaking at the Beverly Wilshire Hotel in Beverly Hills. She left the boys on their own, figuring they'd be OK for a few hours, but she had to wait so many hours to see the Maharishi, she never made it home that night. She called her son Paul and told him to take a bus over to their grandma's on the other side of Pasadena, thinking everything would work out fine, but when Edith DeVine saw her two grand-babies arriving unescorted, that was the final straw. Edith had all she could take of Phyllis's irresponsibility, of her ridiculous meditation, her zany African names—it was all too much. Phyllis was so busy finding herself, she was neglecting the boys, and Edith and Paul Sr. pressured their son to get a lawyer and take permanent custody.

"I didn't have a refrigerator to keep my baby's milk cold. I'd go around to restaurants to get hot food because I was cooking on a hot plate, and Paul wasn't giving me any money," Aisha confided. "So I thought, maybe he'll take care of his kids. I was living off AFDC [Aid to Families with Dependent Children], and I needed to be able to go out and find work. He was remarried at the time, he was stable, he had a big house, and I didn't have anything."

Aisha thought she was making the right choice, hoping that Paul would be able to better provide for the boys, but the whole plan backfired. She says that Paul used the kids against her, and that for years to come, he filled their heads with hateful thoughts about her. His parents pretty much went along with him, because as far as they were concerned, Phyllis was demon possessed. Her TM entailed things like levitation and altered brain wave patterns, and as strict Seventh-Day Adventists, the DeVines certainly didn't approve of this. Then too, they claim Phyllis started living with a woman, hinting that she had turned bisexual—an allegation Phyllis denies, but which nonetheless infuriated her ex father-in-law. He started to believe Phyllis was one with the devil, that she was using the TM as a way to avoid her children, in particular, as a way to escape Phillip's handicaps, and that was just *inexcusable*.

"My own opinion is that Phyllis, in a sense, rejected her son Phillip," Paul Sr. later reflected. "She would always take Paul with her, but she wouldn't want this little handicapped boy with her."

Of course, Aisha's son Paul didn't remember that his mother played any favoritism. Then again, Paul doesn't remember much of his mother from his early childhood days.

He and Phillip were raised by their stepmother, Henrietta, and every weekend, they'd visit their grandparents, Paul and Edith.

"We dealt with Phillip's leg like he was any other child," Edith remembers. "We told him, 'You're no different from anyone else. You can ride a bike or do anything you want to do.' And he did all that. He rode his bike, played basketball, he learned to swim. People were shocked when they found out he only had the one leg. He had just a small limp, and that was it."

In 1984, Phillip moved to Maryland with his dad. Paul had gotten divorced again and was starting life over, having decided it best to live near his sister Denise. Denise had become a successful entrepreneur in leasing and selling computers, and Paul needed her help in raising Phillip. As it turned out, Denise was a tremendous force in Phillip's life. She dressed him in the finest clothes, sent the boy to private schools, had people working with his learning disabilities, and was able to give Phillip a strong sense of self.

During those years, Philip had no contact whatsoever with his mother, who had remarried and had started a new family with Roy McCain, a man she met in the TM group in California not long after her divorce. In the early eighties, the two of them had relocated to Fairfield, the home of Maharishi International University, where people supposedly experienced the deepest levels of their own intelligence through meditation. The university offered a holistic education and a global background that Aisha and Roy wanted to be a part of. The campus, situated on 262 acres of rolling hills, promised to be a place where they could grow in their abilities, could learn to accomplish anything. TM taught that they could spontaneously think and act-free from mistakes—and they believed it, being the complete idealists they both were.

In the mid-1980s, Paul III decided he wanted to come live with Aisha, and she couldn't have been more delighted. Paul became a sophomore at Fairfield High, but as much as Aisha tried to acclimate him, Paul didn't like it in Iowa very much.

For one thing, he had fallen in "like" with a white girl and was being given a hard time about it by the townsfolk, and then it turned out there were no people of color for him to hang with, so he felt isolated.

On top of that, although he tried to be open to his mother's "self-awareness" and was given a mantra, he felt like the spiritual trip was too much. Paul didn't believe in the bubbling bliss of yogic flying or far-out things like that. He heard a lot about people in TM who could fly, or "jet" in the air, but he never witnessed it. After a year in Fairfield, Paul had just about enough, and he returned to his roots in California, eventually marrying a girl in L.A. and settling down with a sales job at Radio Shack.

"My mother is very spiritual," Paul III later admitted. "I must have been like six or seven when she changed her name, and she even tried changing our names, but our father wasn't going for it. My father was real supportive of the eastern philosophy, the meditation. That's more like guru stuff, sort of like Buddhism. But my grandparents thought it was like voodoo. They'd tell me, 'Your mother is practicing witchcraft.'

"All these years, my grandparents told Phil and me something totally contradictory to what my mother was saying," Paul said. "My mother is more in tune, not just with the physical law, but the spiritual law. She's into herbs and rocks and stuff like that. But a lot of that crap, me and my brother didn't embrace."

Back in Maryland, Phillip began to have some typical growing-up problems at home. At the age of seventeen, he had fallen in love, had thought he'd gotten the girl pregnant, and had decided to make it on his own. Working at McDonald's, he felt he could earn enough for himself and his girl to start a family. His grandfather happened to be visiting the East Coast at the time, and he tried to straighten Phillip out, to tell him the facts of life and keep him from making a mistake so young, but Phillip resented it.

"They thought they could rent an apartment, get married, and live happily ever after," Paul Sr. recalls. "He even brought me the newspaper and showed me an apartment he could get for $400 a month, and I had to explain to him that even if he had $400 a month, he'd have to pay for food and transportation and so forth. He did not have the knowledge or the wisdom to sit down and see what these things were going to cost, and in that sense, you might say he was in a dream world."

Just before Phillip turned twenty, he had a confrontation with his mother on the phone, and she explained away some of the falsehoods he had grown up believing. She told him she would always love him, told him of the many times she had wanted to steal him and his brother away from their father, and said she always knew Phillip would come to know who she was down the road. She had been waiting for the day.

His girlfriend had left him, he never could hold down a job, and Phillip decided he was tired of Maryland and the D.C. area. So he called his mom and told her he wanted to give Iowa a try. Aisha didn't force him to go to school. Phillip wanted to work at Hardee's and study at home, on his own, which was fine with her. Phillip liked Fairfield, but he got bored there and went to Job Corps about a year after he arrived.

"Phillip got to know me. Phillip's joy was cooking, and he'd be at home in Fairfield, trying these recipes. He thought about becoming a chef and owning his own restaurant at one time," Aisha reminisced. "He also used to study a lot about spiritual life; he wanted to learn. He wanted to study the Bible in its original text and the original of the Koran and meld the two. He wanted to show people that they worship the same God. They're just looking at different angles."

For Phillip's twenty-second birthday, Aisha took him on a religious pilgrimage to Mother Cabrini's Shrine in Golden, Colorado, a Denver suburb, where apparitions of the Virgin Mary had been seen. Phillip had once told Aisha he had seen the image of the Virgin Mary in a tree outside their Fairfield house. He had some kind of special relationship with the Holy Mother, he told his mom so she knew the trip to Colorado was important to him. By the time his birthday rolled around that year, October 8, 1993, Phil was close to finishing his curriculum as a Job Corps student, but he had come back from Denison to recuperate from a football injury. Phil had broken his good leg playing touch football with a few of the guys and had gone through major surgery to put five pins in his leg to reinforce it.

"He walked up a hundred-something steps with a cast on his leg, and this is his good leg, which means he can't put weight on his artificial leg," Aisha recalled. "It was an ordeal for him to go to the top of the shrine. I was really surprised. He really had to go through a lot of effort to get up there. We took a picture of the two of us at the top."

41

IT WAS DECEMBER 14 WHEN PHILLIP HIT OMAHA. Actually, it was the very same day Brandon had been bonded out of jail. Lisa, Brandon, and Leslie went to pick him up at the station, but as Soon as they got back to Leslie's house, Leslie and Phillip were at odds, and Phil realized he had made a mistake. Leslie had another guy staying over at the house, her buddy Lenny Landrum, and Phillip didn't appreciate it. Phil thought Lenny should leave.

Leslie promised him they were only just friends, but Phillip would hardly listen. As far as Phillip could tell, he needed to get out of Falls City. Still, it was the holiday, so Phil figured he better make the best of it, and the first night, he and Leslie consummated their relationship, which turned out to be a good thing. Suddenly, they felt so much closer to each other, even if Leslie thought Phillip was the most jealous guy she'd ever met.

Before he arrived, Phil had written Leslie saying he was scared to show his feelings, that he didn't want to be hurt, that he didn't want to let his guard down. In his letter, he admitted that he loved her, said he thought they really had each other figured out, and brought up the issue of Leslie's child, Jasmine, reminding her that he always wanted to name his own child that, that he really wanted to be a father to Leslie's little girl.

But Leslie had forgotten about all that by the time Phil showed up. She was too busy being angry at Phil's outrageous possessiveness. Back at Job Corps, she had told him she had a lot of male friends, and he seemed to be cool with that. Now, in Falls City, he couldn't accept it. She didn't think things were ever going to work out for the two of them, and she started giving Phillip a hard time, telling him she wanted to break up. Yes, she would always keep and cherish the teddy bear he'd given her, and yes, she saved the roses from him; they were pressed in a book. Nonetheless, she couldn't see them spending their lives together, not with Phil accusing her of bedding every guy she hung around with.

Phil immediately apologized, told her he'd always love her, said he wanted her to stop playing games, and Leslie finally gave him another chance.

However, as the days passed, Phil was back to his old accusatory ways, and Leslie could hardly tolerate him being around.

She wasn't about to let him interfere with her having fun with her family and friends over the holidays, and by Christmas Eve, as far as Leslie was concerned, Phil was just an extra. He could come and go as he pleased. Leslie just didn't care.

"I'm not used to somebody being nice to me. I have to go clear back, back to the days with one of my old boyfriends, because that's who got me used to the abuse, to the being spit on," Leslie confided. "He used to spit in my face, knock me around, cheat on me, have sex with my best friend, and then come back to me. He even gave me gonorrhea."

Leslie never knew her worth. She only knew pity, anger, sorrow, and shame. Her life has always been one big sob story, filled with incidents that have gotten her locked up in juvenile detention, with thoughts of her personal pain and suicide. She was always nothing but trouble. The constant theme for Leslie is to shift blame on others; it's always someone else's fault.

Leslie even slit her wrists once, at age sixteen, but she was found, stitched up, and placed in her mom's custody for a while until she ran away again. At that age, she hated both her mother and her father; Lana was always her father's favorite. She admitted she started to date black men exclusively just to get back at Leland. In fact, Leslie says when she was seven months pregnant with Jasmine and her father learned of the interracial baby, he disowned his daughter. Leland only began to tolerate Leslie again after she gave the baby up.

"There's so much anger, so much hate that I have inside of me, it's just sad," Leslie admitted. "I don't like to go into my childhood details. All three of us—me, Jerrylyn, and Lana—we've seen men beat our mom. We've seen them throw my mom down, beat the shit out of her. I mean, my childhood, it's fucked. That's why I'm so stubborn.

"I have to give Phillip some credit," she tearfully went on. "He was a nice guy. I had someone that was really good, but it was just that I was so used to the abuse, I wasn't used to the someone being nice to me. Phillip wouldn't hit me. I wanted him to hit me. I'm used to pushing someone to the point where they explode, to the to the point where I'm going to get hit. But Phillip wouldn't do it."

Phillip was a pretty easygoing guy. When he realized that Lenny was going to be at the Tisdels' home, that his objections were going to be ignored, Phil befriended the young man. It turned out that Phil and Lenny each belonged to rival gangs—Lenny was one of the Crips, Phil had once been part of the Bloods—so they were supposed to hate each other. But the feud between those two groups had calmed down over the years, and both of them felt that gangs should work together rather than against each other. They spent their time talking about more important things, like Salt-n-Pepa, Boys II Men,

Michael Jordan, and the Chicago Bulls.

"In lots of places, the Crips and Bloods have joined together; they've become one. A lot of things have been changing. The Crips and Bloods aren't a problem anymore, not as much as other gangs, like the Vato Loco Boys-that's Spanish for crazy dudes," Lenny explained. "You see, the gang I stand in, we are not a gang that goes out to shoot somebody. We are a gang that just kicks back and has a good time. We're not like those other kinds of gangs that want to go out and fuck other people up."

Being a person of color himself, Lenny understood Phillip's uneasiness about Falls City. Then again, Lenny was only half black, so he was accepted a little bit better, plus he had lived there on and off, had even gone to school there for a while. Lenny had become sort of family with the Tisdels—he spent a few months with them the year before—and he'd gotten to know their circle. The people the Tisdels hung around with were OK. They weren't judgmental and narrow-minded; they all seemed nice.

That week, Lenny and Phil hung out with John Lotter and Tom Nissen a little bit. They all went down to Stanton Lake a few times, and John was usually a blast to be around, Tom was a bit of a jerk, but they all drank a lot and made jokes and didn't really pay attention to their differences. It wasn't like Lenny and Phil were being trashed or being called names. Everything was cool.

Actually, it was Lana and Lisa who had become the subject of vicious tongues around Richardson County. People were calling them lesbians; they were shooting their mouths off, saying stupid things. Lana was picked on at the Kwik Shop in Falls City. Lisa was mocked at a barn dance in Humbolt. The two of them suffered in their own worlds—rejected and deceived, yet still believing that somehow none of it was real, that Brandon *had* to be a man.

"Everyone in Humbolt knew about Brandon. Lisa didn't try to hide it," Tammy Dush said. "Lisa couldn't believe something like this happened to her. She made it clear that she was too caring to shut Brandon out. She was mad and hurt about it, but she didn't want to hurt him, didn't want to turn him out on the streets. She was afraid something bad might happen. She thought maybe people from his past might want to do him in."

42

AJAX OF HOMER'S *ILIAD* IS A MAN OF BRUTE STRENGTH. So is the mythical Hercules, who gave Atlas a break by holding up the world. In America, there's Superman, Paul Bunyan, and a little known figure named Antoine Barada of Richardson County, a real person among Nebraska's nineteenth century pioneers, a legend in the region who, they say, would lift stranded boats out of the Missouri River with his bare hands.

Barada Street in Falls City is named after him, and the locals have long known the tales of his he-man strength, of his great machismo. These days, the younger generations have not really grown up on Barada stories, but regardless, there's a general regard for male bravado that prevails in Falls City; it's in the air. It's a sensibility that's pretty much implied.

Like everything in downtown Falls City, Barada Street runs very close to Chase Street; they're just seconds apart.

When you drive down Chase, you pass the Tru-Value hardware store, the Wagon Wheel Restaurant, then Mr. Automotive before you get to the Nissens' white-frame home. Ironically, the house is located right across the street from the Blue Valley Mental Health Center, so Tom probably felt comfortable there in a subconscious kind of way. It's a flimsy little house, with a crooked front porch slanting down to the sidewalk and a wooden heart hanging on the door, engraved with the word Welcome, visible only if you get close enough.

On Christmas Eve a group of people were over there playing cards, drinking, and having a good old time. The Christmas tree was lit, it was lightly snowing outside, and they were all happy to be in a cozy spot, sheltered from the extreme cold and wind outdoors. There was Leslie and Phil, Lana and Brandon, John and Rhonda, and of course Tom and Kandi, Tom's brother, Scott, and the Nissen and Lotter kids running around, who were waiting for Santa—their toys all wrapped and hiding under Tom and Kandi's bed.

For much of the night, people were downing a lot of alcohol—Jack Daniels, schnapps, whatever they could get their hands on, playing a drinking game at the kitchen table. The house was a disaster. There was garbage and empty beer cans and Jack bottles everywhere, and everybody started getting wild and stupid as the night went on, the celebrating having begun in the early afternoon. Actually, some people had started showing up at Tom's as early at 10:00 that morning. His buddies Jason Specht and Eddie Schlicker had popped in around then, which is when Tom and John had started guzzling the first case of Busch Light. The two of them were completely fired up by the time the evening guests arrived.

That night, Lana was looking her best in new tight black jeans with her hair perfectly done and full makeup on. Brandon was dressed down, real casual, like the rest of the guys.

Still very much a couple, Brandon and Lana acted like love birds, constantly kissing and touching each other. The two of them seemed joined at the hip, and some people were rather sick of watching it.

John Lotter was teasing and carrying on as usual, purposely bumping into Rhonda and then saying, "Oops, I didn't mean to do that," getting more and more obnoxious as the evening progressed. By 1:00 in the morning, John wasn't being funny anymore, he was getting vicious, and he started in on Brandon's case, teasing him about being a girl, telling him that he was horny, saying that he wanted to have sex, that he felt like getting laid.

Brandon told John he might as well forget it.

Tom Nissen was also pushing Brandon's buttons whenever he had the chance. Several times that night, he sat Brandon down and said, "Look, I'm tired of hollering at you. Why don't you just tell the truth and get it over with?"

"Brandon, you're going to have to leave," Tom finally insisted. "I know I promised that you can stay here, but in the morning you're going to have to go back to jail because Lana asked me. I asked Lana if I could take you back to jail tonight, and she said to take you in the morning."

"Lana never said that," Brandon argued. "You're so full of shit, Tom, and you don't know what the fuck you're talking about. You can't put me in jail just 'cause you bonded me out. Who the hell do you think you are? The cops?"

The two of them got into a yelling match, and it got hot and heavy for a while. Tom pointed his finger at Brandon, Brandon pushed Tom back up against the wall, and they were both up in each other's faces, both kind of drunk.

The two of them moved into the bathroom, and Brandon pushed Tom again, this time knocking him into a cabinet. When Tom spun and hit the floor, he picked himself up and came back at Brandon with a punch.

At that point, Brandon got himself up over the sink to look at the damage. Of course, Lana was already long gone, already home opening Christmas presents with Leslie and Linda, so there was no one who could save him, no one to step in between the three of them when John entered the bathroom, closing the door behind him.

Actually, a lot of people had conversations with Brandon in the bathroom that night. Scott had gone in to try to talk some sense to Brandon without doing much good. According to Lana's later testimony, Eddie Schlicker, a big tough guy with a chip on his shoulder and a White Power tattoo to prove it, had gone to Brandon and threatened to kill him if he didn't tell the truth about his sex.

All night, Brandon managed to laugh these people off.

"You guys just don't understand," Brandon kept saying. But after a while, none of them would take that for an answer. The guys decided they needed someone to see this guy's cock or else.

Suddenly, with John and Tom locked in the bathroom with him, Brandon knew he'd have to show them, so he unzipped his pants and started pulling them down so they could see that there was something sticking out from behind the zipper.

"Well, what is that?" Tom kept asking. "What is it?"

"That's my dick," Brandon said, taking Tom's hand and guiding it toward the zipper. "See... feel it."

But something about it didn't look quite right, so Tom grabbed Brandon and snatched at Brandon's jeans.

Brandon was wearing a pair of Tom's underwear—Tom had loaned them to him because Brandon had no clean clothes when he got out of jail. Actually, everything Brandon had on—jeans, shirts, underwear, everything except for shoes and jacket—belonged to Tom.

Then Tom reached down toward the underpants, and all he felt was the texture of a belt.

"I wanted to put that belt there so you guys couldn't see what was behind the belt because I'm a little bit deformed from the operation because they haven't finished it yet," Brandon yelped, pulling his jeans back up.

"Whatever, Brandon," Tom said, walking out of the room in disgust with John following behind him.

Days before, Tom and Lana had intimately talked about her sex life with Brandon. She had confided to Toni that Brandon was small but said that she could feel it, even though there wasn't that much there.

Now, Tom didn't know what to think.

John had also heard tales from Lana. She had sworn she'd seen Brandon stand up and pee, and she said something about Brandon using a catheter because of the sex change operation he had. Even Tom had seen Brandon stand up and piss at one of the urinals at the Oasis, so when John and Tom compared notes, that part of the story seemed real.

But Tom and John were confounded. Surprisingly, they had seen this tan-color pigskin belt, and they weren't sure if he was stuffing it down his pants to look bigger or if he was lying or *what*.

Tom was so angry, he called down to the police station and talked with Officer John Caverzagie about having Brandon's bond revoked. Caverzagie told Nissen that it couldn't be done, which just made Tom more irate. Tom told the assistant police chief he was concerned about Lana getting her money back. He said he didn't want to see Lana get in trouble.

By then, Nissen was sick of dealing with the Brandon fiasco—his patience was shot and he wanted Brandon out of his sight. He was hoping to throw Brandon back in jail and kill two birds with one stone—he thought it would also be a help to Lana—but now he realized he was going to have to handle the matter differently. He was going to have to take things into his own hands, and Lotter agreed. The two of them squeezed Brandon back into the bathroom to have another chat.

A few minutes later, everyone out in the living room heard it: there was a loud thump when Brandon got knocked down.

Tom held the hands while John pulled away the pants and everything else, and they both saw *exactly* what she had down there, the lying bitch.

PART FOUR

LOOSE ENDS

43

IT WAS AFTER 2:00 IN THE MORNING, CHRISTMAS DAY, when John and Tom pulled up to the Stephenson Hotel. Brandon had run up there to make a phone call, she was calling Humbolt for help, wanting someone to drive down to get him and instead of waiting outside, Tom had gone into the lobby to grab a pack of cigarettes. When he saw Brandon on the phone, he kept telling her to hurry up.

"You're not going anywhere, Brandon, so just hang up the phone," Tom finally ordered. "You're staying at my house, and I've got a whole bunch of people coming over there, and I need to get back now. So let's go."

Brandon went with John and Tom, and they quickly stopped over at the Tisdels' place. It was close to 2:30 by then. John stayed out in the car while Tom ran in, letting Linda know that Brandon was definitely a girl, which, of course, really infuriated her. She never wanted to lay eyes on Brandon again, and as far as she was concerned, she didn't care what happened to the kid. When Tom told her he had Brandon out in the car, Linda made it known that Brandon was no longer welcome in her house, not under any circumstances. Of course, Lana was down on the basement stairs, overhearing all this, and this time, she knew her mom meant business. If she wanted to continue seeing Brandon, it would have to be on the sly.

When John and Tom got back to the Nissens' place with Brandon, everyone was gone except Rhonda and Kandi, both of whom were asleep, so it was a creepy scene, and Brandon knew more trouble was ahead.

"John and I need to talk to you," Tom said calmly as the two of them shoved Brandon back in the bathroom.

"John turned around and held the door and Tom hit me once and I fell in the tub," Brandon later told police.

"Then I stood back up and Tom hit me again. This time I fell on the floor and he kicked me in the ribs I don't know how many times. Tom stepped on my back, and he picked me up by my coat and carried me out to the car by my coat."

Rhonda woke up from all the commotion, and she caught a glimpse of

Brandon's split lip as they were leaving. It was bleeding badly, and there was blood on Brandon's coat, so it scared her, but she didn't know what she could do. Tom was swaying and could hardly stand up straight—his eyes looked wild, all pink and bloodshot—and John wasn't in much better shape himself.

"If you guys get in trouble..." Rhonda warned in a motherly tone, but her words faded into thin air. The three of them were already out the door.

Teena didn't know what roads they traveled; they became gravel roads. Perhaps they were on the dustless highway, she wasn't sure. All she knew was they ended up on a dirt road, and John was kind of screwing around with the car, driving erratically, when suddenly they got stuck in a ditch next to an old church in the middle of nowhere.

The three of them got out and tried to pull the car out. Brandon and Tom were looking around the building for some bricks or blocks they could use to put underneath the tires, and they tried a few boulders, thinking they'd have better traction, but it was no use. They needed a tow.

It was freezing out, and Tom had no coat, so Brandon offered her White Sox jacket a couple times, but Tom refused. It was all bloody, and Tom wasn't interested in playing buddy-buddy with Brandon anymore. He had other ideas in mind.

When they realized they'd have to find help, Tom walked about a quarter mile to the nearest farmhouse and woke a farmer up. A short time later, Tom and the farmer pulled up in a red pickup truck, which they hooked up to Lotter's Crown Victoria. Tom had to help with the chain, and they had to lock the hubs in, so it took a while. The pickup's headlights were bright, so John held Brandon's head down in his lap and instructed her not to look up. The farmer had no idea someone was being held unwillingly when John rolled down the window and politely thanked the man. The farmer smiled obligingly, thinking he had done his good deed for the day.

After the three of them got back on the road, they headed over toward Falls City, and John was so drunk he was swerving again. They were still drinking beer, and they stopped a few times to take a leak. John almost went into a ditch twice more before he finally came to a place where he turned off the road and parked.

"What are you doing?" Brandon asked them, panicking, but John and Tom were too busy having their own conversation to respond.

"I'm not going to beat on her," John said, "but if you want to, I'm not going to stop you." "Turn the car back on and pull over there by the Hormel plant," Tom said. "There's a couple things I need to pull out of the backseat."

Nissen reached back and grabbed a baby car seat and some toys from the car, swiftly placing them in the trunk.

John grabbed Brandon by the neck, forcing her into the backseat of the car, and all the while she was begging them not to do this, not to hurt her anymore.

When Tom got in the backseat, he was getting madder by the minute, and he hit Brandon again—this time hard in her side.

Actually, they weren't parked by a church. It was a school, because Tom remembers seeing a teeter-totter and a merry-go-round and a sign, District 45. Tom wasn't sure what school they were near, he kept asking John where they were, but John wouldn't answer. Once they had gotten off Barada and Chase Streets, Tom had lost his bearings and he felt kind of disoriented; he couldn't believe they were out there in the fields, out there getting ready to do this to Brandon. "I just asked them if they would quit and leave me alone, let me go and walk," Brandon told authorities. "I never got a response or anything, except for John saying that he wasn't going to beat me anymore. The way they were acting, I knew it was going to happen. Tom kept on grabbing my shoes, and John was sitting in the front seat and I was begging with John, and he goes, 'I don't hear you.'"

"Take off your shoes," Tom ordered.

"Why?"

"Just do what I tell you!"

Brandon started undoing a shoelace.

"And take off your clothes!"

Brandon stopped moving.

"Take them off now!"

"But why? What are you going to do?"

"Just shut up, Brandon, and get undressed."

"Please don't do this. I have asthma. I can't hardly breathe."

"You can either make this easy or make this difficult," Tom finally told her. "I can either beat the shit out of you and get this done or not. It's going to happen either way."

"I was unable to fight and I was scared. He made me take my pants off and he put them up front with John," Brandon later reported. "So then Tom proceeded to rape me, and then when he was done, I asked for my pants back and John said no. Then Tom got up front and John got into the back and did the same thing. I was still crying, and Tom told me to shut up in a stern voice."

When Brandon got her clothes back on, Tom took her outside the car and punched and kicked her again just for good measure.

"OK. We're all done," Tom said, "and no one will find out, right?"

"OK," she whimpered.

"If anyone asks what happened," he quipped, "just tell them we were bumper skiing."

44

"WE WENT BACK TO TOM NISSEN'S HOUSE, AND TOM AND John both told me to take a shower and clean the blood off," Teena wrote in her witness statement. "Tom told me I could not leave."

"When Tom was in his room with his wife and John was on the floor with his girlfriend, I went in the bathroom and turned on the water to make it sound like I was taking a shower. I then busted out the screen window and broke out and ran to Lana Tisdel's house and the police were called.

"It was 6:00 in the morning, Christmas, when Brandon appeared, bloody and battered, at the Tisdels' front door. Lana let him in, and Leslie ran down the block to call the police. When Falls City police Chief Norm Hemmerling arrived on the scene, it was obvious that Teena Brandon had been brutalized: her lips were swollen, she was bleeding from the mouth area, and she had bruised cheekbones.

Teena told the police chief that at approximately 3:00 that morning, John Lotter and Tom Nissen had forced her into a vehicle, bad taken her to a rural county area, and had sexually assaulted her in the backseat of the car.

It took fifteen minutes for the ambulance to get to the Tisdel residence, so Teena gave the first part of her statement while waiting to be transported, then continued it in the Falls City Hospital emergency room. Having accompanied Brandon to the hospital, Lana informed Hemmerling that she was at Tom Nissen's the night before, that at some point, she overheard Lotter ask Brandon what she would do if he raped her. Lana told the officer she had advised John to stop talking like that"

Photos were taken of the injuries to Teena Brandon's face and back, and Chief Hemmerling and Officer Sean Nolte then responded to 1815 Chase, where they viewed and photographed a window that was damaged on the north side of the house.

Later that morning, Hemmerling turned over the rape evidence collection kit to Richardson County Sheriff Charles Laux; the rape was in the sheriff's jurisdiction because it occurred out in the county. The kidnapping and initial physical assault, however, which occurred in Falls City proper, remained under investigation with the Falls City police and was handed over to Investigator Keith Hayes. Hayes received a call at exactly twelve noon—in the middle of Christmas dinner with his family.

When Sheriff Laux was advised of the rape, he made a call to the Nebraska State Police in Lincoln that morning, speaking with Investigator Tom Reinhart, explaining that he had a situation involving an alleged *sexual* assault. Laux told Reinhart that the victim had been jailed earlier in the month, that the person was jailed as a boy, then it was discovered that the boy was really a girl, and that this person, Teena Brandon, had made complaints to both the sheriff's office and the Falls City police. Laux was seeking Reinhart's advice.

Reinhart wanted to know if a rape kit had been done on the victim, and Laux said he wasn't sure. Reinhart told Laux to interview the victim so he could get the names of the suspects and possibly have them arrested, asking if Laux knew who physically assaulted Brandon. The sheriff stated that he did and assured the state police officer that he and his men were trying to find those persons to arrest them.

Again, Reinhart told Laux to interview the victim, to get all pertinent information and names of the suspects. Reinhart also said if the Falls City police were going to arrest those suspects, that he, Reinhart, would be willing to drive down to the jail or to the Falls City Police Department to interview them. Reinhart was very willing to provide backup in any way he could.

"Thanks, I just wanted some information," Laux said as he rushed the call to an end. "Have a Merry Christmas!"

And Reinhart wished Laux the same.

"If you need any additional help, if you need me down there, call me back and I'll be there to assist you," Reinhart persisted.

But Investigator Reinhart received no other phone calls regarding the rape that Christmas Day.

45

WHEN DR. DAVID BORG ARRIVED AT THE FALLS CITY community Hospital shortly after the ambulance, Brandon reported that he had been beat up, so the doctor assessed him and ordered some X rays. Actually, it was the X-ray technician who identified Brandon as a female. The technician had heard local gossip about this person, Brandon, and he told the nurse on duty to ask Brandon to undress completely, so they could find out for sure. Nurse Lori Moore recalled that Brandon became shaken and emotional about this request but was willing to comply.

"Who told you I was raped?" Brandon asked, guessing that because she was asked to disrobe they wanted to do a rape test.

"Who did this to you?" the nurse prodded, a bit unnerved herself. Lori Moore was surprised to hear a rape was involved. She hadn't even guessed it.

As soon as Nurse Moore realized the physical assault on Brandon included a sexual assault, the whole protocol in the emergency room changed. She immediately bagged Brandon's clothing. She set up another examining room for a vaginal exam, and Dr. Borg was called back to reexamine the patient. The admission form at the hospital was also changed; the word *male* was originally circled, so it had to be crossed out and switched to *female*. The name on Brandon's chart initially identified her as Charles Brandon, so that had to be corrected.

Dr. Borg later admitted that he had no idea this person was a female until Nurse Moore told him. At that point, specimens of blood and clothing were taken, and examination of the genitalia was completed—standard rape-kit procedure.

The doctor noted swelling and bleeding from the vaginal area, along with some trauma to the vagina, consistent with sexual penetration. Brandon denied ever having previous intercourse, and because she was bleeding from the hymen, Dr. Borg imagined she was telling the truth about that—she was a virgin. The doctor noted that the patient was very reluctant and non-cooperative—she was afraid of the examination, apprehensive—but then, that wasn't unusual for someone who had never been through a pelvic exam.

Around 7:30 that morning, the minute Teena was allowed to dress and leave the examining room, she called Tammy from the hospital pay phone. In a quivering voice, she told her sister she had been beaten up and raped. Tammy was flabbergasted, but she tried to keep her cool for Teena's sake.

"Is anybody there with you now?" Tammy wanted to be sure.

"Lana and Leslie."

"Did you already get examined?"

"Yeah."

"Did they do a rape kit?"

But Teena gave no answer. She didn't want to discuss it anymore.

During that first call, Teena was very upset and hard to understand, so Tammy didn't press it. Teena had given the names Nissen and Lotter, and Tammy recognized them both. Nissen was someone she had met once at the Village Inn, where she worked in Lincoln. Lotter she had only heard about. She had met his sister Michelle, Teena reminded her. but Tammy could barely recall it.

Tammy just couldn't believe "friends" would do something like this. She knew Teena was in distress, she knew her sister had nowhere to go, that Teena was basically stranded in this weird place, this no-man's-land near the Kansas-Missouri border, and she was angry that people weren't trying to help. Teena said she had been kicked out of the Tisdels'.

"Do you want me to come get you?" Tammy finally asked.

"No, I'm going to find a way home. Somebody here'll take me," Teena promised.

As soon as she hung up, Tammy dialed her mother. Of course, JoAnn was shocked and outraged at the news, and her asthma kicked in, so Tammy cut the information short, assuming it was better if their mom knew fewer details for the moment. That week, however, they both heard more of the story as Teena continued to make her SOS calls.

"It's probably the second time she called from the motel that I questioned her why she seemed so agitated and so anxious to get away from there," JoAnn later told police. "She discussed the threats then, and she also said that she felt Lana Tisdel had set her up for the rape."

But Tammy didn't have a way to get down there to pick Teena up, and although JoAnn and Molly offered to do it, no one seemed to find their way to Falls City. Instead, JoAnn had gotten Lisa Lambert on the phone; and after a number of calls back and forth, finally, on the day after Christmas, Lisa agreed to go rescue Teena.

"Teena seemed really hyper and kind of scared," JoAnn would later remember. "I spoke with a gentleman who was staying at Lisa's house, I think his name was Shane, and at that time I told him that she was scared because she'd been threatened, and he guaranteed me that she would be safe out there on the farm with Lisa."

46

TO DR. BORA, TEENA BRANDON DENIED THAT SHE HAD been anally penetrated. But later reports from Cellmark Diagnostics concluded that there were sperm fractions found both on the anal and the vaginal swabs police had submitted in the case. The DNA obtained showed that Nissen could not be excluded as the source for the sperm fraction found on the anal swab and that Lotter could not be excluded as the source for the sperm fraction found in one of the condoms discovered at the crime scene.

On Christmas afternoon, when Teena went down to the sheriff's office to file the official complaint, she was interviewed by Charles Laux and his deputy, Tom Olberding. In her deepest voice, Teena described all the events with Lotter and Nissen of the night before—that they were all at a party drinking, that the guys depantsed her and then forced her in their car. She said they went past the dustless highway, they got stuck in a ditch, that John made her keep her head down when the farmer came to help, that Tom forced her to take her clothes off and let her know he was going to rape her.

Laux needed more details. He needed to know every little thing.

"Let's put it real bluntly what they did to you. We're here to investigate this and the only way we can investigate is if you tell us exactly what happened," Laux said in a stern voice.

"He penetrated me without my permission."

"He penetrated you? Which one penetrated you first?"

"Tom Nissen."

"Tom Nissen? Did he penetrate you in the front or back?"

"In the back first, at first."

"In the back first," Laux echoed.

The questioning went on, with Laux, an overweight mid aged man, extricating each sexual particular as fully as possible. Young Deputy Olberding, in his twenties, asked a few sensitive questions, but mostly he was there to listen, to provide support for the sheriff. When Teena said she was a virgin, Laux huffed. Evidently, Laux had the impression that she was sexually experienced, so he grilled her about it.

As this line of interrogation went on, Teena was becoming more obviously upset—the deputy could see that—so he tried to end the interview as soon as possible. Deputy Olberding wanted to let the poor girl go home. It was Christmas after all, and she had been through enough.

But Laux wasn't through with Teena Not at all. As soon as Olberding dismissed himself, Laux got back to the subject of the rape and depantsing. He held his own private interview with Teena one on one, which he tape-recorded to keep on public file.

"When, ah, which one of the guys jerked your pants down to find out if you were a boy or a girl?" Laux began.

"John."

"OK. He did that before all this other stuff took place. I thought you said that John was holding the door and Tom was the one beating on you?"

"He did."

"And then, ah, John undone your pants. Right? And pulled your pants down how far?"

"Past my knees."

"And what did you have in your underpants?"

"I don't know if you're talking about earlier when I had a sock but not when he pulled my pants down. I didn't"

"You didn't have a sock," Laux growled. "Do you run around once in a while with a sock in your pants to look like a boy?"

"Yeah."

"How come you forgot to tell us about this?"

"Well, I didn't see it as important."

"Well it's all important when we're doing an investigation," Laux said, using his most official tone. "We asked you to start at the beginning, and you skipped half of it. Now we don't know if we're in the middle of daylight and dark. We don't know what is up or down. All right, so, after he pulled your pants down and seen you were a girl, what did he do? Did he fondle you any?"

"No."

"He didn't fondle you any, huh? Didn't that kind of amaze you? After he pulled your pants down and had wanted to take you to bed and you told him no and that you was a boy. Doesn't that kind of, ah, get your attention somehow, that he wouldn't put his hands in your pants and play with you a little bit?"

Teena's response was inaudible.

"Well, it doesn't make any difference," Laux said. "Now, you were all half-ass drunk, and knowing these guys, it wouldn't make any difference to John what he did in front of everybody else. He would think it was funny, huh? I can't believe that he pulled your pants down and you are a female, that he didn't stick his hand in you or his finger in you."

"Well, he didn't."

"Can't believe he didn't." Laux paused. "Who pulled your pants back up?"

"I did."

Eventually, after Teena described being picked up at the Stephenson Hotel, after she detailed being stuck in the ditch again, and she repeated being hit and kicked by Nissen, she finally got back to the scene at the Hormel plant and the issue of the rape.

"So when they got ready to poke you," Laux asked, "how were you positioned in the backseat?"

"On my back."

"You were on your back. Where did they try first at?"

"My vagina."

"They tried sinking it in your vagina, and you say you never had sex before. Is that correct?"

"Right."

"And which one tried doing it first?"

"Tom."

"Tom," Laux echoed. "And Tom couldn't get it in you?"

"He said he couldn't get it in, but all I know is it hurt, so I couldn't tell the difference. Whatever he was doing, it *hurt*."

"How did you have your legs positioned when he was trying to do that?"

"He had them positioned on each side, and he was positioned in between my legs."

"You had your legs, ah, your feet up around his back or did you just have them off to the sides or what?"

"I had one foot on the floor and the other on the seat."

"OK, so then after he couldn't stick it in your vagina, he stuck it in your box, or in your buttocks, is that right?"

"Yes, sir."

"How long did he do that?"

"Long enough. I didn't time it."

"I mean, did he, did it seem like a *lifetime* or what?"

"It seems like it took forever."

"All right. Did it feel like he stuck it in very far? Or not?"

"I don't know how far." Teena's voice quivered. "It hurt." Then Teena described the switch, when John took his turn in the backseat while Tom went up front. She capsulized things by saying that John took his pants down, that when John finished, he got out of the car and went back up in the driver's seat.

"Well, ah, let's back up here for a second," Laux told her. "First of all, you didn't say anything about him getting it out. Did he have a *hard-on* when he got back there or what?"

"I don't know. I didn't look."

"You didn't look. Did he take a little time working it up? Did you work it for him?"

"No, I didn't."

"Did, when he got in the backseat, you were already spread out back there, ready for him, waiting on him. He, ah. . ."

"No, I was sitting up when he got back there," Teena corrected.

"Did he play with your breasts or anything?"

"No."

"Well, was he fingering you?" Teena's answer was too faint to hear.

"He said he couldn't get it in?" Laux prodded.

"He said I was tight."

"And you have never had any sex before?"

"No."

There was a dead silence.

"Why do you run around with girls instead of guys, being you are a girl yourself? Why do you make girls think you are a guy?"

"I haven't the slightest idea."

"You haven't the slightest idea," Laux mocked. "You go around kissing on girls?"

"The ones that know about me."

"The ones, the girls that don't know about you, thinks you are a guy, do you kiss *them*?"

"I don't know what this has to do with what happened last night."

"Because I'm trying to get some answers here so I know exactly what is going on. Now, do you want to answer that question for me or not?"

"I don't see why I have to."

By then, Tom Olberding had reentered the room—he had been sitting in on the last part of the interview—and so the deputy interrupted, reminding Teena that she didn't have to answer, that all the information she gave was voluntary. Teena told them she was experiencing a sexual identity crisis, but when asked about it, she couldn't explain what that meant. Teena eventually signed the complaint, said she would testify against Nissen and Lotter, and Laux promised to get the reports "done up" to pass along to the county attorney. When Teena Brandon left, she thought something would be done about this and quickly. Lotter and Nissen had threatened to kill her if she went to the cops, and Teena might possibly have conveyed that to Laux, hoping to speed things up. Of course, no one will ever know exactly what Teena reported, because part of the tape from her interview with Laux—the last few minutes—was accidentally erased.

47

LATE IN THE AFTERNOON ON CHRISTMAS, INVESTIGATOR Hayes arrived at the Falls City Police Department to review witness statements that had been obtained referencing the assault case. These statements were signed by Falls City Officer Sean Nolte, who, at that point, was the only law enforcement person handling the Brandon complaint.

The sexual assault was left pending—in cases where something's considered a close call, the decision to arrest can be procrastinated—and Sheriff Laux had opted to let county attorney Doug Merz make the call about arresting Nissen and Lotter. Of course, based on the rape-kit evidence submitted, Laux *could* have arrested the two suspects immediately.

Lana and her mother were still present when Hayes got over to the police department. The two women were visibly shaken, having just signed their statements. Hayes talked to them both, interviewing Lana in depth, discovering, among other things, that she had *not* asked Nissen and Lotter to depants Brandon, that the guys had taken it upon themselves to do so.

"I was staying at the house, Tom Nissen's, because Brandon was there. Tom and John bought some stuff to drink so we all started to have a good time," Lana said in her statement. "Well, John wanted all of us girls, me, Kandi, and Leslie, to go pick up Rhonda, and he told us to take our time doing it, so we did because of the roads. We left at 9:00 PM and got back at about 9:45 PM. And we went inside the house and John and Brandon weren't there.

"Well, shortly after that, they came walking in the back door," Lana continued. "John wanted to talk to me, so we went into the bathroom, and he started talking to me about Brandon being a girl. Then Tom came in and told me to get out, so I did for about an hour. Tom and John was in the bathroom with Brandon, and finally, they let me in. John took Tom to the side and said something to him. Then Tom grabbed Brandon, and John pulled Brandon's pants down to his knees and made me look to see what was there." Lana reported that she saw John touching Brandon on the chest and between the legs, that Brandon told him to quit, but John wouldn't. Later that night, John got really mad at Brandon, and while they were all sitting on the couch, he grabbed Brandon by the neck and started to choke her. Lana told the officer that she managed to pull John's hands away.

Throughout the interview, Lana insisted she wasn't in the house when Brandon had been beaten up—Tom and John had already taken her home. In the end, the attractive strawberry blonde stated that by the time she got back to Tom's early Christmas morning, the only people left were Kandi and Rhonda.

"I went upstairs to answer the door, it was between 2:30 and 2:45 AM this morning," Linda Gutierres told Officer Hayes. "I answered the door. It was John Lotter and Lana. John was trying to leave, telling Lana to remain here and talk to me. She was very reluctant, and finally I said if she really needed to go back to Tom's and talk to Brandon, I would take her down there."

"I asked her why it was so important that she needed to talk with Brandon," Linda continued. "She said she knew that Brandon was a girl now, that after this was proven to her, she thought the best place for Brandon was to go back to jail."

"The only thing I heard was Brandon fall on the floor when Tom nailed her one," Hayes read in Rhonda McKenzie's witness statement. "Tom came out of the bathroom and had Brandon by the front of the coat and they were headed outside. Tom was in front of Brandon, and John was in back of her, and then they left and came back a little bit later. John and Tom told Brandon to go clean up, so she did. John came to bed and woke me up and told me he did not do anything to her, and that was all that was said. And I finally got back to sleep."

On December 28, at 8:00 in the morning, John Lotter and Tom Nissen showed up at the Falls City Police Department to answer questions about the alleged physical assault and abduction of Teena Renae Brandon. When Investigator Hayes asked Lotter to come back into his office and advised him of his Miranda rights, Lotter waived the warnings. Lotter knew Nissen had already been interviewed, so he wanted to set the record straight. The fierce young man quickly signed and initialed the form and handed it to Deputy Olberding, who was sitting in on the interview.

The first thing Lotter said was that he didn't know if he could recall much about Christmas Eve. Everyone had partied quite a bit at Nissen's house and he had consumed his fair share of alcohol that night. Lotter began by explaining that a couple days before the party, Lana had contacted him and asked if he could find out what sex Brandon was. He told Lana he would if he had the opportunity. Then on Christmas Eve, he and Nissen spent a lot of time talking to Brandon, trying to convince him to tell everyone what sex he was. Lotter admitted that while he and Nissen were with Brandon, one of them told him he could either show them or *they were going to find out*. It was then that Brandon said he would show John, but he wanted to go outside with John alone.

John told Brandon he "didn't really give a damn" what sex he actually was, but since there were some people who wanted to know, he'd go out to the garage. Once they got out there, Brandon pulled down his jeans and underwear, but the garage was not too well lit, so John couldn't really see.

John thought he was looking at something that had the shape of a penis, but when he reached to touch it, Brandon advised him to wait. Brandon explained that he had a sex change operation so it was going to feel funny, warning John that it was going to feel flat. Brandon confided that in order for him to get an erection, he had to pump it up.

Lotter told Hayes he touched this area and felt something "flat and slippery," but he was unable to determine what it was. Because he'd never seen or read anything about a sex change operation, he didn't know what to make of it.

According to Lotter, about a half hour later he came back inside with Brandon, Tom and Lana dragged Brandon in the bathroom to try to determine his sex. Ten minutes later, John entered the room and saw a rolled-up sock lying on the floor next to Brandon. He picked the sock up, noticed it had a stripe of blood on it, and wondered why it wasn't at all like the thing he had seen and touched earlier. When be asked Brandon to explain it, there was no comment. Hayes advised Lotter that Nissen had already confessed about the two of them depantsing Brandon in front of Lana, but John denied this, insisting he didn't go into the bathroom until *after* Teena's pants were down. He denied being present when Teena was beat up, saying only that he heard a thump and walked in to find Teena lying naked on the bathroom floor with

Tom hovering over her.

Lotter claimed he helped Teena off the floor, and at that time, Nissen said he was taking her back to jail. By his account, the three of them left the house willingly in order for Teena to make a phone call from the Stephenson Hotel. Once she made the call, they drove out in the county roads somewhere north of Falls City, got stuck in a ditch, and were rescued by a farmer, then stopped at a few different locations to go to the bathroom although Lotter didn't know exactly where they had been.

Hayes wasn't officially handling the sexual part of the assault—Olberding was—and when that subject was broached, Lotter was cavalier about it. He denied raping Teena Brandon. Lotter was advised that a doctor's examination had been performed, that police had conclusive evidence that intercourse did occur, but Lotter had no idea who might have slept with her. Lotter said neither he nor Nissen had sex with Teena that night Lotter's explanation about why, upon their return to Chase Street, he and Tom told Teena to go take a shower was: "Teena had blood on her face from when Tom hit her."

John reported that they heard the water running, and after a while, Rhonda got up to check in the bathroom. When she came out, Rhonda informed them that Teena was gone, that the window had been busted out, and John said that was the last he heard of Teena Brandon.

Lotter was asked to take a polygraph exam, but he refused. He also objected to giving authorities voluntary samples of his blood and hair. In fact, when those requests were made, John became extremely irritated, said he didn't want to talk anymore, and abruptly walked out of the department. When he left, he was confident that it was his word against Teena's, that the cops didn't have anything on him at all. But that view changed later in the day, after Lotter compared notes with Nissen and discovered what a *blabbermouth* his buddy really was.

When Nissen had been interviewed by Hayes and Olberding, the lawmen had shown him a pair of rolled-up gray socks, which Olberding and Laux collected from the scene at the Hormel plant—and Nissen recognized them as the socks that fell from Teena's underwear in the Chase Street bathroom. Through Nissen, authorities also affirmed that he and Lotter were drinking Busch Light that particular evening, linking them to the empty beer can found alongside the two used condoms at Hormel.

Nissen denied having sex with Teena, telling police it was Lotter who had intercourse with her. When asked to explain why two condoms were recovered from the crime scene, Nissen said it was because Lotter couldn't keep a hard-on and that possibly one of the condoms fell off him and he had to replace it.

Of course, Tom couldn't say for sure, because he was alone in the front seat while John and Teena were undressing quietly in the back. He denied ever turning around and looking to see what was going on back there, admitting only that he heard Teena say, "Don't hurt me," and "It hurts."

According to Nissen, he never heard Teena say stop. In mulling things over with Tom late that day, John was able to determine that his pal had given a pretty explicit statement. Moreover,. Nissen had offered to deliver his pubic hair and blood samples, had agreed to take a polygraph, and had promised to return for questioning the next day in order to participate in yet another taped interview regarding the sexual assault.

Tom assured John he was trying to throw the cops off track, that he wasn't about to cooperate, but Lotter was getting nervous. Before dawn, the two of them were making concrete plans, having hush-hush meetings in the Chase Street bathroom to discuss how to take care of their *problem*.

48

IT WAS NEW YEAR'S EVE, JUST AFTER 3:00 P.M. ON December 31, when Officer John Caverzagie received a call from the dispatcher at the Falls City Police Department asking if he could come into the department in uniform to assist in an arrest and search of a residence. Caverzagie arrived forty-five minutes later, speaking with Chief Hemmerling and other officers who were in the lineup room discussing how the arrest would be handled. Because police had yet to discover conclusive evidence that would allow them to arrest the two individuals for the triple homicide in Humbolt—there were no fingerprints, no tire tracks at the scene—John Lotter and Marvin Thomas Nissen would be arrested and held on the pending sexual assault and kidnapping charges. County Attorney Merz was in the process of issuing the warrants.

Shortly after the briefing, Officer Caverzagie knocked on Nissen's front door, and Lotter answered, clueless that a SWAT team had the tiny place surrounded, not only the doors and windows, but all blocks and alleyways leading up to it.

"John, would you please come outside?" Caverzagie ordered, his gun drawn at his side.

As soon as Lotter opened the screen door, Caverzagie grabbed him, turning him over to rookie cop Greg Cowan and then to Roger Chrans, who had bolted from his Blazer the moment Lotter crossed the threshold.

Caverzagie simultaneously directed Tom Nissen to come out of the residence, and Nissen hesitantly complied, immediately being placed in a prone position beside Lotter.

The other people inside the Chase Street residence—Kandi, Bobbie, and Tiffany Nissen and Tom's friend Jason Specht—were later brought to the police department for questioning. Falls City police knew that Jason Specht had his own troubles with Nissen. The week before, Specht called down from the Oasis because he and Nissen had gotten into a fight. When cops got to the scene, Specht was covered in blood and Nissen was angry and drunk. They hoped Specht would be motivated to give them some information, that he would be able to provide some leads, but the kid said he knew nothing about the homicides, that everything had been quiet and normal at the Nissen house.

When Kandi was interviewed, investigators ran into the same problem. She too had been mistreated by Tom—she had been beaten up numerous times—and they hoped that she might be willing to cooperate in some way, to see justice served. Instead, it seemed she was keeping as close mouthed as possible. They could see Kandi was obviously upset, distraught, concerned about the events of the day—she was crying and shaking throughout her brief talk with them but rather than getting leads, police found themselves consoling Mrs. Nissen.

Kandi did sign a written consent form to search the Nissen home. However, that turned out to be a dead end. Two state policemen along with Deputy Tom Olberding, had gone back to Chase Street and had turned up nothing more than a pair of white Spalding high-top tennis shoes belonging to Nissen. Evidently, that was the only thing in the house that might have been linked to the murders. Nissen and Lotter obviously ditched all clothing and other items that would have contained traces of blood.

At 10:15 PM on New Year's Eve, when Investigator Chrans and Investigator Hayes interviewed Marvin Thomas, Nissen wasted no time in coming clean about his involvement in the murders. Without much prompting, Nissen admitted to being there that night, to witnessing John Lotter shoot three people in Humbolt. He detailed their every move on the evening of December 30, 1993, insisting it was Lotter who wanted to "take care of Brandon." He also mentioned that immediately before they took off for Lisa Lambert's, he and John stopped at Lana Tisdel's place—he did not remember what time it was. Nissen said they were there for about five minutes.

After Nissen gave his rendition of what occurred on the night of the homicides, he was asked about what happened to the gun and gloves. The minute he told investigators that one pair of gloves went over the Nemaha Bridge—they had been thrown into the Nemaha River along with the gun and gun box—Chrans excused himself from the interview and contacted NSP Investigator Jud McKinstry by radio.

The Nemaha River is approximately a mile south of Falls City on Highway 73, and McKinstry had already been down there searching for the weapon. It was a logical place to look, and the first time around, he and Olberding used flashlights as they went along the river, walking the north and south banks. They knew they were looking for a .380-caliber pistol because they had recovered casings from the crime scene. But they came away empty-handed.

Actually, McKinstry and Olberding had spotted something gold lying out there in the darkness—it was way out on the ice, about twenty feet off the south bank, sitting on a part of the river that had frozen over. The more the lawmen focused, the more they could make out what it was: a pair of yellow work gloves. But neither thought to retrieve them.

Now, with this news from Chrans, McKinstry, Olberding, and NSP Sergeant Ron Osborne all hastened back down there. McKinstry offered to slide along the twenty-foot patch of ice to fetch the fuzzy yellow work gloves, and as soon as he picked them up, *bingo*, he felt a box inside and heard metal items jingle. Once safely back on land, McKinstry turned the package over to Osborne, who opened the wedged gloves to discover a blue box containing a Bryco Arms pistol and a sharp folding knife in a leather sheath with the name *Lotter* written on it.

49

THAT SAME NIGHT, NEW YEAR'S EVE, MR. AND MRS. William Edward Bennett walked into the Falls City PD to report a stolen gun. Bennett described the handgun as possibly being a Bryco brand, .380 caliber. He had bought it for fifty dollars cash plus two engine blocks, and his friend Jerry Sanders had just fixed the thing, having put in a new firing pin a week prior. Bennett said the last time he saw the pistol was the day before, December 30, at about 9:30 AM when he opened his dresser drawer.

When Bennett was questioned, the young man informed Chrans that the night before, around 9:00 P.M., his buddy John Lotter had stopped by. Bennett said his friend came in without knocking, which was unusual, and he seemed to be antsy. Instead of joining those watching in the living room, Lotter asked where Bennett's wife, Amy, was, and he disappeared into kitchen to chat with her. He also asked for Yvonne, a cousin of Bennett's John was seeing on the side, but Yvonne wasn't around.

"When John Lotter came in the kitchen behind me and gave me a hug, he asked me if I heard about the rape charges," Amy Bennett wrote in her witness statement, "and I said, 'Yes, you ought to be ashamed of yourself.'"

"John said he didn't rape her," Amy continued, "and if he wanted to rape someone, he has Rhonda McKenzie. He said he wasn't going to jail for rape, and he was going to take care of it."

While Amy made herself a cup of coffee, John excused himself to the bathroom. He was gone just two minutes, then he quickly said his good-byes to everyone in the living room, giving Amy's boob a fast squeeze. He walked over to William on the couch and shook his hand, saying thank you before he headed out the door.

"Not one of us thought to get up and look to see if he was in his car or with someone else," Amy reported. "He was drunk, and we didn't think anything except he was acting strange."

Lotter's total stay at Bennett's was under ten minutes. During that time, Nissen waited out in the car, anxious to get on with things.

Bennett reported that the day after he bought the gun, Lotter was over at his place, that he showed it to John. Bennett said he knew for a fact that John was aware of where the gun was kept. He told Investigator Chrans he found his gun missing just an hour or so earlier that night.

He had gone to look for it after Rhonda McKenzie came by to report a wild rumor that police had searched John's car for a gun because three girls got killed in Humbolt.

* * *

On Sunday, January 2, Keith Hayes assisted Investigator Reinhart with the second interview of Marvin Thomas Nissen. The day before, New Year's 1994, they had tried to interview Lotter, but he was remaining silent. He wanted to talk to a lawyer.

Actually, the second time around with Nissen, Hayes had to do almost all the questioning because Reinhart had laryngitis. Also present during the interview was Richardson County Deputy Jon Larson, a real Mr. Nice Guy. Earlier that day, before the formal interview had begun, Larson had spoken to Nissen about the knife. Nissen acknowledged in an off comment to Larson that a knife was somehow involved. Now, Hayes and Reinhart needed to get Nissen to talk about the knife after being reminded of his Miranda rights.

When the interview began, Nissen told police that on December 30 he remembered going by Lotter's house and that sometime after Lotter showed him a knife in the car. Nissen said when they left Lotter's place, they drove up to the Tisdels' house, parking down at the end of the street, about a block away. The two of them walked up to the Tisdels' wearing gloves, Nissen claimed, "because it was cold." Before they went inside, Lotter showed Nissen Bennett's gun and then placed it back in the box.

While at the Tisdels' residence, Tom talked to Linda, discovering that Brandon was staying in Humbolt. He also asked about Phil, learning that DeVine was possibly in Humbolt as well. Supposedly Phil owed Tom twelve dollars from a poker game on Christmas Eve, and Tom was mad about it. He wanted to collect his cash.

While Tom was busy with Linda, John went downstairs to talk to Lana for a minute. He soon came back to the living room and started teasing Leslie, biting her on the tit in front of everyone. Lotter was drunk, Nissen recalled. They did not spend very much time at the Tisdels' house. They took off for Humbolt after having been there no more than ten minutes, leaving Falls City at about 1:30 in the morning. Nissen drove, getting directions from Lotter on how to travel the back route through Humbolt. Nissen told police Lotter wanted to avoid being seen in the downtown Humbolt area.

On the way, Lotter showed Nissen the knife again, this time taking it out of the leather pouch. Nissen said that he only remembered a knife was involved after Jon Larson had mentioned it. To Hayes and Reinhart, Nissen admitted that Lotter handed him the knife with the blade open, that he took the knife from John. It was a small buck knife, and after John told him he had gotten the knife from his dad, Tom handed the knife back. According to Nissen, Lotter closed it, placing it back in his coat pocket.

For the record, Nissen stated he never saw the knife used at the Lambert farmhouse during the homicides. He reiterated that he did not touch Brandon and did not do anything to Brandon, that John Lotter was the one who had shot her and the girl who was in the bed with her and had also shot Phillip. Nissen told investigators that he actually did not hear the first shot to Brandon, and in fact, he didn't even know she had been shot when she was bent over on the side of the bed and it looked like she was holding her stomach.

By Nissen's account, he saw the next shot, to Brandon's head, and saw Brandon fall back on the bed. He also saw the third shot, under her chin. Nissen said he took the baby from the other girl, then he heard a shot but didn't know if the girl had been hit or not When he heard a second shot, he knew she'd been hit for sure because he saw some stuff coming out of her eye. He then observed John shoot Phil, and again, he wasn't sure if Phil had been hit the first time, but the second time, the shot hit. He saw it hit Phil in the head, and Phil slid to the floor between the couch and the coffee table.

Nissen further implied that Lotter wanted to kill the eight month-old baby, that the two of them argued about it, and finally Lotter told him to shut up, at which time Tom put the little boy back in his crib.

Nissen made a drawing of Lisa Lambert's house, putting X's by the names of the murder victims, pointing out where the door was kicked in and where they had parked the car.

He also marked where the baby and baby crib were in relation to the two girls.

Before the interview ended, Tom mentioned that while they were at the Tisdel house, just before they left for Humbolt, he overheard a conversation between Lana and John during which Lana stated that her father said he would pay to have Brandon "taken care of" or "taken out and left standing in the street." He also alluded to a comment that Leslie made: she said she was through with Phil, that she didn't want anything to do with him, that she didn't love Phil anymore.

But Nissen said he didn't take the Tisdels seriously. He insisted that the only thing he knew John was trying to do, in going to Humbolt, was to scare Brandon to stop her from pressing charges against them.

50

RUMORS THAT AUTHORITIES WERE INVESTIGATING A multiple homicide that occurred in a house just outside Humbolt started circulating through Richardson County on Friday morning, New Year's Eve. Of course, the Tisdel girls had been out there; they had seen the outside of the crime scene. Although they had no confirmation on the identity of the bodies, they were pretty sure who had been killed.

On the way home from Humbolt, after they had been questioned by Investigator Wanda Townsend, the two young women ran into Michelle Lotter, telling her every detail they knew. Michelle had already heard about the killings over the CB radio. Actually, that's how most locals heard the news, on CB's and home scanners and by word of mouth. Naturally, people in Richardson County were on top of it long before the state and national news organizations got hold of the story.

Unfortunately, however, the Brandons first heard about the murders in Humbolt on the Lincoln evening news. Even though no names were mentioned, they had a horrible feeling that Teena was one of the three people killed. They had been calling out to Humbolt all day, getting endless ringing and no answers. Teena had been updating them all week on what was happening with the investigation, and they knew she was dealing with some rough characters. They were really worried about her.

In fact, on December 30, at 6:43 in the evening, Teena called JoAnn to report that she had missed her appointment with the sheriff's department. She said she was supposed to go down to identify a pair of socks and do a follow-up interview, but when she got there, Lotter and Nissen were parked right by the courthouse steps, and she was afraid to go in. JoAnn said she didn't blame her.

"Honey, would you *please* come home?" JoAnn begged.

"Mom, I'll be home on the third, and everything will be all right."

That was the last time JoAnn ever talked to her daughter. JoAnn had wanted to see her for Christmas, for New Year's, but Teena never made it back.

Teena had also called Tammy the night of December 30 twice. In the first call, at 7:17 that night, Teena told her sister that she and Lisa were having problems with Lisa's other housemates, Carrie and Mike Lang. Evidently, the housemates were angry that Lisa had allowed Brandon to move back in, and Teena felt lost.

The second call—at 12:00 midnight—was a desperate cry for help. Teena was scared; she wanted Tammy to come get her right away. Tammy could hear the fright in her sister's voice, but Teena had been asking Tammy to drive down for days—always changing her mind. She had cried wolf.

Now, Tammy wasn't about to get in her junky old car in the middle of the night and try to find her way to some farm road in Humbolt. As they spoke, Tammy could hear the TV in the background, and Teena seemed to calm down when she asked about what she and Lisa were watching on the tube. Finally, Tammy ended the conversation, telling her sister she had to get to bed, that she'd talk to her the next day when she got off work. The two of them spoke for about ten minutes, which was an expensive collect call for Tammy. "I'll try to get down there tomorrow," Tammy told her, hurrying off the phone.

"OK, well, I better let you go," Teena said, the disappointment evident in her voice.

Before the day was out, December 31, 1993, authorities contacted both JoAnn Brandon and Aisha McCain in person, telling them the grievous news. Of course, it wasn't necessary for anyone to call on Anna Mae Lambert at her tiny white-shingled house in Pawnee City, just minutes away from Humbolt. Indeed, she was already being comforted by family and neighbors, and the arrangements for Lisa's aunt, Maggie Barrens, to take custody of baby Tanner were already in progress. Actually, Keith Hayes's wife, nicknamed Snooks, was Lisa's aunt as well, so Anna Mae had plenty of law enforcement people checking in on her, perhaps more than she could bear.

For JoAnn, the knock on her door was a nightmare beyond belief. Seeing this strange man in uniform with a grave expression was all she needed. She knew what words would be following next.

Because of the cross-dressing aspect of the case, media in Nebraska and Iowa gave the triple slaying a tremendous amount of coverage, so the families of the victims couldn't mourn in peace, couldn't have the dignity of privacy. From day one, the press was crawling all over them, especially the Brandons.

Right away, the story was picked up by *The New York Times*, the *Chicago Tribune*, and a host of other big-city papers. That first week, ABC's *Prime Time Live* along with the *Sally Jesse Raphael* and *Maury Povitch* shows were already contacting Richardson County court clerks in an attempt to gain victims' names and numbers. Two tabloid reporters even went so far as to comb JoAnn's garbage, desperate for information when she refused to talk.

The public, chagrined by the unusual circumstances surrounding the homicides, at the same time felt the media were cashing in on the sensationalism of a hate crime involving a transvestite, which was what Teena was being referred to as. Entire reports seemed to focus on Teena Brandon and her sexual identity. Many were appalled that so little was mentioned about the other two victims; DeVine and Lambert were presented as innocent bystanders who just happened to be in the wrong place at the wrong time. Even in Iowa, where DeVine was buried, only a small amount of space was devoted to him in news stories. No doubt, it was much more interesting to focus on this female-to-male transsexual.

It was the *World Herald* in Omaha that carried the first scoop on the triple murder, reporting that two men were being held without bail on charges of sexual assault and kidnapping and suspicion of criminal homicide.

"I just couldn't believe it happened to Lisa, because she didn't have an enemy in the world," the story quoted Tammy Pohlman, a bartender at Big Mike's Tavern in Humbolt.

The news article mentioned that people in Humbolt were having a hard time dealing with such an atrocity in their quiet little town, reporting that on New Year's Day, as folks were watching bowl games and eating Big Mike's homemade turkey soup, they dropped coins and dollar bills in a tin can labeled Lisa's Baby Trust Fund.

People were sad. They loved Lisa. Everyone in town knew her because she worked part-time at Big Mike's, so many would see her there at night and on weekends. She would be missed by everyone. A senior citizen from the Colonial Acres Nursing Home lovingly described Lisa as "a little bitty thing who worked hard but took the time to joke with residents."

The first day the news hit, January 1, 1994, a press conference was held by county attorney Doug Merz, who had announced that although Brandon had posed as a man, "there was no evidence the killings had anything to do with bias based on Ms. Brandon's sexual identity."

Merz said Ms. Brandon had told law enforcement officers about the alleged Christmas Day rape, but he was uncertain about when she had reported it. The county attorney declined to say whether revenge for the rape report was the motive for the shootings, trying to sway a mounting public opinion that officials were somehow largely to blame for the deaths of three young people.

"You're not too successful if all you have is 'He did it,' and they say, 'No, we didn't,'" the *World Herald* later quoted Merz. Apparently, the elected official wanted to assure people that authorities had been pursuing the rape investigation, that part of the problem was that Ms. Brandon failed to show up for a scheduled December 29 meeting with investigators in Falls City.

Another statewide paper, the *Lincoln Journal*, depicted Teena, JoAnn, and Tammy Brandon as helpless victims of a mishandled investigation. "Teena told us they threatened to silence her permanently if she reported that they raped her," one lead-in said. Readers were mortified that two career criminals had been kept on the loose.

The Brandons made public statements that the slaughter was a hate crime and that gay bashing was the motivation. JoAnn disclosed that Teena was particularly upset because Sheriff Laux had asked her why she preferred women and why she pulled her pants down for Nissen and Lotter. JoAnn insisted that the two men should have been arrested earlier, that Teena "gave the authorities what they wanted, and they never picked those guys up."

"You can call it an it as far as I'm concerned," Laux had told the Tisdels at the time the rape report was filed. And the day following the murders, the Lincoln paper actually reported that statement, which just added more fuel to JoAnn's fire.

"No matter what she'd done in her life, she didn't deserve to get beat up and raped," JoAnn tearfully told a Lincoln reporter. "She didn't deserve to be ignored by the sheriff and she didn't deserve to die."

Later, Sheriff Charles Laux was reached by the Falls City Journal for comment, and he took the opportunity to express his thanks to the state patrol officers, the Falls City police, and the sheriff's deputies, who all helped in the investigation. of a "lengthy and complicated case." The sheriff reiterated his position that at least one more full-time deputy was needed in his department, saying he would go before county commissioners to present his request for more manpower.

Meanwhile, Laux had his hands full dealing with all the media in town. Barbara MacDonald, a reporter from News Watch 2 out of Saint Joseph, Missouri, had a run-in with him when she arrived in Falls City to cover the story.

"When we first got there, I went up to the sheriff and introduced myself as a reporter," MacDonald explained.

"He knew who I was; he knew where I was from because I had a big van parked outside that said News Watch 2, KQTV. And when I came out of the arraignment, *my van was gone*. They decided to tow my van away."

MacDonald and her female co-worker went to the sheriff for assistance and were basically told, "Sorry, can't help you.

You're on your own. "She had to call the station for assistance, someone tracked the van down, and then she and her co-worker walked across town to Armbruster's service station, getting misdirected for blocks, carrying heavy camera equipment the whole time.

"Criticism and blame should be directed at those who allegedly committed the crimes, not those who have conducted the investigations of the events that culminated in a triple murder in a farmhouse south of Humbolt," Doug Merz told reporters following arraignment hearings that took place on Monday, January 5, at the Richardson County Courthouse.

"I know law enforcement officers took matters seriously and tried to develop a case despite lack of cooperation," the *Falls City Journal* quoted Merz. "It is not enough to simply arrest a suspect for detainment, then see him or her go free," Merz insisted. "Arrests without convictions do not deter crime."

The paper reported that Merz cited inconsistencies and a lack of corroboration as reasons for the holdup in the sexual assault investigation.

"I don't know what a hate crime is," Merz told reporters.

"I don't know if we have laws against hate crimes in Nebraska."

In Falls City, when people saw news accounts of Teena Brandon's dual sexuality, when they read the inferences about the connection between the murder and the rape, many became puzzled. They didn't understand why something like this would happen in such an unlikely place as their town. It made no sense. And what was someone like that doing around the corn-fed kids of rural Nebraska?

"She said she felt like a man inside, but she was a female outside," twenty-one-year-old Michelle Lotter told a reporter from the Associated Press, trying to explain things away. Michelle said she believed Brandon was a lesbian, that her brother and fellow murder suspect Tom Nissen were both "angry after learning about Brandon's deception and seeing her dressing and acting like a man."

"My brother went off the deep end, got obsessed, when he found out that Brandon was a girl," Angie Lotter told the *World Herald*. "John just kept building stuff in his mind, which he is good at doing. He just snapped, I guess."

Locally, people who knew John Lotter could easily see how he might be involved in a murder. Lotter had been a troublemaker all his life. It was almost his destiny to do something as heinous as this. At the outset, almost all conversation in the local stores, in the coffee shops, even on street corners, centered around the killings. The topic actually eclipsed the Cornhuskers' two-point loss in the Orange Bowl on New Year's night. It was a terrible tragedy. But then, people figured it would all blow over soon enough.

They were ready to get on with their lives, to start fresh with a new year.

No one could foresee the incredible amount of attention the story would eventually warrant. Not only did the murders appear on the front pages of statewide newspapers for months, the savage crime was receiving a lot of television coverage as well. By Monday, January 4, the story went national: *A Current Affair* began taping from the Humbolt farm. That same night *Paul Harvey* talked about the homicides on his radio broadcast.

In Nebraska, people were inundated with the gory and scandalous details of the case. For days, the headlines told the sad, outlandish news:

BIZARRE STORY ENDS IN MURDER... GENEROSITY MAY HAVE LED TO DEATH... FALLS CITY MEN CHARGED WITH THREE COUNTS OF MURDER... BRANDON FIT PROFILE OF TRANSSEXUAL... FRIENDS SAY VICTIM PLANNED SEX CHANGE.

Before it was all over, some began dubbing the Teena Brandon saga a "mini-OJ phenomenon." State newspapers revved up the controversy by highlighting the sexist attitudes of law officers toward women's complaints of domestic violence.

Nebraska's Clay County Sheriff Richard Marsh, who had himself formed a group for victims of sexual assault ignored by police, spoke out officially to local reporters.

"If it's happening in my neck of the woods, it's happening elsewhere," Sheriff Marsh said. "You almost think that if this young lady hadn't been murdered, nothing would have been done."

To gay, lesbian, and transsexual people, it was more than just a hate crime, it was more than just a problem with police: "Brandon Teena" was fast becoming an *icon*. Right from the start, the National Gay and Lesbian Task Force had joined forces with transsexual and transgender groups in putting pressure on Nebraska authorities to officially recognize sexual bias as the motive for the slayings. They wanted the crime to be reported under the Federal Hate Crimes Statistics Act. But there was more.

Before the crime happened, few had even heard of transgender people. Now, all of a sudden, "Brandon Teena" was putting transgenders on the map. Of course, it was of no concern to them that there was no such name as Brandon Teena. That was a minor detail. It didn't dawn on many of the transgender or gay activists that Brandon would probably never have used Teena as a last name, because it would have called up too many questions. Activists were satisfied with the local rumor: a bartender in Humbolt had told a member of the press that Brandon had come in and signed his last name as Teena, which may possibly have been true.

But since they needed to call him something, Brandon Teena was going to be it. Later, when it came to activists' attention that JoAnn Brandon had set up a trust fund for the purpose of getting her child's headstone, some were willing to help out, but not if the headstone read Teena Brandon. Really, all that mattered was that the activists had their martyr. For them, Brandon Teena was a latter-day Joan of Arc.

51

WHEN RHONDA McKENZIE WAS INTERVIEWED BY investigators following the arrests of December 31, she gave a rundown of what was going on at Nissen's the previous night, talked about when the guys left for the Tisdels' place, and said she fell asleep trying to wait up for John. She stated that she was awakened at approximately 3:30 AM by John and Tom's return, and at that time, John's instructions were "If the police ask what time I got home, I was here between midnight and 1:00 in the morning."

Rhonda said she asked John why he wanted her to lie, to which he replied, "You're already in it from the mess that happened on the 25. Don't worry about it, everything is already in hand." That was the extent of the conversation before she lay down to go back to sleep. Just as her eyes were closing, Rhonda happened to look over at the clock on the VCR—the time was 3:35 AM.

When Kandi talked to police, she initially reported Tom and John had gotten home at 1:00 AM that morning. Ever the dutiful wife, she didn't change her story until she was interviewed a third time. On the second interview, police were looking for Tom's Woodings Verona jacket, an article of clothing that Patrolman Greg Cowan had noticed in the Nissen house the night of the arrests, which, unfortunately, police had left at the arrest scene. Now they needed to locate it.

By January 4, which is when investigators realized their oversight, Kandi had already moved out of the Nissen residence, taking Tom's clothing with her. For days, Kandi was nowhere to be found in Falls City, but Chrans finally tracked her down in Beatrice, Nebraska, where she was staying with her brother. It happened that Kandi was wearing the jacket when she answered the door. She told Chrans she wanted to keep it because she could still smell the cologne that Tom wore on it, and she wanted to feel closer to Tom while he was in jail.

Investigator Chrans informed Kandi that she was not obligated to hand him the jacket, but by the third interview, she did turn it over along with the shirt Tom had been wearing the night of December 30-31. By then, Kandi must have had a change of heart about Tom, because in the third go around with police, she finally came clean about what time Tom got home that particular morning. It was somewhere around 3:00 AM.

She also recalled that at about 12:30 or 1:00 AM., when Tom and John came back from Rulo that night, she noticed something about Tom's eyes that "didn't look right," that his eyes changed colors, which was what happened when he was very mad or upset.

At that time, her husband asked her to fix him a sandwich, which she did, and while she was preparing his late supper, Tom said something to the effect that "it would be taken care of soon," but she wasn't really sure what he was talking about.

He left and returned at 3:00 in the morning, and when she heard Tom come to the back door, she went to unlock it for him. She thought it was strange because Tom never used the back door; he always kept the front door unlocked. The minute she let the guys in, Tom asked her to go get bleach so he could wash his hands, and she poured the Clorox while Tom stood over the kitchen sink. She said it was dark, that she didn't see any type of blood. Actually, she didn't really see his hands at all. When Chrans asked why Tom would use bleach on his hands, Kandi said she thought maybe he and John had car trouble, mentioning that Tom had used bleach on his hands in the past, usually when he was working on his car.

Kandi also advised that her husband had an agreement with Lana that he would let Brandon stay at his house "only if Brandon would reveal what sex he was." She further stated that, somewhere between December 24 and December 31, Tom had told her he would kill himself if he ever had to go back to prison.

Just two days before Kandi's last interview, Michelle Lotter had been in for questioning by John Caverzagie, during which she reported an incident that occurred on December 23 when John had come by to see her at Angie's house in Tarkio. The Lotters had all gathered there to celebrate an early Christmas, and Michelle recalled how upset John was because Teena Brandon had lied to both her and Lana. Michelle told the officer that John jokingly asked, "Would you like me to take care of Brandon for you?" But she said she was a big girl and could take care of herself.

Michelle gave Caverzagie a history of her involvement with Brandon, starting from the time she became acquainted with him on December 12, describing the two trips she and Lana had made with Brandon to Lincoln: one time they had gone to Big John's to play pool, the other time, they went up there because Brandon had some sort of court date. Michelle ended her statement by admitting she knew Brandon was a girl from the day she and Lana went to see him in jail, December 15. She described sitting across the visitor's table from Brandon, stating that they both could see down Brandon's V-neck prison shirt, and it was clear that this person had breasts.

When he was done with Michelle, Caverzagie went to see Linda Gutierres, who described in detail the few minutes when Lotter and Nissen stopped by in the early morning of December 31. Linda told Caverzagie that she had a close relationship with both Tom and John, that the boys even called her Mom.

She said that apparently Tom was looking for sympathy over the sexual assault allegations, because she and Tom had a talk about it while John was in the basement with Lana, and Linda assured Tom that no matter what, they would still be friends. In thinking about it, Linda would later realize that it seemed Tom was trying to tell her something, like he was trying to apologize in advance for something, but he never came right out and made himself clear. At the time, she knew Tom was drunk, so she just blew it off.

To Caverzagie, Linda revealed that after John and Lana came upstairs, Lana pulled her aside and whispered, "John just said he wanted to kill someone," but none of them took him seriously. John was always talking like that, always bluffing and threatening.

While at the Tisdel place, Caverzagie spoke briefly to both Leslie and Lana, first getting Leslie's account of that same early morning visit by Nissen and Lotter, during which Leslie admitted that there had been some conversations about Brandon that morning. Leslie stated that before the guys left her house, John had made the comment "I'm going to put a knife in my hands because I'm crazy and I'm going to kill someone."

In Lana's interview with Caverzagie, she acknowledged that she and John had a talk while Brandon was in the Falls City Jail, and she told him, "Well, I guess the only way we're going to find out Brandon's sex is to pull his pants down and look."

Lana then went through the events of December 24 and 25, about being taken home by John and Tom and being woken up by Brandon at 6:00 in the morning, essentially giving him the same story she gave Hayes. Lana told Caverzagie that she had been sick December 27 and 28, and when she recovered, Brandon secretly came down to Falls City to spend the night. She drove him back to Lisa's in the early morning of December 30, at about 6:00 AM.

In talking about Lotter and Nissen's brief early morning visit, Lana said it was Leslie who heard John's comment that he wanted to kill someone, insisting that she never paid any attention to what John had been saying that night. She stated that her next contact with Lotter was the afternoon of December 31, around noon, when he stopped by her house to bring over some clothing of Brandon's.

Lana said John was cool and collected. He handed her a paper bag full of Brandon's stuff in exchange for a pair of Tom Nissen's jeans.

52

ACTUALLY, LANA HAD ALREADY BEEN INTERVIEWED twice by Investigator Wanda Townsend before she talked to Caverzagie. Apparently the rookie investigator wasn't satisfied with the answers this nervous young blonde had given at the crime scene, so Townsend drove to Falls City on December 31, re-interviewing Lana down at the police department.

When Lana was asked if Tom Nissen or John Lotter would have any idea where Lisa Lambert lived, she said that she and Tom had stopped off at Lisa's just before Christmas when they went to pick up Brandon and give him a ride to Lincoln. Lana told Townsend she had only been to the Lambert residence three times—the last time would have been on December 30 at 6:00 or 6:30 AM—when she and Missy Wisdom drove Brandon and Phillip out there.

But that wasn't the last time she had seen Brandon and Phil in person, Lana explained, because they had shown up at her house in Falls City at around 4:00 in the afternoon on December 30. Brandon had driven Lisa's car down, they stayed for about twenty minutes, and actually, Brandon waited out in the car while Phil went in to say good-bye to Leslie. Lana tried to skip through all those personal details, she didn't want to get into it with Townsend. Lana claimed she couldn't remember.

Before Townsend was through, she discovered that in the early morning of December 31, Lana was downstairs playing a card game with her half-brother Terry Torrance when she heard John and Tom's voices upstairs. Lana recalled that Lotter seemed drunk and Nissen looked suspicious. She told the investigator that Nissen was real nervous, and he was rubbing his fingers together. Lana noticed that both he and Lotter were wearing gloves, which she thought was odd. No matter how cold it got, she had never seen either one in gloves before—ever.

On January 13, Lana was interviewed once again, this time by Roger Chrans and Keith Hayes, who advised her there were some issues that needed to be clarified in regard to her previous statements. The lawmen handed Lana her witness statements, asking her to look them over to make any corrections that might be necessary, and Lana did, initialing them in a few places and handing them back. Afterward, she submitted herself to fingerprinting and further questioning, giving investigators the complete chronology of her relationship with Brandon.

Right off the bat, Lana confided that she and Brandon had sex about four days after they met. She insisted that she had no idea that Brandon was a female, stating that she even saw Brandon stand up and pee once, that she didn't know how he did this. She said she later heard that Brandon used some type of catheter. Lana was asked if she knew who Gina was, and she told the officers that Brandon had been engaged to her. Although the two had never met, Lana had seen the photo album of their engagement party and had heard a lot about the girl. Somehow, Lana was also aware that Gina had ended the engagement after discovering that Brandon was not a male.

Regarding the night of December 30-31, Lana told police that she had been out with her friend Jason Fitts, who dropped her off at Tom Nissen's at about 10:00 PM. When she knocked on the door, however, Lana was not allowed in the Nissen residence—Kandi didn't want her there—so Missy came out on the porch to chat, informing Lana that John and Tom were in Rulo. Lana again described her visit with John and Tom at 1:00 AM, finally admitting that she bad heard Lotter say, "I feel like killing somebody," qualifying that he then added, "and *you're* next."

Lana told police she had no idea what John meant by this. According to Lana, before he walked out the door, John turned to her and said, "I'm sorry, I hope you all don't hate me."

But Lana swore she never knew anything like this was going to happen to Brandon or anybody else.

On March 23, after police had almost completed their investigation, searched Lotter's car, seized additional materials from Nissen's house, returned to the crime scene to look through photo albums, pocketbooks, and notebook folders, and interviewed everyone under the sun, Tom Nissen casually dropped a bombshell: he leaked to authorities that "she was in the car."

It was Officer Tom Olberding who Tom confessed to while Olberding was transporting Nissen back to Lincoln after a hearing in Falls City. It was 2:58 in the afternoon, and they were driving along quietly as usual—that had become the routine with all the motions and hearings. Nissen and Lotter were always being transported between the two places, usually by Falls City lawmen who they both felt comfortable with.

Suddenly, Nissen blurted, "She was in the car and she went to the door and knocked on the door, but no one would come to the door, so she came back to the car." Then under his breath, Nissen stated that after she came back, he and Lotter went up and kicked the door in.

"Did she go into the farmhouse with you?" Olberding asked without thinking, not having advised Nissen of his rights.

"She stayed in the car the whole time," Tom told him.

Up until that point, the prisoner had volunteered all this new information, so the officer explained that he would have to file a report on it. Nissen asked him to wait as long as possible, explaining he was trying to make a deal with the state, and Olberding said he would.

Then Nissen divulged that "she" had just visited him in the Richardson County Jail, that she was trying to find out whether the cops knew about her being in Humbolt.

Of course, Olberding filed the report the same day, causing all hell to break loose, especially with Special Prosecutor James Elworth, who was handling the highly publicized triple-murder case for the state of Nebraska. Elworth needed police to get the dirt on Miss Lana Tisdel, and *fast*.

PART FIVE

TRUTH AND CONSEQUENCES

53

IN LATE MARCH, LANA AND LESLIE TISDEL, ALONG WITH their mother Linda and Michelle Lotter, all boarded a jet for New York—the first trip to a big city for any of them. They were going to tape a segment of *The Maury Povitch Show*, having been wooed by producers for a shot at their fifteen minutes of fame. Also on that flight were Daphne Gugat and Lindsey Oassen. It would be a good show; it was great TV in the making, producers promised. As far as they were concerned, the Teena Brandon story was a talk show waiting to happen. What better thing to make audiences scratch their heads and say *what?*

JoAnn and Tammy Brandon were also invited on, but the day they were ready to fly, they backed out at the last minute, having their Lincoln attorney, John Stevens Berry, contact the show with regrets. For starters, the Brandons figured they had bigger fish to fry, and their publicity-hungry lawyer thoroughly agreed. They all had high hopes that the story would be featured on *60 Minutes* or some other nighttime program; they were only interested in dealing with shows that had some real clout.

As it happened, the Brandons probably made the right move in their decision not to appear because they really wanted to have their own stage—they didn't want Teena's story to become trashy and sensationalized. If JoAnn and Tammy had arrived in New York to learn the Tisdels were being included on the show, there would have been an ugly scene. The Brandons and Tisdels had already done battle—they hated each other. At Teena's funeral, they were practically reduced to a cat fight. After the service, they chased each other down to a nearby Taco Bell, where Sara Lyon wound up in a screaming match with Leslie. In the fast-food restroom, idle threats were made from both sides.

More than ever, after having spoken to special prosecutor Elworth, JoAnn and Tammy were certain that somehow, Lana Tisdel was to blame, that *she* was the mastermind behind the murders and the rape. They were outraged that Lana had gotten away with it all, and were further incensed that she was behaving like some kind of "movie star," suddenly to become the toast of the town in New York City.

As Povitch's somber theme music played in the background, the talk show host recapped the unusual story of twenty-one-year-old Teena Brandon, who "posed as a man" and wound up paying the ultimate price because of it. Footage from Lana speaking on *A Current Affair* was shown, with the sultry blonde calling Brandon a gentleman and one of the best guys she ever met.

Linda talked about how much she had approved of her daughter's new love, bragging, "He bought Lana flowers, teddy bears, perfume. He was a very polite young man."

"He talked like a man, acted like a man," Lana told America. "Everything a man does, Brandon did."

Footage aired of the Richardson County Courthouse, the Humbolt farm, and of Lotter and Nissen in shackles. As the story unfolded, Lana explained how she discovered Brandon's sex, describing the day she visited Brandon in the Falls City Jail.

Even though she wore plain jeans and a simple black top, Lana looked beautiful in the stage makeup. Her hair dyed blonder than ever, her face glowed as she described her "boyfriend." When Maury asked if the two of them were intimate, Lana claimed they did nothing more than kiss. She described the depantsing, claiming that in the bathroom, she tried to cover her eyes, but John and Tom made her look. Linda, also looking her best—heavily made up, hair done, wearing a classic blazer with jeans—described the night of the rape, revealing that in the early-morning hours of Christmas, she and Lana had stayed at the Nissen house until 5:30 AM, waiting up for Brandon.

The information must have seemed damning to people like the Brandons who later watched the show. Why would Lana Tisdel be at Nissen's until 5:30 and then appear back home by 6:00 AM, just in time for Teena to arrive all bloody and battered? Also, if Lana and her mom were at the Nissens' until 5:30 in the morning, how could it be that the guys brought Teena there, asking her to shower?

Of course, the logical explanation is that Nissen and Lotter were watching the house, and seeing Linda's car there, they waited for Linda to pull away before entering with Brandon. If Linda left at 5:30 and the shower scene only took a few minutes, it fit perfectly that Brandon would show up at the Tisdels' in the six o'clock zone. But that's not how the Brandons saw things. Once the show aired, JoAnn and Tammy and their attorneys became even more convinced that the Tisdels had been in on it all along.

For the viewing audience, Linda described Brandon's demeanor on Christmas morning, telling Maury that Brandon was scared, that "he" didn't want to report the rape, that she had to talk Brandon into pressing charges. Linda wanted Brandon to enforce his rights. Now the only thing she felt guilty about was that she had closed her house to "him." If she hadn't thrown Brandon out on the street, Linda admitted, Brandon would most likely still be alive.

When Leslie finally spoke—she did not get much air time—she described how her boyfriend had been shot execution style, using her fingers to show how close the gun had been held to Phillip's head. It was eerie; Leslie shed no tears at all. She even defended Michelle Lotter, making sure people knew she held nothing against her childhood friend. Lindsay and Daphne came on in the final segment, both dressed in prissy starched white tops, looking highly virginal, with Lindsey describing Brandon as "a nice, caring loving person."

"Everything you wanted, he would buy," she added, her voice slightly quivering as memories of her "best friend" flooded her mind Lindsay confided that she dated Brandon, even that she kissed him, saying that Brandon was just like any guy she went out with: he was jealous, very possessive, he didn't want other guys around her.

When it was Daphne's turn, she explained that the reason she liked dating Brandon was that she could talk to Brandon "more as a friend, as someone who would listen." The TV audience looked shocked when Daphne described Brandon as "the best guy I could have ever met in my whole life."

Cameras zoomed in on one audience member, capturing the woman's puzzled yet titillated expression as Daphne talked about Brandon having been raped, always referring to her friend as he and him even after she admitted that she knew Brandon was a female a week after they met.

Brandon told her that he was a hermaphrodite, the caption read under Daphne for the benefit of viewers at home.

Michelle Lotter, sporting a new hairdo—a two-toned blond and brunette style that was cropped, almost shaved, in the back—sat quietly in center stage, flanked by the Tisdels on one side, Brandon's "girlfriends" on the other.

When Michelle finally spoke, she admitted that her brother's anger may have festered but maintained she couldn't picture John raping or killing anyone. Of course, John had brutalized Michelle countless times over the years—but she ignored his violent side, and she always defended him.

"He liked Brandon," Michelle assured the national TV audience. "It was hard for John to get angry at Brandon. Even after John found out Brandon was a girl, it still really didn't really seem to bother him that much."

Obviously, Michelle wanted her brother acquitted, and this was one way to try to help him, to possibly win public support. From his jail cell, Lotter was itching to get on TV himself. In fact, he wanted his case tried in the media rather than in the courtroom. Lotter insisted he was innocent, and he wanted to tell his story and let the people decide.

When Michelle was pressed by Povitch, the talk-show host putting her on the spot about John's possible guilt, she finally recognized that even though she couldn't see her brother doing something like that, people do change.

"He was drinking a lot through that week," Michelle rationalized, "and that changes people. You know how that works on people, and a lot of things could have been going through his head." As Michelle spoke, the camera panned over to Leslie Tisdel, who was shaking her head in sorrow. Leslie was the only person on the show to express remorse for what happened to Lisa Lambert and concern for the little baby, Tanner. Clips of Leslie in tears at one of the funerals flashed across the screen.

If Teena hadn't reported the rape, would she still be alive? Maury wondered. The TV host had an activist with the Anti-Violence Project of New York City on the show to talk about women who are afraid to report violent crimes. The activist stated that, unfortunately, many women become revictimized or retaliated against when authorities don't take their reports seriously.

Audience members asked about Brandon's family, wondering why Brandon had no place to go after the rape. Daphne explained that Brandon felt forced to stay away from his family because they would betray his sex.

A male member of the audience wanted to know what it felt like to kiss Brandon. Didn't these girls know she was a *female*? "No," Lindsay claimed. She didn't find out Brandon was a female until after the murders.

"It didn't feel different at all," Daphne threw in. "At the time, you're thinking that you're kissing a man. It doesn't change your feelings."

A kiss is still a kiss.

54

IN THE MONTHS TO FOLLOW, THE COURT-APPOINTED attorneys—Pete Blakeslee for Nissen and Mike Fabian for Lotter—spent hours and hours deposing everyone they could get their hands on. The big issue: Nissen and Lotter were arrested without proper warrants, they were taken out of Nissen's home without search warrants, thus the attorneys were trying to prove that the arrests were illegal.

Even county attorney Doug Merz, the chief law enforcement officer of Richardson County, was deposed pursuant to Judge Robert Finn's order that he answer questions in connection with the issuance of arrest warrants in the case.

In a sworn statement, Merz told defense attorneys he first viewed the Brandon rape reports in the late afternoon of December 30. Merz said he directed Laux to pursue the investigation when Laux first contacted him about the case on December 25, stating that the sheriff did not request the authority to arrest at that time. Merz explained that after he reviewed the reports, he had a phone conference with Police Chief Norm Hemmerling in the early morning of December 31, but at that point, he gave no opinion as to whether or not arrest warrants should have been sought on the suspects.

At around 10:30 that same morning, December 31, Merz received a second call from Hemmerling, this time notifying him about the homicides. Merz immediately proceeded to the crime scene, having no idea who the suspects were. That early on, Merz hadn't connected the murders to the rape investigation at all. For all he knew, he could have been dealing with anything, including suicide. Nothing had been ruled out, because the initial information he had was vague.

Merz claims he made no decision to seek arrest warrants while at the farm; he returned to Falls City without issuing permission to law officers to effectuate any arrests. It wasn't until he was back at his office that the county attorney determined Nissen and Lotter could be arrested on sexual assault and kidnapping charges, that probable cause *did* exist based on these individuals' dangerous history of assaultive conduct. Merz said he discussed probable cause with Hemmerling, telling him he would seek a magistrate or judge to issue the warrants, insisting he did not advise Hemmerling the individuals could be arrested without the warrants in hand. But that's exactly what happened.

In fact, Lotter and Nissen were placed under arrest at 4:15, December 31, yet it wasn't until after 5:00 PM that Merz presented the affidavit and application for arrest at a hearing before Richardson County Judge Curtis Maschman.

In his deposition, Merz told the defense attorneys he wasn't aware that the arrests had already been made when Deputy Tom Olberding went before the judge to present evidence of the rape and assault of Teena Brandon. In front of Judge Maschman, the officer never mentioned that the two suspects were already in custody, being held one floor up in the sheriff's department.

In the end, however, Merz conceded that the warrants had indeed been issued after the fact, and now Blakeslee and Fabian planned to make the most of the blunder.

In late October 1994, the defense attorneys held a drawn-out suppression hearing, arguing before District Judge Robert Finn that the evidence pertaining to the five cases against their clients was obtained illegally, without warrant, that statements were taken illegally; thus nothing was admissible in court. Blakeslee and Fabian wanted all evidence thrown out.

The two of them put on a pretty good show for the court, especially as they interrogated each and every one of the police officers involved, roasting them for participating in an arrest without warrants. Some, like Investigator Roger Chrans, testified that he would not have stepped foot on the Nissen property had he known the warrants weren't in hand.

Apparently, the decision to arrest without warrants was made by Falls City Assistant Police Chief John Caverzagie, who failed to tell state police about it. Caverzagie knew Lotter and Nissen were flight risks. Lotter in particular had been arrested for escape numerous times; Falls City police had been involved in high-speed car chases with him. So at 4:00 PM on December 31, when Caverzagie issued the order to move out, he felt justified in having the team of officers approach the sexual assault suspects without warrant. Besides, Caverzagie had been told by Doug Merz that the warrants were forthcoming.

Through it all, Blakeslee and Fabian were trying to show that if these officers believed probable cause existed on the rape charges, it would have existed on December 25, long before the homicides. It followed, then, that since these two had not been arrested prior to December 31, police officers did not feel they had probable cause. So, why, suddenly, after three homicides were committed in Humbolt, did law enforcement decide that probable cause on rape charges did exist, that they could arrest these guys on stale charges without warrants? The sexual assault charges were just the excuse police needed, defense attorneys argued, in order to arrest their prime homicide suspects, hold them in jail for questioning, and eventually draw a confession out of Nissen that resulted in both young men being charged with three counts of first-degree murder.

"Obviously, you're taking the position now, sir, that you had probable cause on the thirty-first when you went to arrest Mr. Nissen without a warrant, correct?" Blakeslee asked Caverzagie in cross-examination.

"Yes, sir," the officer responded, almost in a whisper.

"So it is of some significance when you developed that probable cause, isn't it?"

"Yes, sir."

"And you'd rather have it be the thirtieth than the twenty-ninth, wouldn't you?"

"I don't see what difference that would make."

"Well, it makes a difference, sir, for this reason," Blakeslee sneered, "the reason being that if you've got probable cause for a serious crime like sexual assault and a serious crime like kidnapping, you don't want to wait around. You go to pick these guys up, don't you?"

"This is correct"

"So it's kinda hard to argue probable cause on the twenty-ninth and not do anything until the thirty-first, isn't it?"

"Yes, sir."

"Probable cause is getting stale, isn't it?"

"Yes, sir."

"But it looks a little better if you say, 'Well, I read the report on the thirtieth, and the early morning hours of the thirty-first, and I found out there was probable cause. And now, on the thirty-first, I arrested them.' That sounds pretty good, doesn't it?"

"Yes, sir."

"But you didn't, after reading the reports, go try to find these guys, did you Officer Caverzagie?"

"The early morning hours of the thirty-first? No, sir," Caverzagie said, squirming.

"You went home, didn't you? Went to sleep?"

"Yes, sir."

Still, no matter how bad the defense attorneys made the cops look, special prosecutor James Elworth argued that the arrests were proper, that all evidence should be allowed in, offering the court these theories: (1) the arrests had been made pursuant to probable cause; (2) the warrants were, in fact, issued shortly after their arrests; (3) these warrants were served *prior* to any questioning or any evidence being recovered.

Of course, in the end, it wasn't only the police who had some egg on their faces, it was Blakeslee and Fabian as well, because they found themselves in the unfortunate position of having to try to knock out the validity of Brandon's rape charges as a way to prove that probable cause *didn't* exist for the arrests. The two lawyers had to do this because they knew that if they could in some way discredit the sexual assault charges, the prosecution would lose their argument that the primary motive for the killings was to silence Teena Brandon. If defense could destroy the motive, prosecutors would have a real tough time winning these cases.

Of course, when Fabian started to ask questions about the rape, which he did right at the start of the hearing as he cross-examined Nurse Lori Moore, people in the courtroom were appalled. JoAnn and Tammy Brandon felt especially violated by the attorney's insinuations that Teena might have been sexually assaulted at all.

"So you made contact with the patient, and during the first part of the conversation, this individual related to you that she was physically assaulted?" Fabian asked the nurse.

"Yes," Moore stated blankly.

"And no mention was made of sexual assault?"

"Not at that time."

"It was only when you asked the individual to remove her clothes because you received information from the X-ray technician, that this individual then said, 'Who told you I was sexually assaulted?'"

"Yes."

"So this individual at no time volunteered this information and said, 'Please help me, I've been sexually assaulted'? It was only after you instigated the questioning and asked her to remove her clothes?"

"Yes."

"Were you advised of anything by Ms. Brandon regarding anal penetration?"

"No, I wasn't."

"Were you advised by Ms. Brandon anything about being sexually assaulted at more than one location?"

"No, I wasn't"

"Do you have any personal knowledge as to other statements made by Ms. Brandon and whether or not they are consistent with the statements she gave you?"

"No."

The idea was to make it seem like maybe Teena Brandon engaged in consensual sex with her buddies, Lotter and Nissen, but this line of questioning from Fabian seemed to be going nowhere. When Fabian was through, Blakeslee took his turn, even trying to reject Nurse Moore's professional judgment, bringing up the fact that she had never worked a sexual assault case in her brief nursing career. Indeed, Nurse Moore testified that she had only been a hospital worker as of July 1993. Prior to that, she was an employee at a lumberyard.

As if that was supposed to mean anything.

The upshot of the week-long event: the warrantless arrests became a nonissue as District Judge Finn ruled all evidence would be admitted.

Trial dates were set and prosecution and defense teams now prepared to do battle. There would be a long road ahead. Nissen's trial would not begin until February 1995. Lotter's would follow a few months later, in May of that year. In the meantime, the media frenzy continued, with news reporters and national TV shows hounding the court, the victims, all other relevant parties—even the alleged killers.

Secretly, Tom Nissen was most intrigued by the publicity. He was hearing from the *Oprah* show and everyone else in TV, but it was *Playboy* that really got to him. Soon after the suppression hearing ended, Nissen decided to give *Playboy* a full-blown interview. He loved the idea of seeing himself in print, in one of his favorite places, no less.

55

WHEN TOM NISSEN BEGAN CALLING ERIC KONIGSBERG from prison, feeding the journalist explicit information for the *Playboy* piece, they talked about romance and sex at the outset Tom described his sexual relationship with Lana, which he said ended right before she started dating Brandon. The two of them spoke five times altogether—once for an hour and forty-nine minutes—and the freelance writer took extensive notes, clearing the content of his article with one of *Playboy's* attorneys before it ran in the January 1995 issue.

Of course, Nissen wasn't sure about cooperating at first, so before the phone calls, the two had exchanged a number of letters, Konigsberg always writing on *Playboy* stationery, trying to coax his prey like a hunter with a decoy.

"I need to know I can trust you," Nissen finally wrote. And Konigsberg wrote back, bluntly assuring him, "I promise not to betray your trust, not to fuck you over, to listen carefully to what you have to say." Konigsberg had already read the newspaper accounts, had talked to law enforcement people, and had spoken to members of Nissen's family. He was quite familiar with the story, he told Nissen, and it wasn't long before Tom started to feel close to the journalist.

They had become a strange sort of pen pals.

After the suppression hearings ended, Nissen called Konigsberg to let him know police had revealed that two condoms were found at the Hormel scene, one of which proved most definitely to have Lotter's semen in it. During that conversation, Nissen confessed about his involvement in the rape, telling Konigsberg, "I went first, then John. I think it just sort of happened. I'd never done it before. I don't know that it wasn't more of an ego thing.

"I felt like I'd been fucked," Nissen went on. "Me and Brandon had a long conversation that evening, and Brandon started to feed me another line about how he was going to have a sex operation. John was really upset with the whole situation. Maybe he still wished he was going out with Lana."

In another phone conversation, Nissen expressed his fear of Lotter, claiming that after the murders, John was behaving irrationally toward him. He confided that Lotter made a threat about nobody snitching on him and getting away with it.

When the article appeared in *Playboy* in December 1994, released a month early, as magazines always are, Nissen's attorney was aghast. Nissen's trial was just weeks away, and Blakeslee had no idea that his client had spoken to anyone about the crime, much less a reporter. To Konigsberg, Nissen had admitted that he was the one who knifed Teena Brandon that night in Humbolt.

Of course, murder and rape weren't the first things on *Playboy* readers' minds. They were interested in the *she* that became a *he*, in following the evolution of Teena into Billy and then Brandon. They were getting juicy tidbits about this person's tangled sexuality and the deception that went on.

"Teena liked to begin sexual encounters with extended foreplay—lots of kissing and ear nibbling, undressing her partners, sucking on their breasts," the article reported, "but she never allowed anyone to undress her. With all but a few girls, she kept her undershirt and boxer shorts on."

"One time I tried to go down on him and be stopped me," *Playboy* quoted an anonymous female source, noting that Brandon wanted to return the attempted favor, giving the girl great *head* and the first orgasm she ever had in her life.

"After that, I don't think there was a time with him when I didn't come," the anonymous girl was quoted, "orally, going all the way, even dry humping."

"I noticed that he could go a long time, and he usually pulled out as soon as I had my orgasm," another anonymous source said. "It wasn't until after he said he had the sex change operation that I noticed it stayed hard afterward. When I asked him about it, he said it was because the only options for him after surgery were to be hard all the time or for him to use a pump."

"Still it was funny," the girl went on. "Sometimes I'd feel through his pants and it'd be small, and sometimes it felt like he had a lot more."

The article was quite thorough, and although there were some minor inaccuracies in the article (for example, he said a revolver was used in the homicides when it had been an automatic), there was still a very clear picture of the crime, the victims, and the killers—one that led everyone to raise their eyebrows. What no one could believe was that Nissen had confessed to the crime right there in national print—it was a dream come true for the prosecution.

"The stabbing [of Teena Brandon] well that was me," Nissen had admitted. "It just kinda happened so fast. I couldn't tell if she was already dead. I honestly don't know. You ever get caught up in the moment before?"

Just days after *Playboy* hit newsstands, Konigsberg was contacted by the state of Nebraska, becoming a star witness for special prosecutor James Elworth. Actually, Nissen had already confided to one of his prison mates about stabbing Teena Brandon, so the prosecution had one such confession before the article appeared. Nissen had admitted to it early on, in March 1994, when he was chatting in the jail's exercise room with a kid named Harry David Foote.

Now, Konigsberg would be a second source—and a much better one at that. He couldn't be discredited by the defense as having something to gain by snitching, as having a criminal past that might tarnish the truthfulness of his statement.

Even though certain journalists thought the *Playboy* writer shouldn't have put himself in the middle of a trial, Eric Konigsberg was the very last witness the jury would hear before they went into deliberations, and his testimony was convincing. When it was all over, jury members admitted that the writer became key in their decision to convict.

56

WITH ALL THE PUBLICITY, THE HYPE, THE SUPER awareness about the case in Nebraska, Falls City was swamped with media when the Nissen trial began in February 1995. Not only were there reporters for print, TV, and radio, the story had also enticed two crews of documentary makers from New York, a couple of Hollywood producers, and a half-dozen people claiming to be writing books, one of whom had actually quit her job in Colorado after the *Denver Post* ran a long piece on Teena Brandon. She said she had a vision of Teena in a cowboy suit, beckoning her to Nebraska.

Of course, the small town had never seen that kind of influx before, and locals were not used to dealing with so many demanding outsiders. Between the sequestered jury and the media army, the Hotel Stephenson couldn't accommodate everyone, so people were staying in the two other smaller motels in town, in places outsiders called fleabags, and the rest had overflowed to Hiawatha, which was actually a preference for some—the accommodations were good, and being twenty miles away, it was more low key.

In Falls City, after the same faces kept appearing day in and day out, everyone had started to feel like they were on a stage. It became a cast of characters living a bizarre drama, everyone watching each other's moves—who ate with whom, which journalists had an in with lawmen, which victims befriended each other. It was a regular soap opera, complete with gossip and rivals and archenemies.

The waitresses and management in the Stephenson Hotel had their hands full, especially with all the requests for special meals, faxes, Fed-Exes, photocopies, just about anything and everything you could think of, which locals couldn't always supply. One of the reporters, Pia Martinez from the Associated Press, even installed a private line in her hotel room in an effort to circumvent the antiquated hotel telephone system. Others spoke long distance on their cellular flip phones, an eye-catching sight in an isolated, economically depressed farm town.

Whether Falls City liked it or not, the twenty-first century was knocking on its door. People had to rise to the occasion, and actually, they did. Shop owners worked hard at supplying extra services whenever possible, happy for the new business.

Witnesses are usually not allowed to watch court proceedings, but an exception was made for JoAnn, Aisha, and Anna Mae, who were about to be called to identify the bodies of Teena Renae, Lisa Marie, and Phillip Elliot.

Throughout the Nissen trial, officials kept using the name Teena Ray Brandon, which really disturbed JoAnn, but then, everything about the trial upset her. Between all of her hysteria and outbreaks, she didn't remember to correct the court about Teena's name.

On the first day of Marvin Thomas Nissen's trial, February 21, 1995, the benches throughout Judge Robert Finn's courtroom were filled to capacity, but Nissen's parents weren't there, nor was Kandi. Sitting at the defense table with him were his attorneys, Peter Blakeslee and Mike Cruise, both of whom Nissen hated. He had filed motions to get rid of Blakeslee but was turned down. Cruise had the extra bonus of handling the Nissen divorce, which gave Tom more ammunition to dislike him. The divorce was something Kandi wanted, not Tom. More than ever, Tom wanted to stay married to her, to continue seeing his three kids. While Tom was locked away, Kandi had given birth to a third girl, and Tom hadn't even seen her yet.

It was bright and early in the morning, a snow-swept windy day, when Jim Elworth began his opening statement, speaking to the jury in that folksy way of his. It didn't hurt that he had a solid frame and good looks. His blue eyes flashing at the jury, he was definitely easy to look at. Behind the scenes, women commented about how handsome he was, and secretly, JoAnn Brandon was developing a bit of a crush on him.

The young prosecutor got a little choked up during his highly prepared speech—an unusual and endearing display that had emotional impact on everyone in the courtroom, even more so because it was so obviously unintended. Most people didn't know that Elworth had recently lost one of his own children, a three-year-old girl. Between that and the Nissen case being the first homicide Elworth was entirely responsible for, things must have gotten to him.

He began by giving a vivid picture of the isolated farmhouse, of the back bedroom with the water bed and the baby crib next to it. He talked about the "through and through" wounds the victims suffered, about the defendant herding Phillip DeVine into the living room, listening to the young amputee plead for his life. He described the blood-soaked pillow found under Lisa Lambert's head, which was later produced as evidence for the jury to smell, to touch. He brought up the package found on the frozen Nemaha River, which would be in evidence, then focused on the Clorox poured over Nissen's hands and Tom's comment to his wife that his "problems were now over."

"You'll hear from a firearms expert with the Nebraska State Patrol who will tell you that the slugs recovered from the bodies of the victims, the slugs recovered from the farmhouse, were, in fact, fired from the gun of William Bennett, which was recovered from that frozen Nemaha River," Elworth told members of the jury. "You'll hear testimony that the knife with Lotter's name on it had bloodstains on it when it was recovered and that the blood was tested, tested against a known blood sample of Teena Brandon, and found to be the same type—type A blood."

Elworth promised that before the trial was over, the jury would hear about the calculated acts performed by defendant Nissen, that they would be convinced beyond a reasonable doubt that the defendant, whether he pulled the trigger or not, was legally responsible for the senseless brutal deaths of three innocent people.

Peter Blakeslee then rose, his receding hairline and somewhat disheveled suit making him not nearly as impressive to the average eye. When he spoke, there was nothing that would necessarily make people sit up and listen. If anything, his introductory remarks seemed lifeless, as colorless as his dark blue suit and the monotone of his voice.

Ultimately, Blakeslee told the jury that the evidence was in Nissen's favor, that the evidence didn't show that "they" did it—meaning Nissen and Lotter—instead, only one person committed the murders, and that was *John Lotter*. He was certain the jury would find that his client, Marvin Thomas Nissen, did not bear any legal responsibility in this terrible crime, asking them to put all their emotions aside when trying to reach their decision.

"Are you ready with your first witness?" Judge Finn asked from behind his high-back chair, swiveling toward the jury box.

"If any of the jurors get uncomfortable or need anything," he told them just as things started rolling, "just raise your hand, and we'll excuse you for a while, OK?"

An imposing character, Finn, with his silver-white hair, handsome face, and gravelly voice, was no stranger to death penalty cases. Of the eight people on death row in Nebraska, Finn was already responsible for two: Willie Otay, a man convicted of a brutal rape and murder, and Mike Ryan, the cult torturer from Rulo whom people in Nebraska had been anxious to electrocute for ten years. Of course, neither man had been put to death yet—although Otay was about to be electrocuted. Many Nebraskans were fed up with the system. Some were trusting in the recent laws that had passed that were intended to hasten this kind of thing. It was part of the whole national push to get tough on crime, and certainly the majority of victims in this triple homicide were hoping it would work. JoAnn Brandon, in particular, wanted to see Nissen and Lotter fry.

Months earlier, John Lotter had written to her from his prison cell, sending his condolences for her family's loss, describing himself as a nice guy who would have stopped this terrible crime from happening if only he could have.

John presented himself as a friend of her daughter, as someone who Teena trusted with her secret about being a girl. He hoped Teena would rest in peace and that God would bless the Brandon family. Of course, reading that only incensed JoAnn more.

It was Anna Mae Lambert who first took the stand, a middle-aged woman with wire-rimmed glasses, slightly overweight, wearing polyester slacks and a pullover shirt. She spoke clearly and distinctly as she described for the court, in the most matter-of-fact way, the gruesome scene she came upon the morning of December 31. She talked about discovering a "Negro" dead on the floor in the living room and then seeing her daughter lying in bed with someone else. She couldn't look at them, she said. She was only concerned with baby Tanner at the time. She revisited picking him up out of the crib and fleeing from the bedroom, explaining to the jury that she had been trained as an emergency medical technician, so she knew what to do when arriving at a crime scene, and she didn't disturb anything.

Anna Mae's voice was businesslike. The only time her stern face quivered was for a brief moment when Elworth apologized and held up a poster-size color photo of Lisa Lambert in a prone position, bright red blood oozing from her mouth and left eye socket.

"This is marked as Exhibit 74, and I'll ask you," Elworth coaxed, "if you would, please, just take a look, and can you identify your daughter in this picture for me please?"

"Yes, that's her," Anna Mae said as her eyes shot a glance at it.

JoAnn Brandon was next, slinking to the stand in five-inch high heels and a long black dress, looking rather youthful. She briefly mentioned her daughter's sexual identity crisis and began to get into Teena's childhood, mentioning the sexual molestation, but JoAnn's testimony was objected to and sustained, and then it came time for her to I.D. the photo of Teena. It was a grisly poster of her daughter's face, a close-up with a bullet wound to her chin with Teena surrounded by a current of blood. JoAnn shrieked, saying,

"Yes, that's Teena," and she ran from the stand, tears streaming from her face. She was sobbing uncontrollably, and Tammy had to take her out of the courtroom so she could compose herself.

When it was Aisha McCain's turn to get up there, draped by a designer scarf and heavy jewelry, she came off almost like a professional witness, although there was something about her—she was radiant, light emanated from her face.

It almost seemed as if Phillip was still alive when she spoke of him. For the jury, she wore a mother's proud, happy face, detailing her son's recent achievements as a representative of the Job Corps.

But then she looked at the picture of Phillip. Aisha was a whole different person after she saw the gory poster of her baby, his legs twisted and deformed under a heavy coffee table, his white shirt drenched in blood.

57

THROUGHOUT THE FIVE DAYS OF PROSECUTION testimony, Peter Blakeslee rose repeatedly to challenge the state's witnesses on the same grounds: the evidence was derived from the violation of the defendant's rights, outlined in the defendant's motions to suppress evidence because of an unlawful arrest and an illegally obtained warrant. Of course, Blakeslee was categorically overruled, so the continual objections only had the effect of being disruptive, which is maybe all Blakeslee could hope for—to break up the flow of expert testimony.

Roger Chrans was the first witness on day two, explaining to the jury that it was his case, and as chief investigator, he was responsible for all assignments given to him by prosecutors. Right off, Chrans established that Nissen had been read his rights verbatim, that the defendant had waived them, unquestionably, without any promise of a deal in exchange for his cooperation. Nissen had signed the papers twice. He hadn't been coerced, hadn't been intoxicated or impaired in any way at the time.

Chrans went back and retraced what Nissen told him about the night of December 30 and the morning of December 31, then he described the entire course of police work in the homicide case. Among other things, they had sent out a team of investigators on horseback to cover the roads of Humbolt and Falls City, looking for the pair of missing gloves and any other discarded bloody clothing. They had also searched Lotter's car a number of times, unfortunately without turning up any blood, and they had checked for fingerprints in the car and farmhouse to no avail. But none of that mattered because it was the golden gloves, with the knife and the gun inside them, that Elworth zoomed in on, lifting up a giant poster of the gloves being recovered from the ice for Chrans to identify.

To members of the jury, Chrans outlined the police protocol in handling evidence—the bloody pillow, the casings and bullets. Most of it was kept in the Richardson County evidence vault, with Roger Chrans in sole possession of the key. Other than bringing the items to court, Chrans explained, these things had been kept untouched in the locked facility.

With certain evidence, for instance, the knife that had to be disassembled in order that it be properly tested, Chrans personally received the item from the State Patrol Criminalistic Laboratory in Lincoln and then flew to Washington, D.C. to hand deliver it to Cellmark Diagnostics. Chrans then talked about the inventory and submittal sheet, all the paperwork involved in handing information and evidence. When he was finished with all the technical mumbo-jumbo, the investigator identified the person they'd been speaking about all morning: defendant Marvin Thomas Nissen.

"He's seated on the far side over there, dressed in a white shirt and a sweater, blondish hair, no beard," Chrans pointed out.

In cross-examining him, Blakeslee tried to get Chrans to talk about Nissen as being emotional and intoxicated the night of the murders, to get Chrans to help paint a sympathetic portrait of his client. Blakeslee pointed out that Nissen vomited in his bathroom after they returned from Humbolt, that he cried during his interview with police, that he was the poor chap who was *scared* of Lotter the night they were out there at the Humbolt farmhouse.

Chrans couldn't totally reject Blakeslee's key points, but in redirect exam, Elworth made sure to clear the matter up.

He wanted the jury to understand that in no way was Nissen a passive bystander, accompanying Lotter out of fear.

"Does it say anywhere in your report, or do you have any recall, that he ever said he was scared of John Lotter?" the prosecutor asked.

"Specifically that, no," Chrans said.

"Was he asked specifically if he'd been threatened?"

"By Investigator Sergeant Osborne, yes."

"What was his response?"

"He had not been threatened."

What followed Chrans's testimony was a string of law enforcement officers—Osborne, Hayes, and Reinhart—all of whom were asked about the chain of custody regarding evidence. Each detailed the dates the evidence had been collected, how it was all precisely marked, in what order, and Elworth introduced hair, blood, and fiber samples along with bullets and casings as exhibits. When it was his turn, Hayes described the "scenic drive" he took on January 2 as he followed the exact route Nissen had described in his December 31 statement. Hayes had recorded the mileage on the return trip as approximately forty-six miles, and of course, Elworth used this to show the jury that Lotter and Nissen were not intoxicated that night out at the farm. In fact, they were thinking so clearly, they traveled this lengthy alternate route to find places to dispose of evidence and make sure that no one was following them.

When the prosecutor shifted gears and began to question Hayes about his interview with Nissen on December 28 regarding the rape of Teena Brandon, Blakeslee objected on the grounds that it was not relevant, but he was overruled. Blakeslee was right about one thing: since Nissen hadn't been convicted of the crime of rape, the exact details couldn't be discussed in open court. However, because Teena Brandon's rape went directly to *motive*, the judge allowed Elworth to establish that complaints had been filed by her, alleging Nissen had committed sexual assault and battery.

"Did you specifically tell this defendant, Marvin Thomas Nissen, that he was a suspect in these alleged crimes?" Elworth asked. "Yes, I did," Hayes responded. "And did you relate certain information and certain specifics to Nissen about the crime?"

"Yes, sir," Hayes said as his face hardened, making his crisp law enforcement uniform seem all the more threatening and authoritative.

58

AS HE SAT THERE WATCHING A PARADE OF WITNESSES testify about his using the knife, about his leading authorities to the gun, about everything that linked him unquestionably to the homicides—Nissen showed emotion only when Kandi stood up to testify on the state's behalf.

For almost a year, the two had exchanged letters, proclaimed their love for each other, and agreed they'd hold their marriage together. But that had all changed. Kandi filed for divorce in October 1994, which just about killed him. He tried to commit suicide in his cell, slitting his wrists, but was discovered and sent to the hospital just in time.

In her early letters, it was obvious that Kandi still loved him. She wrote every day, making sure he knew how much he was missed. She had especially wanted Tom to be there for the birth of their third child, Angie Lynn, delivered February 15, just weeks after he had been carted off to prison.

In those early days, in the weeks following the arrest, Kandi fawned all over Tom in countless letters. She constantly told him how sexy he was, how much she wanted his touch and needed him in her bed. She told him she was in a rut without him, that she kissed his picture every night, wore his clothes, and just waited for the mail, hoping a new letter would be there for her.

In the beginning, Kandi had felt so bad about everything.

She felt down on herself, blaming herself somehow, and she just couldn't face people. When she finally had the nerve to leave her brother's place and return to Falls City, she moved from Chase Street into a trailer and wouldn't see anybody—not even her parents. She told Tom he was her drug, spending hours every day dreaming about being in bed with him, remembering how he treated her like a queen. She wrote and told him she had created a Marvin Thomas Nissen shrine at home.

What made matters worse was that the children were heartbroken without him, and she complained that she couldn't manage them alone. She told Tom she couldn't keep the house clean and she was afraid she was going to lose them if she didn't get help.

Of course, Tom wrote and assured her that he'd be out of jail soon, swearing that he didn't have anything to do with this terrible atrocity. John Lotter was the culprit, he told Kandi, and the truth would come out before long. Even if there was a trial, he would be set free, Tom was certain.

In the meantime, he was obsessed with Kandi. In one letter, for example, he wrote the words "I love you, I miss you" 100 times. He promised that no matter what happened, even if he lost her as his wife and friend. he'd never lose her in his heart. He loved Kandi "so fucking much" that he was willing to do anything to be with her.

Kandi had high hopes.

While he awaited trial in the Diagnostic and Evaluation Center in Lincoln—a criminal facility surrounded by yards of barbed wire, TV surveillance, and cement watch towers—Tom always encouraged his wife, telling Kandi to consider taking college courses, to find a good job, to put the girls in day care, to get her act together so things could be good for them again when he got out. But Kandi never paid any attention. She was too busy living in a dream world, watching movies like *Ghost* and hoping that somehow Tom would materialize out of thin air, just like Patrick Swayze's character had. She actually wrote and asked Tom if he could maybe come back and at least haunt her and the girls.

Whenever the Humbolt murders were on the news, Kandi would write to inform Tom that the girls recognized his picture on TV and they wanted to know where their daddy was. Was he ever coming home? Kandi thought Angie looked just like Tom and couldn't wait until she could show him his new daughter. But when would that be?

Sometimes Kandi put nude pictures of herself in her letters, so Tom could remember what he was missing. For Valentine's Day, she sent him a mushy card and a handmade Valentine from Bobbie. Tom cried when he saw it.

"What do I say to her about where you are?" Kandi asked in their first prison visit. But Tom had no answer.

Eventually, however, as weeks rolled into months, Kandi started seeing someone else.

Actually, it was his brother, Scott, she first slept with, which absolutely devastated Tom.

She had written to tell him about it, asking him to please forgive her, that it was a mistake. When Tom confirmed Kandi's claim, he disowned his brother, but it didn't matter much. By then, Kandi had moved on to a new guy, Chuck, and now she seemed to want little to do with her kids, which enraged Tom even more. Whenever possible, Sharon told him, Kandi pawned them off to whoever else would take them.

In her letters, Kandi no longer asked for Tom's opinions on new outfits; she no longer kept him up-to-date about things like Tiffany's potty training. In fact, she cut him off completely from every aspect of her life. Now she would write only hate mail. Kandi's eyes had finally opened to the truth when she discovered that not only did it look like he was sleeping with Lana around the time of the murders—something Lana continued to deny—he was sleeping with Lana's aunt, Missy, as well.

Tom had even written to Missy from prison, asking her to marry him when his trial was all through, and Missy had shown the letter to Kandi, who verified the handwriting.

When she read that Tom was offering to *adopt* Missy's baby, that was the last straw. Kandi was through with him forever.

Tom made certain to write Kandi to let her know about his suicide attempt, that he had been sent up to Lincoln General, that he was put in a room with nothing but a toilet and a blanket, that hospital workers had to place him in a five-point hold in order to get sixteen stitches in his one arm. Kandi had a momentary change of heart, writing to say how sorry she was.

Kandi told him she hadn't meant to drive him to it, that she didn't want to hurt him anymore. Still, they just couldn't stay together. More than pitying Tom, Kandi pitied her own miserable existence. She saw herself as just another face in the crowd who no one cared about, no one at all.

Back in July 1994, Social Services had come and taken her three children away, placing them in foster care because of the numerous reports about the filth and unhealthy surroundings they were living in with their mother. Kandi had written Tom about it, and he was sickened by the news.

Couldn't she do *anything* right?

Now, in front of reporters, lawyers, God, and everyone else, he watched Kandi waltz up to the witness stand. She was wearing Tom's favorite jean dress with little black heels, looking cute as a button. How Kandi could get up in front of everyone in court and betray him even further, Tom just didn't know.

"What's the present nature of your relationship with the defendant?" Elworth asked.

"Divorced."

"Have you gotten a divorce now, at this time?"

"We're in a six-month waiting period," Kandi quipped.

Kandi Nissen told Elworth everything she knew about the night of December 30, explaining that just before he left for Rulo, Tom said he was going to see his mom to try to get power of attorney over Tiffany "in case anything happened." She told the jury about him coming home at 12:30 AM on December 31, at which time she made him a sandwich and he told her, "Our problems are over."

"Had you asked him, or had you been discussing with him, anything about problems you were having before that statement was made?" the prosecutor asked.

"No."

"Was that just out of the blue to you?"

"Yes."

"Did you ask him what he meant by the statement 'Our problems are over'?"

"No. He left right after he said it."

Kandi didn't ask where Tom was going. She testified that she didn't see her husband again until 3:30 in the morning, which was a strange time for someone to be knocking on her back door. She gave details about washing his hands with Clorox, told the jury that Tom had asked her to supply an alibi, and stated that in no way did she believe Tom to be drunk when he returned at that time.

In cross-examination, Blakeslee tried to show that the couple did have financial problems, insinuating somehow that's what Tom might have been referring to when he said the word *problems*. Then the attorney reminded Kandi that in her deposition, given months earlier when she and Tom were still a couple, Kandi had confirmed that Tom was extremely intoxicated the night of the murders.

"You knew I was asking you about this critical event on December 31, didn't you?" Blakeslee prodded.

"Yes."

"And in fact, you told the truth in that deposition, didn't you? You said that your husband was intoxicated, and he was, wasn't he?"

"Yes."

"Ms. Nissen, it was you who filed for divorce, wasn't it?"

"Yes."

"I believe that's all the questions I have," Blakeslee snapped, giving her a nasty look.

Blakeslee was trying to establish intoxication to use as a possible mitigating circumstance, and now Kandi was undermining that. Blakeslee must have been at the end of his rope by then. For weeks, Nissen and Blakeslee had fought incessantly over a plea deal the state was offering. Tom had refused to sign the thing, absolutely unwilling to admit any guilt even though the state was willing to drop the rape charge as part of the deal.

On top of that, Tom had publicly filed a motion to remove his attorney, asserting that Blakeslee had gone on a verbal tirade over the plea agreement. Of course, the state newspapers picked that up, which couldn't have made Blakeslee too happy.

When it came time for Blakeslee to put on a defense, Nissen, of course, chose not to speak on his own behalf. The defense rested without having called any witnesses. Everyone was floored. Early on, Blakeslee had filed a motion to transport one of Nebraska's most notorious criminals in to testify on Nissen's behalf. Apparently, Roger Bjorklund, who had been incarcerated for the brutal murder of young Candice Harms in Lincoln, had been willing to act as a character witness for Nissen.

But Blakeslee changed his mind at the last minute. Maybe he thought bringing Bjorklund in would have been more trouble than it was worth. No one really knew what the Lincoln attorney's logic was in resting before he even began. But one thing was sure: the defense didn't have to prove anything, the prosecution did. And in Blakeslee's mind, the state hadn't really proven that Nissen shot these three people.

In any event, people had been expecting a show, and they didn't get their money's worth. Now, the men and women of the jury would decide the defendant's fate. And a conviction of three counts of first-degree murder meant Nissen would be facing the electric chair.

59

"IF YOU FIND THAT THE STATE HAS FAILED TO PROVE beyond a reasonable doubt any one or more of the foregoing material elements, it is your duty to find the defendant not guilty under count I." This was the last jury instruction and the one that stood out in certain jurors' minds. Because of reasonable doubt, there were some who were actually considering a conviction of manslaughter.

"You will allow no sympathy or prejudice to influence you in arriving at your verdict," the instructions said. "The law demands of you a just verdict influenced by any considerations outside the evidence."

Of course, that was easier said than done.

For starters, the jury felt they had to grapple with whether Nissen had anything to do with the shooting of DeVine and Lambert. Because no one had actually been able to prove that, the jurors had a problem. Then there was the issue of the baby: a couple of them felt that since Nissen *held* the baby and perhaps saved the baby's life, maybe he wasn't a totally bad guy.

On the issue of the knifing: Dr. Blaine Roffman had performed the autopsy and testified that there was no way to know definitively in what sequence the wounds were inflicted. Nissen could have killed Teena by puncturing her liver; then again, Lotter might have shot her dead first. There was just no telling.

Jury instructions are always lengthy and complicated, and in this case, the twelve members seemed to have difficulty understanding them, coming back to Judge Finn with questions more than once. In terms of ability, it was clear from their occupations that these jurors were capable; they had reliable jobs in computers, high school education, bookkeeping, and the like. They were good solid citizens representing most walks of life.

But that didn't mean they understood the intricacies of the law, especially once this concept of felony murder had been introduced. Felony murder was another option allowing them to convict Nissen, which actually should have made their decision cut and dried.

In his closing argument, Elworth had taken great pains to explain the felony murder theory, making clear to jurors that a conviction of felony murder would be equivalent to a conviction of first-degree murder, at least in terms of the penalties it would carry. The thing Elworth needed the jury to understand was that even if they didn't feel the state had proven premeditation—that is, Nissen and Lotter went to Humbolt with the intent to kill Brandon, and as part of their crime, they had preplanned the killings of any witnesses—*even if jurors didn't believe this*, Nissen could still be found guilty on three counts of felony murder.

By law, John Lotter and Marvin Nissen were both guilty of three homicides, no matter who held the knife, who held the gun, no matter who did what. Under felony murder, if a person dies in your hands while you're in the process of committing an underlying felony—in this case, breaking and entering the farmhouse—then you're guilty of murder just by being there.

It was that simple, Elworth told jurors, and he reminded them to check out the pictures of the door jamb, to look at the shattered door of the Lambert house. There was no question that these two guys broke in, Elworth reiterated, and no question that they committed murder while already in the process of a felony.

If the jury could only come up with three counts of felony murder, that would suffice. Nissen would still stand a good chance of being executed. But obviously, the prosecutor wanted to see Nissen convicted of three counts of first-degree murder—anything less would fall short of true victory.

"I submit to you that the intent to kill Teena Brandon was formed over that period of days, December 28 through the point where she was actually shot," Elworth explained. "The intent instruction will also tell you that intent can be formed instantaneously as long as it's being formed prior to the act being done. And so while they may not have had the precise intent to kill Lisa Lambert or Phillip DeVine when they walked into the home, before Lisa Lambert and Phillip DeVine died, the intent was formed. It sure didn't take long, but there could be no witnesses after Teena Brandon was shot."

Much to everyone's surprise, the jury deliberated for two and a half days. It was hell on all those concerned; people were standing around, not knowing what to do with themselves. Ed Nissen and his wife, Pam, showed up during that period, having made the drive from Mississippi. They kept a low profile and spent as much time with Marvin as the sheriff would allow. By then, Charles Laux had been voted out of his job; Keith Hayes now held the office. And even though Hayes's own niece was probably the most tragic victim of the three—dying with her baby beside her, not knowing if Tanner would be killed or tortured—the sheriff still found it in his heart to have compassion for Ed Nissen. In fact, Sheriff Hayes allowed Ed Nissen special visiting privileges with his son, watching the two of them console each other in the bleakness of the Richardson County Jail. No doubt, Ed was hopeful that his child would be found not guilty.

Because of the conflicting information in the jury instructions and the strong personalities of certain jury members, the jury was headed in three different directions from the start: first degree on Brandon, manslaughter on DeVine, and not guilty on Lambert. That first day, no one could seem to agree firmly on anything, and tempers began to run high.

"The only thing we all pretty much acknowledged was that he stabbed the first victim," juror John Jacobson later recalled. "There was zero evidence on Lambert, and with DeVine, we all felt there was a strong possibility that the defendant became somewhat of a victim himself after the first murder."

"We thought Nissen seemed to indicate he was scared of Lotter," Jacobson said, "and if Lotter is obviously killing people, standing there like a madman shooting people, Nissen could be kind of a victim too. If he starts to say, 'Hey, knock it off or I'm gonna report you,' he's gonna get killed too."

On March 3, 1995, just after having returned from lunch break, Marvin Thomas Nissen buried his head in his hands waiting for jury forewoman Barbara Fajen to stand up and read the verdict.

Nissen was found guilty of first-degree murder in the death of Teena Brandon, guilty of second-degree murder for the part he played in the death of Phillip DeVine, and guilty of second-degree murder for the death of Lisa Lambert. In Nebraska, the first-degree murder charge carried with it a penalty of life in prison or death in the electric chair. The second-degree murder charges each carried a penalty of ten years to life in prison.

Nissen's eyes welled up as he learned that his sentence would be pronounced by a special three-judge panel in Omaha, the sentencing date to take place after John Lotter's upcoming trial. "I want him to get the chair," JoAnn Brandon told reporters, the media swarming around her as she stepped outside the courthouse. "You take a life, you should give your own," she told the news cameras. Aisha McCain wasn't there for the verdict. Tammy Brandon had promised to call her, but what could Tammy say?

That the jury felt Phillip's life wasn't as important as Teena's? Of course, even if that wasn't the case at all, the victims couldn't help feeling that way—especially Anna Mae and John Lambert. Lisa's parents were crushed when the verdict came down; you could see it written all over their faces.

Then there was Elworth, Merz, and Chrans—none of them looked too happy either. Chrans had threatened to quit his job if Nissen didn't get convicted. Now he had to settle for a lesser conviction, and in the face of the massive work still ahead in the Lotter trial, it was a bitter pill to swallow.

After court was adjourned, Judge Finn went into his chambers where he had instructed the jury to wait. When he got there, it was obvious that certain jury members were unsettled by their resolution—some of them were crying, and a few even looked like they were on the verge of a nervous breakdown.

"I just want you all to know that the decision you made was the right decision," Finn assured them, "because the jury system is the best system in the world."

And even though they didn't know what the judge really meant, jurors later confided they were grateful for his encouraging words. Even so, that didn't mean they weren't queasy about the verdict—a couple of them still weren't really sure they had done the right thing.

"Everyone got kinda lost there at the end and got kind of very discouraged," juror Kay Buhrman admitted. "The last time we took the vote, there were several of us holding hands. When it all came out twelve and zero, there weren't very many dry eyes in the room. I mean, I think the conviction was correct. But for me, personally, I have a hard time with the death penalty."

"A wrongful conviction was going through my mind," Jacobson conceded, "I mean, I didn't want to send this guy to the chair if he wasn't guilty of these things."

60

THAT EVENING ON THE NIGHTLY NEWS, THE conviction of Marvin Thomas Nissen shared headlines with O. J. Simpson and the latest skirmish in the court of Judge Lance Ito.

Of course, that was only in Lincoln and Omaha; even as close as Kansas City and Chicago, the Brandon story hadn't been picked up, at least not on TV. Newspapers across America, however, ran the story, albeit in very small print. It had been sent through the Associated Press wire services, which was enough for the transgender people to get hold of it. Their movement was picking up speed, and this news was now being bounced around their circle—on the Internet, through E-mail, and every other possible channel they had available.

Expectedly, transgender people didn't feel the verdict was sufficient. They wanted a conviction of three counts of first-degree murder. As they started to state opinions and get organized, they realized the best thing they could do was to become a *presence* at the upcoming Lotter trial. If nothing else, at least they could get some publicity and have something positive result from this horrible travesty.

Meetings were held in New York and California, with transgender representatives from both coasts agreeing to participate in some kind of action. It took weeks, but they finally decided to hold a memorial service for Brandon at the Unitarian Universal Church in Kansas City, after which they would caravan up to Falls City, where they'd spend the day holding a peaceful demonstration. Organizers like Riki Anne Wilchins, were really looking forward to the event. Riki Anne was tired of being ignored by gays, of being pushed around by lesbians; she wanted to establish herself as a separate force, and she had started the Transexual Menace activist group for that purpose.

Finally, Riki Ann was getting noticed. Because of her activism, her picture had appeared in the April 1995 issue of *Esquire*. She was right up there with Tula, the *Playboy* pinup, and Jaye Davidson of *The Crying Game*. They were all pictured in an article entitled "The Third Sex," which focused on the professional debate over "the transgendered" and their sex reassignment surgery. Was it a neurosis? Or a perversion? Or was it, as the piece seemed to suggest, "a brave rejection of oppressive gender categories?"

It all began with George Jorgensen, the young WWII veteran who underwent surgical castration in 1952 to become Christine. Now, over forty years later, *Esquire* reported that transgender people were calling for the abolition of gender distinctions in America. Suddenly, Riki Ann and others were being contacted by the producers of *20/20*. They were *hot* and planned to make the most of it.

Indeed, at the memorial service for "Brandon Teena" in Kansas City, the gender hate crime had people up in arms. Speaker Leslie Feinberg (a self-proclaimed "stone butch") suggested the elimination of all categories of male and female, insisting that gender distinctions should be dropped from things like driver's licenses, passports, and bathrooms. The activist asked people to replace the pronouns *he* and *she* with gender-neutral words like *heesh*.

Heesh was greeted with loud applause.

"I'm talking about respecting and supporting our transsexual sisters and brothers," Feinberg said, "whether they are non-operative, preoperative, or postoperative beings. We, the transgender people in this civic center, are crossing the boundaries of gender that we were expected to have when we were born. That's what those pink hats and blue bonnets are all about."

Unfortunately, transgender people were being treated more like freaks than like real people, so they were hoping their involvement in the "Brandon Teena" case would give them some political pull, and they were right. A number of them organized National Gender Lobby Day and held a demonstration on the steps of the Capitol. But lobbying senators in Washington wasn't enough.

As it turned out, transsexual and transgender persons at the Brandon Teena action made it clear that they weren't very pleased by the way they had been depicted in the media overall. They felt they were misunderstood, misrepresented by the money-making entities on Madison Avenue and elsewhere. Following the publication of the Esquire piece, for instance, transgender activists attacked the magazine for being bizarrely fascinated with transsexuals and their "quasi divine" status. Riki Anne Wilchins was particularly miffed, telling *Esquire* to "get a life," to "try taking the challenges we face seriously."

Although it was a serious piece on the transgender revolution, indeed there were some sensationalistic punches. The article highlighted things such as "ample estrogen-induced breasts" and preop men, who, the night before the sex change operation, have been known to "perform a ritualistic farewell masturbation."

What *Esquire* didn't report was that Riki Anne Wilchins had conceived of the Transsexual Menace organization as a direct result of the Teena Brandon case. It all started in April 1994, when a lengthy piece on Brandon ran in *The Village Voice*. After Wilchins read what she considered to be trash about a fellow transgender person, she decided she had had enough. She got a group of a dozen or so people together, printed up T-shirts with the words Transsexual Menace, and went down and protested outside the trendy magazine's New York office.

The *Voice* article, aptly called "Love Hurts," featured large-sized pictures of Brandon's girlfriends—Reanna Allen, Daphne Gugat, Lindsey Oassen, and Gina Bartu. Then there was a ten-by-ten-inch blowup of Brandon and Lana with the caption "He knew how a girl liked to be treated."

It was quite a story:

"Two days after Brandon arrived in Falls City, every teenage and young adult woman in town was after this pool player with the jaw-line of a Kennedy, who could often be seen in a White Sox jacket and slicked-back hair," Donna Minkowitz wrote. "Sometimes he'd call a limousine to take a girl to work or, with Elvisesque extravagance, give a girl his entire paycheck."

Obviously, that wasn't the kind of thing Riki Anne and her followers objected to. They had no idea what the facts were on Brandon's dating habits, and it didn't really matter anyway. What Wilchins was furious about was the writer's refusal to acknowledge this person, Brandon, as a male.

With blurbs like "I've seen him pee" and information about Brandon's "equipment" looking real, Riki Anne complained that the story was belittling the *agony* this person had suffered. Moreover, the writer of the piece was presenting Brandon as a butch, which was totally insulting to Wilchins and the transgender community.

"However they classify Brandon, everybody wants her," the *Voice* reported, "from photos of the wonder-boychik playing pool, kissing babes … Brandon looks to be the handsomest butch item in history—not just good—looking, but arrogant, audacious, cocky-everything they, and I, look for in lovers."

After the Menace protest, Wilchins tried calling Minkowitz, but she couldn't get the Voice freelancer to print any type of retraction.

A year later, with the Lotter trial pending and a political action under way, Wilchins and others were busy with their mission: printing up T-shirts, posters, and flyers to take to that dreaded spot on the map, that place they'd all heard so much about: *Falls City*. Among the attendees was a transgender cop who had flown in from the west coast of Florida, Tonye Barreto-Neto.

Deputy Barreto-Neto had driven up to Falls City in advance of the protest, just as a way to smooth things. He flashed his Hillsborough County badge, introduced himself as a deputy sheriff, and told one of Hayes's deputies what he was there for—a peaceful vigil.

"We'd like to let you know up front what's going on,"

Barreto-Neto explained. "We don't want any trouble, so if there's any ordinances you need us to know, let us know." The Richardson deputy was very cooperative. In fact, he was almost apologetic for what had happened in their community. He told Barreto-Neto that Falls City authorities had no problem with a demonstration, that Sheriff Hayes and other uniformed officers would be there to protect the demonstrators. He also promised the group could rest whenever they wanted to, said they didn't have to keep moving, and invited them to come and sit in on the trial. Barreto-Neto went back and told the people in Kansas City that everything would be fine.

It was Mother's Day, Sunday, May 14, 1995, and those preparing for the action were getting to sleep early, planning to wake up at 6:00 AM to make the two-hour drive and be there at the very start of the Lotter trial the next morning.

Forty of them made the journey. It would be the first national transgender demonstration ever.

All of them were there for heartfelt reasons, but the outfits that some of them had come up with, between leather and plastic and lace, promised to create a huge spectacle.

Most straight, regular folks looked at them in disbelief. Maybe it was just the kind of thing the trans people wanted.

In January 1996, Deputy Barreto-Neto appeared on *20/20* as part of a story on transgendered cops. The Brandon Teena demonstration was featured, the Falls City Courthouse was shown, and the blood in the Humbolt farmhouse was discussed. Other hate crimes against transgender people were mentioned. No mention was made of the two other people killed in the Humbolt farmhouse. John Stossel and Hugh Downs talked about the strangeness of it all. In the end, Barbara Walters seemed much more at ease talking about George Burns and his 100th birthday celebration.

61

AS TWENTY-FIVE TRANSGENDER PEOPLE HELD UP Brandon Teena signs outside the courthouse, inside district court, the three mothers came before a new jury to identify their slain children. It was May 1995, and the jurors learned about the bitter cold day when Anna Mae discovered the crime scene; retrieving a baby blanket from the living room to cover her half-frozen grandson. As the testimony began, John Lotter was looking unusually subdued, sitting there like a quiet little angel.

Up until then, Lotter had been a behavioral problem—bursting out in curses at the suppression hearing, ripping out sinks in the Richardson County Jail, starting fist-fights in the Diagnostic and Evaluation Center—even, officials suspected, sending unsigned death threats to Nissen, the Tisdels, and McKenzie. Officials eventually resorted to putting the twenty-three-year-old in a stun belt.

They tried it out during jury selection in Omaha, and it seemed to work pretty well. It was funny that from a distance, John looked almost like a bridegroom with it on, his black slacks and starched white shirt set off by this big wide black band. It was a very peculiar cummerbund, the kind that could deliver 50,000 volts of electricity to the defendant's body at any given moment.

But once the trial began in Falls City, Fabian argued the belt wasn't necessary, that it would prejudice the jury against his client. Lotter had promised to calm himself and was therefore required to wear only ankle cuffs. As had been done in the Nissen trial, black satin fabric was draped around the defense and prosecution tables to keep the jury from seeing the prisoner in chains.

Day one of the trial was circus-like, between the cast of transgender people floating in and out-men looking like women, women looking like men—and the farmers in their overalls, the assorted law professionals in sharp suits, the bodyguards in plainclothes with gun bolsters, the other officials in police uniforms. It was colorful, to say the least.

Then, of course, there were the victims and their entourages, some dressed with the news cameras in mind, others haggard and sloppy. In front of them sat two rows of media, with laptops and note pads ablaze.

When that first day was over, after the transgender demonstrators and apathetic spectators were gone, things were more intimate, and it was down to business as usual in the court. The jury watched the flock of experts stepping forward to reel off their credentials, to show evidence, to answer questions. To the remaining courtroom audience, it was all the same stuff that went on at Nissen's trial. It was *deja vu*.

One person who was easy to listen to was Dr. Reena Ray.

In explaining how they tested the bloodstains found at the Lambert residence, she used the analogy of a Jell-0 mold.

Apparently, the human hemoglobin is boiled, put into a mold, and tested for a positive reaction, and in that way, Dr. Roy identified a match to Teena Brandon's blood type on the knife handle. This doctor knew how to explain technical things, how to reduce them.

On day three, a local schoolteacher brought a junior high class into court to witness the proceedings, but that was about as far as it went concerning new onlookers in the courtroom. Locals weren't interested in being there anymore; they were sick of it.

Of course, there were the fresh faces of the Lotters: Michelle and Angie were present most days; their father, Terry, only appeared on the day he had to testify, then the ever devoted Donna was sitting front and center throughout—always wearing her work uniform, standard black polyester pants and nurse-type shoes.

As it usually happens, it was slow going in court for the most part, the action coming in spurts only after hours of grueling testimony. When Lana Tisdel got up to the stand, John showed no emotion at all, and neither did she. John hardly looked at her, and Lana refused to glance his way.

They were like two lovers just after a spat.

"Miss Tisdel, do you recall talking to Assistant Chief Caverzagie on the second day of January 1994?" Fabian asked on cross-examination.

"Yes," Lana said, her voice barely above a whisper.

"Can you explain why Assistant Chief Caverzagie would put in his report of January 3, 1994, the statement 'Lana told us that she did not really hear this'?"

Fabian was referring to John's alleged statement that he wanted to kill somebody, made on the early morning of December 31.

"I don't know why he put that in there," Lana said, her voice flippant.

"So if he put that in there, he's mistaken or lying?"

"He's mistaken."

"Let me ask you a question about the evening of December 30, the day before the homicides. You had an individual in your home by the name of Lenny Landrum, did you not?" Fabian reminded her.

"Yes, we did."

"And when police officers questioned you about who was present in the home the night of the thirtieth, the early morning hours of the thirty-first, you never made any mention of Lenny Landrum, did you?"

"No, I didn't."

"You *lied* to state patrol, to investigators?"

"Yes, I did," Lana mumbled.

"And you talked about that lie, did you not, with your mother and your sister and your brother, that you weren't going to tell anyone that Lenny Landrum was there?"

"I don't remember sayin' that." Lana paused. "We talked about it."

"You talked about it? And you talked about it to your little brother?"

"Yes."

"And you didn't suggest to him to say this statement that 'I feel like killin' someone?' You didn't suggest that statement that you couldn't remember on the third of January?"

"No."

Rhonda McKenzie testified as well, and again, there was the same non-reaction from Lotter. He was just blank, watching the mother of his child forsake him without the slightest reaction. For months, Lotter had tried to control Rhonda from his prison cell, writing letters, making phone calls, promising to love her forever, insisting on her loyalty in exchange. Now he realized that was all a waste of time. Obviously, these pieces of the puzzle were critical for the jurors to hear—that John asked Rhonda for an alibi, that he told Lana he felt like killing someone—but to everyone else in the courtroom, it was just old hat. People were jaded by then. They thought they knew it all, heard it all before. As far as Lana's involvement was concerned, the state had apparently concluded that she had not participated in the murders and that she was not in the car. She was never charged.

But just as the prosecution was about to wrap up its case, an amazing thing happened: in the eleventh hour, Marvin Thomas Nissen decided to cut a deal with the state. In order to save his life, Nissen was willing to roll over on his partner and *tell all*.

When Nissen walked in, everyone was wired, people were on the edge of their seats. What shocked everyone was how meek the convicted killer and accused rapist looked as he sat up there. He was so fragile looking he almost seemed dainty, his thin blond ponytail dangling behind his soft narrow frame. It was hard to believe he was responsible for such monstrous deeds.

Of course, Nissen didn't really want to snitch; he didn't want to be up there at all. That was why he hadn't cut a deal earlier. He was concerned for his own safety, scared of what Lotter and his jailhouse cronies would do to him. He knew people in prison were beaten to death with mop ringers, stabbed, *burned* for doing things like this. No one likes a double-crosser—

least of all hardened criminals.

"Snitches don't work well in prison," Tom had argued to his attorney. "What kind of lifestyle would I have in protective custody? I'd just get out one hour a day. I wouldn't be able to lift weights and walk yards."

Yet Nissen knew it was necessary for him to testify, so he used that to the hilt. To Blakeslee, he presented the theory that John could get up and say he was passed out drunk in the backseat of the car, that John could even say he had no idea Tom had driven to Humbolt.

John could claim he never woke up until Tom parked the car on Chase Street, Nissen contended, and since there were no fingerprints on the gun, on the knife, or in the farmhouse, Lotter just might go free. Nissen had them. He knew Elworth, or Jimmy Boy as he called him, needed some juicy testimony to convince jurors. But Nissen wasn't going to come easy. For one thing, Lotter was threatening to kill him after the trial was through, so Nissen was struggling with that.

People involved in the case pleaded with Tom. No one could understand why he would want to take all the blame, why he wouldn't want the chance to stay off death row. Nissen did a lot of thinking about it and in the end decided that maybe he *could* help the state win its case. He agreed to be transported to Falls City to tell his version to the jury—this time, promising not to leave anything out. It would be the truth, the whole truth, and...

As he started, he Pointed his finger at John Lotter. There was the guy who shot Brandon, Lambert, and DeVine.

"Sir, have you entered into an agreement today to receive some sort of benefits in exchange for your testimony?" Elworth asked, putting all the cards on the table.

"Yes," Nissen said, nodding his head.

"To the best of your recollection, would you recite that agreement please?"

"That I testify truthfully about the matters that are here today and that I agree to be sentenced to three life terms, to retain my appeal rights, and to be transferred to another prison out of Nebraska."

"Anything else that you can recall at this time?"

"That nothing I said could be used against me," Nissen said without a hint of a smile.

Marvin Thomas Nissen gave a rundown of the ride to Humbolt December 31, of the alternate route they took to Lambert's when they reached the city limits. He told the jury there were just two people in the car—himself and John Lotter—that they were both wearing gloves and had with them a gun and a knife. He said the two of them talked on the way up there, agreeing that they'd have to kill whoever was with Brandon as well.

In the recent past, he had lied to police, to fellow inmates, and to *Playboy*.

Now, he said, he wasn't lying anymore.

Nissen described entering the farmhouse, looking for the lights, and approaching the back bedroom, where he asked for Brandon. He told jurors he was watching the baby standing in his crib, and at that point, John shot Brandon, then handed him the knife. Tom testified he stabbed Brandon "to make sure she was dead."

"As far back as Christmas Day, did you know you might be facing some trouble?" Elworth quizzed.

"Yes." Nissen nodded.

"At that time was Lotter living at your house?"

"He was staying there, yes."

"And at that point, did you begin to talk about what to do about this possible trouble that you might be in?"

"Yes."

"Are you able to say, from the twenty-fifth of December through the thirtieth of December, how many of these conversations you had with Lotter?"

"I couldn't give you a number. There was a lot"

"Were they behind closed doors?"

"Yes."

The killer outlined the plot the two of them had come up with to slay Teena Brandon, which they had put into action on December 26. He told jurors that on that day, the two of them drove up to Lincoln, using Brandon's address book as a guide. He admitted they staked all three different residences while there, waiting for Brandon to appear, planning to force her into Lotter's car, then murder her.

"Did you discuss how you were going to kill her?" the prosecutor asked, a slight strain in his voice.

"Yes."

"What was that discussion?"

"To chop her hands and her head off," Nissen said methodically. "Why were you going to do that?"

"In order that the body couldn't be identified."

"Had you taken any materials with you to Lincoln in order to accomplish that?" "Took a hatchet, a rope, and a change of clothing."

"Why a change of clothing?"

"In the event that blood was on the clothes."

Upon further examination, Nissen testified that both he and Lotter had a change of clothes, that the rope was a white nylon clothesline from home, that the hatchet was a roofing-type hatchet Tom used around the house. He explained that before they drove to Lincoln, the two of them stopped at the Lambert house, but nobody was home. Just to be sure, they drove back into downtown Humbolt and called Lisa's from a pay phone. No one answered.

"Did you, on December 28, after talking to Keith Hayes, step up your discussions regarding what to do about Brandon?" Elworth asked, having brought up the rape investigation.

"Somewhat, yes."

"Did you know for certain you're in trouble at that point?"

"Pretty good idea."

"So tell me, if you're able to, any specifics of what you talked about from the point of December 28 on into the time of the evening of December 30."

"Really started discussin' it at more length, of killing Teena Brandon." Nissen fidgeted. "Any question in your mind that you knew you were going to kill Teena Brandon at that point?"

"There was no question in my mind."

"Was Lotter aware, and was he part of the plan as well?"

"Yes," Nissen said, looking straight at the defendant.

"You mentioned Lotter was staying at your house. How did you two spend your days?"

"Mostly with drinking."

"And how did it happen during these time frames that you would end up in the bathroom or the kitchen talking between yourselves about Teena Brandon?"

"We'd be settin' around my home, just talking about something, and Teena Brandon's name would come up."

"Do you remember what specifically was talked about?"

"By that time, the nature of the conversation was always the same."

"And what was that?"

"How to kill Teena Brandon," Nissen squarely admitted.

"Were you discussing particular ways?"

"Me and John Lotter discussed a whole bunch of different ways."

"Tell me what those ways were if you recall."

But Nissen *didn't recall*.

62

THROUGHOUT NISSEN'S TESTIMONY, EVERYONE HEARD the precise and chilling details of the murders. Nissen was so graphic about it, explaining each death in a step-by-step fashion, people felt like they'd almost witnessed the event, like they'd been there for each horrifying moment.

Mike Fabian—the kind of guy who exudes an aura of success, with looks and demeanor resembling those of Jack Nicholson—now found himself completely stumped by the prosecution. Before he could let Nissen off the stand, Fabian's only hope was to perform a complete character assassination. If he could make Nissen look like a sniveling weasel, Lotter still might stand a chance.

"Mr. Nissen, did Mr. Lotter ever forcibly sexually assault Teena Brandon?" Fabian began in recross, very deliberate in his tone.

"I don't know," Nissen said flippantly.

"Did *you*?"

"Yes," Tom said.

"Did Mr. Lotter ever beat or kick Teena Brandon?" the defense attorney wondered.

"Not that I know of."

"Did *you*?"

"Yes, I did. Well, excuse me, I don't ever recall kicking Brandon, but yes, I hit Brandon."

"Did you knee her in the stomach after the sexual assault?"

"Yes, I did."

"And when that was all over, you pointed the finger at Mr. Lotter and said you didn't do anything," Fabian sneered.

"I said I didn't do anything, yes."

"You have also been granted immunity. Anything you say today under oath cannot be used against you. Right?"

"Yes."

"So you can say anything you want today, and no one can do anything about it"

"I suppose you're correct by sayin' that," Nissen quipped. "You've got no liability as you sit up there today. You can tell the biggest lie in the world, and nobody can prosecute you. Right?"

"Well, unless I'm found to be lying."

"And that's something you negotiated for, is it not? That whatever you say wouldn't be used against you?"

"Yes."

"Even though you were going to come in and tell the truth?"

Under this line of questioning, Fabian thought he really had him. The sharp attorney felt hopeful the jury would see through Nissen's lies and find Lotter not guilty of first degree murder.

There was only one little problem.

Lotter was insisting on taking the stand, he wouldn't listen to reason, and Fabian knew his client could quite possibly hang himself under cross-exam. But Lotter had made the choice against the advice of counsel, and he was constitutionally entitled to testify on his own behalf.

Just after lunch, Wednesday, May 24, Fabian requested that Lotter's leg irons be taken off so he could appear as everyone else had, as a regular citizen, speaking in his own defense.

The jury filed in looking tired and humdrum, but they immediately snapped to attention when they heard John Lotter's name called. The defendant was quickly sworn in, and under direct examination by his attorney, Lotter testified that he never planned the death of Teena Brandon, never shot Teena Brandon, and never shot Lisa Lambert or Phillip DeVine. Lotter called Tom Nissen a liar and, in essence, was letting jurors know he'd been sitting in prison for seventeen months, serving time for something he hadn't done. He was a victim of circumstance.

On cross, Elworth started by asking John about his day on December 30, taking him back to 1993 and his drive to Rulo with Tom, retracing their stop at the Old Tyme Bar, things like that. John talked about hanging out at Camp Rulo and listening to karaoke music that night, but he denied telling Jim Morehead that he was in trouble again, denied saying that if he ever went back to the penitentiary, "it would probably be for a very long time."

Morehead, a local farmer, had already testified about their conversation, and in light of that, Lotter's statement seemed kind of flimsy. There was something about the quality of his voice; it just didn't ring true.

When the prosecutor brought up their detour to William Bennett's house, Lotter admitted he had gone there with Nissen but denied stealing any gun. Lotter tried to make it look like maybe Nissen had taken it, bringing up the fact that on December 31, Bennett had reported that his back door was somehow busted out.

The defendant absolutely denied making any comment to Lana that he felt like killing someone and swore up and down that he never discussed any kind of alibi story with Rhonda. *That was a lie*, just her *opinion*, he said.

In fact, Lotter claimed he spent the entire morning of December 31 at the Nissen house, stating that, in fact, *he never went to Humbolt at all*.

"So you didn't have a series of meetings with Nissen starting on December 25, either in his kitchen or bathroom or in the car, talkin' about Teena Brandon?" the prosecutor snidely asked.

"No, I did not," Lotter said emphatically.

"Did you go to Lincoln with Nissen on December 26, looking for Teena Brandon?"

"No, I did not."

"Were you in Lincoln on December 27?"

"No, I wasn't."

"This is Exhibit 128. Do you recognize it?" Elworth held up a piece of paper for John to view.

"Yeah, I recognize this," Lotter said. "That's my signature."

"That's *your* signature?"

"Yes," Lotter said, looking stunned as Elworth unfolded the top portion of the document, revealing the claim stub from a pawn shop.

"And doesn't this exhibit, in fact, show that on December 27, 1993, at 10:00 AM, you pawned fourteen CD's at a pawn shop in Lincoln, Nebraska?"

"Yes," Lotter had to admit. "So, you did go there." "Well, I guess I did."

Elworth offered Exhibit 128 to the court, and Fabian could make no objection. On redirect-exam, Fabian pointed out that pawning CD's has nothing to do with murder, but it was to no avail. The damage had already been done. Surrounded by a half-dozen sheriff's deputies and security guards, Lotter maintained his innocence right up to the very moment he was led from the courtroom.

"Nissen's a little fucking liar," he yelled as he was being escorted to his jail cell.

"He should go to the chair," John Lambert told reporters, insisting there wasn't a doubt in his mind that Lotter killed his daughter, disgusted that Lotter didn't show any remorse whatsoever.

On Friday, May 26, it was front-page news all over the state:

LOTTER CONVICTED OF FIRST-DEGREE MURDER...
LOTTER GUILTY...

The ten women and two men of the jury had found him guilty after only five hours of deliberations. Lotter was found guilty of burglary and three counts of using a weapon to commit a felony, and they had convicted him of three counts of first-degree murder, reaching the verdict under the felony murder provision.

As soon as the verdict was in, the case was automatically up for appeal; that was standard, as it had been for Nissen. In fact, by then, Nissen's appeal was already under way. Under the terms of his plea agreement, Nissen had been sentenced to serve three consecutive life sentences, which translated into zero chance for parole for at least twenty-seven years. Obviously, Nissen felt he could get that lessened. He had been studying law books for over a year in the prison library, hanging by a thread of hope, but when the matter went before the court, Nissen's appeal was denied.

Before court was adjourned, Fabian asked for additional time to prepare for a sentencing hearing, and that being granted, a two-week slot was scheduled for the weeks surrounding Thanksgiving, meaning the judgment on Lotter would be dragged out until the end of December 1995 or even beyond.

When Thanksgiving week finally rolled around, a three-judge panel sat in the Richardson County Courthouse listening to Fabian present the mitigating circumstances in this life-or-death situation. Of course, before the sentencing hearing even began, people had their hackles up; victims and their families were horrified by the anticipation of such an event.

Most couldn't believe Fabian would dare try to make Johnny Lotter look like the poor victim of life's circumstances. After the Menendez decision in California, where killing one's own parents had been excused via this kind of twisted-victim logic, people were losing all faith in the United States justice system. Now, this was another potential low blow.

If Fabian, by parading a bunch of Lotter family members around and a host of hired shrinks, could somehow get Lotter off the hook, that would be the final straw.

63

WHEN DONNA LOTTER TESTIFIED ON HER SON'S BEHALF, she had the whole town feeling sorry for her. This was a woman who had been dealt the wrong cards in life, people knew.

They had seen how hard she had worked, how she had tried to keep her family together, but she just couldn't combat her husband's drinking, her husband's irresponsibility. No one wanted to blame her; as far as locals were concerned, she was the nicest person in the world who would do anything to help someone in need.

Of course, admitting an eight-year-old into a mental institute is quite unusual, but Donna didn't seem to have a choice back then. Her son was out of control in public school, his counselors suggested an institute in Omaha, and because there was nothing like that available in Falls City, she had to send her child away. It was for his own good.

Unfortunately, though, John always received mixed messages from his mother. On the one hand, she wanted him back. On the other, she allowed her husband to control that decision, and Terry wanted nothing to do with the kid. It was a very sad thing to hear Donna get up and testify that after John was born, Terry looked at him and said, "He doesn't belong to me." It was even sadder however, to discover that John had been diagnosed with craniosynostosis, meaning that the soft spot on his head hardened up too fast, and as a result, his brain wasn't able to develop fully. Because of that condition, John had an IQ of 84, had a learning disability from the age of four, and was mocked by other children. More devastating, little Johnny was ridiculed by his own father, who John said used to call him retarded whenever he had the notion.

As far back as 1979, when John was in the North Elementary School in Falls City, his behavior was rather typical of an emotionally disturbed child. Part of the problem was that Johnny's world was inconsistent and unpredictable—his father often gone, his mother always working—so he was becoming increasingly antisocial and disruptive in public.

On May 23 of that year, a conference was set up with Donna to try to develop a meaningful plan for John's future, to change his handicapped condition from "specific learning disability" to "emotionally disturbed." The school psychologist wanted her to learn more productive ways of creating stability for Johnny, but unfortunately, according to the psychologist's report, the mother didn't show up that day, and it was too late in the school year to reschedule.

Donna's pattern as a no-show became directly related to John's levels of increased disturbance. She seemed to have no clue about how to deal with him, and in trying to show him love, she was unable to discipline him. From the time he was born, Donna considered Johnny a problem. She told mental health workers that he was different as an infant because he never wanted to be held and he never really slept.

"No matter how much I held him or loved him, he cried," Donna confided during a psychiatric evaluation on October 17, 1980, when John was just nine years old. Donna said she didn't buy the idea that because she was working so much, Johnny was developing problems. "He always knew where I was," Donna insisted, citing the fact that her two girls didn't have any problems, that *they* were left alone just as often.

In January 1980, John was sent to the Nebraska Psychiatric Institute (NPI), where he stayed until May 13. After he returned to Falls City, when asked her opinion about her son, Donna told health workers she thought he was worse. "Perhaps it's just because I was without those problems for four months," Donna told them. "Perhaps I just notice it more now."

Actually, John Lotter had wound up in NPI as a result of his having taken a bicycle from the Falls City community pool. While at the police station, authorities caught him going through cars in the police parking lot, which got him in more trouble, and the next thing little Johnny knew, he was being hauled off to the looney bin. It was a decision his parents could have stopped but didn't. Psychologists later speculated that Lotter shouldn't have been placed in that kind of setting at such an early age, that his problems were strictly behavioral in those days. What he really needed was extra attention.

By 1980, when John started getting into more trouble for minor law violations, a Blue Valley mental health care worker sent an evaluation to the Richardson County welfare office, as per their request. In it, John was viewed as having an "unsocialized aggressive reaction of childhood," as being openly disobedient, and it was recommended that the boy be placed in a group setting, somewhere that he could receive inpatient treatment.

He was referred to the Children's Inpatient Service in Omaha, where staff child psychiatrist Dr. Sungdo Hong suggested John receive "individual expressive psychotherapy" and a "structured classroom with high supervision." The psychiatrist wanted John placed in an atmosphere where there would be "powerful rewards," where "punishments are consistently maintained and non-emotionally dispensed."

Apparently, in order to get little Johnny to listen, Donna would often resort to crying. More than one report indicated that the mother would break down in tears, begging John to behave, which only confused the kid about authority.

Though his parents had legally divorced when John was just three years old, his father continued to live in the house with Donna for another five years. This always posed a problem for John; he didn't understand why his dad mistreated his mother, why Terry didn't love her. For a while, Donna let John wear her *wedding band*—the two of them united as some kind of strange couple. When a psychiatrist later pointed out that perhaps the ring was inappropriate, Johnny took it off and threw it across the room.

Then there was always the problem with payment of child support. Terry Lotter was unable or unwilling to make the $280 monthly payments, forcing young John to be placed under the supervision of the Nebraska Department of Social Services.

The continuing bizarre relationship of his parents had a wild effect on John. He never knew if they were honestly together or not, and things became especially confusing when Donna and Terry reunited in marriage on December 10, 1982. The weird part was, they still weren't man and wife—Terry always had girlfriends and he hardly came home. When he did appear, Donna refused to sleep in the same room with him. She lived in a codependent situation, supporting the family on her measly pay checks while Terry pissed his money away.

In school, teachers recognized that part of John's predicament was that he had difficulty expressing himself verbally. He had poor motor skills and a faulty command of the language. Because he couldn't communicate his feelings, he would become upset; he would cry and carry on like a baby.

One educational therapist, Nancy Dugan, found that when Johnny would get upset to the point that he was out of control, he would do much better when she would just hold him. After a while, he would break down in tears and be more willing to talk about what was bothering him. Unfortunately, though, John was soon removed from Dugan's arms, his behavioral problems dictating that he receive higher levels of care.

One of the things that bothered John was the fact that he had been placed a year behind his age level in public school. His handicap necessitated that placement; John was unable to keep up in areas like reading and math. But the boy never understood why he was left behind, so he slammed desks, intimidated other children, and cursed out his teachers because of it.

At his sentencing hearing, it was revealed that Lotter had stolen 300 cars over the years, always trying to go home. This information came from his primary psychiatrist, Dr. Paul Fine, a professor emeritus at Creighton University who had cared for Lotter during an eight-year period, starting from the time John was age nine. Dr. Fine cared about Lotter.

Way back in 1983, the doctor had noted in a report that "John wants to do right, and when he doesn't, he *can't.*"

"He really comes across like Cool-Hand-Luke, flippant, but really full of despair," Dr. Fine wrote. "He really cares. Get him to cry and talk about it."

In the Richardson District Court, Paul Fine testified that Lotter was a "confused lost child" who had a high probability of organic damage to his brain, which directly correlated to Lotter's dismorphy, to his misshapen head. The Omaha psychiatrist testified that *since birth,* Lotter had more than one mental disorder going on, that a myriad of conditions manifested themselves in "unpredictably impulsive feelings and behavior."

The psychiatrist, who had reevaluated Lotter the night before—after not having seen his former patient for almost nine years—told the court that Lotter would "very possibly react violently if he were tricked by someone or if he were made to look foolish."

Under examination by Fabian, Dr. Fine testified that if Lotter was overwhelmed during the murders, "he might not have known what he was doing at the time he was doing it."

When questioned by Elworth, however, the doctor agreed with the psychological profile of Lotter as "manipulative, selfish, rebellious, unreliable, and nonconformist." Eventually, Fine characterized Lotter as "someone who blames others and won't accept the consequences of his actions."

Another mental health professional who testified at the hearing, psychologist Timothy Jeffrey, chairman of the psychology department at the University of Nebraska Medical Center in Omaha, said Lotter had "tried to improve his behavior as a child" but had been "discouraged by consistent failure."

In having reviewed Lotter's psychiatric history, Dr. Jeffrey said the convicted killer "acted impulsively" with an "escalation of anger" toward those who wronged him. Timothy Jeffrey cited as an example the time when John's little school chums made fun of Donna, which set Lotter off into a psychotic rage.

Fabian had brought Dr. Jeffrey in, primarily to have him testify about Lotter's limited ability to reason between right and wrong and his smaller understanding of the standards of society. After expert testimony regarding Lotter's incapacity to understand his crimes, the defense attorney was hoping the three-judge panel would show mercy on his client and not sentence John Lawrence Lotter to die in the electric chair.

"John Lotter is programmed differently," Dr. Jeffrey told the court. "He gets caught up in the anger." The psychologist stated that Lotter's "reaction to threats is to be aggressive and not think of the consequences." But under cross-examination, the psychologist had to admit that disposing of the murder weapons would indicate that Lotter *did*, indeed, know that the crimes he committed were wrong.

When the hearing was all said and done, the three-judge panel, headed by Robert Finn, pretty much knew they could only come up with one outcome. Although the actual pronouncement wouldn't be until late February 1996, the judges were already bound by previous case law: in Nebraska, no one in history had been found guilty of a triple homicide and been sentenced to anything less than *death*.

EPILOGUE

IT WAS ODD. THE MEDIA HAD EXPECTED CRUSHING crowds for the Lotter and Nissen trials; they expected the town to be out in full force, up in arms about this horrible crime. One reporter wrote a story on it. He couldn't believe that more people were standing around the Stephenson Hotel lobby following the O. J. case than were in the courtroom gallery, across the street. Locals were just ignoring it.

"I don't think this case had a lasting effect on the people around here," admitted Scott Schock, managing editor of the *Falls City Journal*. "A lot of the attitude around here revolves around the crop; we're almost a hundred percent dependent on farming," Schock explained, "and a whole lot of people in this town didn't know any of these people at all. It's not like the Tisdels, Nissens, or Lotters were a part of the Future Homemakers of America."

Future homemakers indeed.

Even though there wasn't a snowball's chance in hell, Lotter would spend his Christmas '95 wondering, praying that, against all odds, his life would be spared. Partially, he was concerned for his daughter, Rochelle, who was being raised under Rhonda's harsh rule. Then again, with Lotter's limited brain capacity, it would be hard to tell what he really cared about.

He had other things to worry about. Rumor had it Lotter had been raped a number of times in prison.

In Humbolt, there had been talk of burning down the Lambert farmhouse, but no one had gotten around to it yet. It still stood there, off the beaten path, a couple of dilapidated sheds out back, a barbecue grill turned over and rusted out front.

Inside, the place looked frozen in time, everything exactly as John and Tom left it, save for a few items Brandon's friends had managed to steal. People broke into the place just weeks after the murders, trying to recoup the remnants of their loved ones. Brandon's black cowboy hat had been taken, and a few of Lisa's clothes were gone, but other than that the Honeycomb boxes stood upright on the kitchen counter, the dirty laundry was piled next to the washing machine—everything was untouched.

It had become a spook house.

Police had altered very little when they combed the place.

They retrieved only the necessary evidence, but after the trials did return some remaining personal belongings to the victims' three moms. Aisha took a box of Phillip's things back with her to Iowa. Anna Mae had received the important papers for Tanner—his Social Security card and other documents. It was JoAnn who was left with very little of Teena. There were just a few items of men's clothing, and they were things she hardly recognized.

Of course, no one would ever know for sure what happened in there that night, but Investigator Jack Wyant would later surmise that Nissen's testimony was a total lie, that his confession had all kinds of holes in it. For one thing, Wyant thought it seemed obvious that DeVine was shot first, because the killers probably stumbled on him as soon as they broke the door down. They got him out of the way, then made their way to the back bedroom to kill the girls. It was just Wyant's hunch.

* * *

By the time the personal items were returned, Aisha had already reconciled the death. Phillip was in a better place, she was sure. Her spirituality left her with no questions.

Anna Mae had all of Pawnee City rooting for her; people even tied yellow ribbons around trees for Lisa. No one could do enough to help her get through it—everyone going out of their way, that is, except for Troy Newburn, Tanner's deadbeat dad. Newburn didn't bother to show up for Lisa's funeral and, although under court order, refused to pay any child support.

As for JoAnn, she still hadn't put up Teena's tombstone, afraid it might get vandalized as a result of the publicity.

Already, hate-crime groups had gathered at Teena's grave site. A crowd of seventy-five had been there on Columbus Day, calling for an end to discrimination against gays, Jews, American Indians—the list was endless.

At times, JoAnn would think back and remember Teena's dream—not the dream to have her sexuality accepted, but the dream she remembered Teena had when she was just a girl: that she would die violently one day. JoAnn could hardly believe it was true. None of it was real to her.

Then there was Tammy, who had become engrossed in her own life with her husband. She had recently wed Brian Schweitzer; they had one child in May 1993, Baileigh Lynn, and now they just had their second girl, Alexis, in the fall of 1995. It was a handful for the two of them, and between the murder trials, the press, their work and family, they lived with a lot of anxiety.

Of course Tammy was also stressed out for other reasons.

There were things she felt guilty about; for instance, she had once spoken to Tom Nissen on the phone, insisting to him that Teena was going through a series of sex change operations. Tammy hated to lie, but Teena had pressured her to do it. Now Tammy wondered if maybe she shouldn't have.

There was also the phone conversation Tammy had with Aisha. They had spoken just after the murders occurred, and at that time, Aisha reported that when Phillip called from Falls City, he seemed nervous and frightened on the phone.

"They want me to do something bad," Phillip had said in an uneasy voice.

"What is it? Why don't you just come home and get out of there?" Aisha had pleaded.

But DeVine never explained what he meant by the comment. Now, all Tammy could figure was that more people had been involved in this ordeal than the public would ever know.

Of all the families of the victims, only the Brandons filed a wrongful death suit with Richardson County. JoAnn was seeking a cool $1 million, alleging negligence by Sheriff Charles B. Laux. With all the money local government had already spent on the trials, people in Richardson County worried about what would happen if any judgment came out in Ms. Brandon's favor. As it was, they suffered from such a poor economy, between the sad shape of farming and the overall lack of jobs for young people in the region, they just couldn't afford it.

Meanwhile, Tom Nissen was feeling sorry for himself in jail, writing letters to evoke sympathy from anyone he could.

More than ever, he hated that his kids had been placed in foster care again. He learned that Kandi had been given a second chance by Social Services and had lost the girls again.

It was casually, in the days after his appeal was denied, that Tom finally talked about his urge to kill. He said he didn't remember much, except that at first, it had been birds—later, it was dogs. Nissen felt bad about killing the dogs—his friend in Mississippi made him do it.

On the one hand, he insisted he wasn't some kind of natural-born killer. On the other, he swore he didn't kill Brandon as part of a hate crime.

Who knows what motivated Nissen? His blatant racism had been brought up in court, but even if he'd been a member of the KKK, jurors believed that the killing of DeVine was just some weird coincidence. One African-American juror said Phillip was just a "bonus" for Nissen, that DeVine's race didn't make a damn bit of difference.

As for Brandon's girlfriends, most of them moved on.

Heather Kuhfahl and Daphne Gugat each had babies, both giving birth out of wedlock, perhaps to let the world know just how *heterosexual* they could be.

And some of the young girls built scrapbooks around Brandon, keeping all the news clippings, following the story in the media, remaining, as they had from the start, more curious than anything else.

Then there were those who faded into the woodwork—or at least tried to.

Lana Tisdel moved out of Falls City to a place called Fremont. It was still in Nebraska, but it was a couple of hours away from the constant harassment. Back home, she was still being called lesbian, she was mocked, and she was tired of all that.

Regardless, she was constantly drawn back there, to her old friends and old habits, although her relationship with Michelle Lotter would never be the same. She and Michelle didn't see eye to eye about things anymore.

But of everyone, perhaps, not surprisingly, it was Gina Bartu who seemed the most affected. She had to go through therapy to deal with it all, and she never really wanted to let go of Brandon.

"If he had the money, he would have had the operation in a heartbeat, just so it wouldn't have been an issue that would have come up later on," she reflected. "But just the fact of *saying* he would do it was different than actually having it done. I think it may have scared him. All I know is, when I was with him, everything was just too good to be true."

Yes, it certainly was.

PHOTO ARCHIVE

Tammy and Teena Brandon at ages five and two. A mother couldn't ask for two sweeter girls. *(courtesy JoAnn Brandon)*

Teena's first communion. She's in the front row at the far right, all dolled up in white knee socks and ruffled veil.
(courtesy JoAnn Brandon)

Teena, at center, and her girlfriends put on a song-and-dance as The Sex Pots in 1984.
(courtesy JoAnn Brandon)

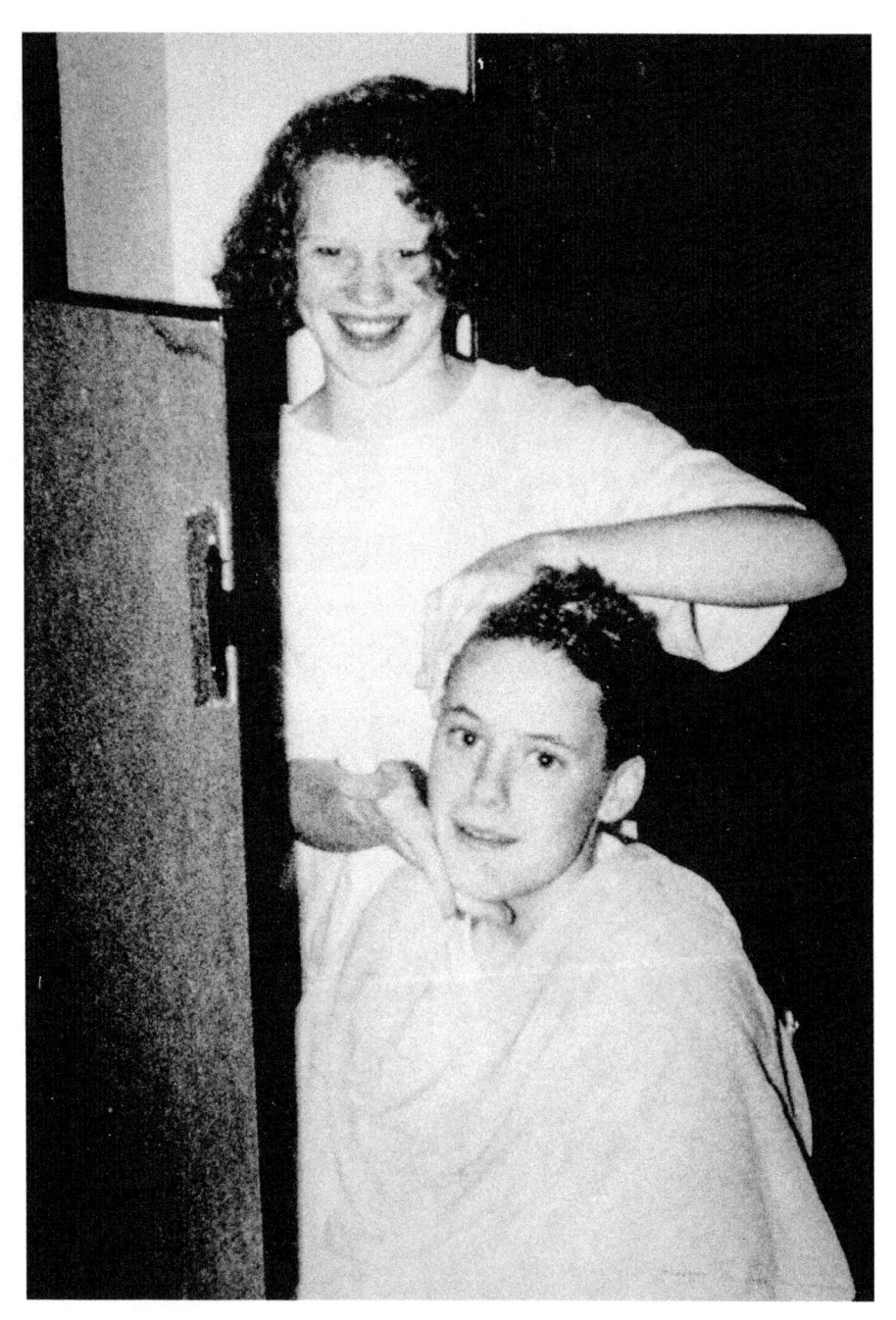

*Heather Kuhfahl cuts and dyes Billy's hair.
(courtesy Heather Kuhfahl)*

Gina Bartu, the proverbial girl next door, fell in love with Brandon and eventually agreed to marry him.
(courtesy Gina Bartu)

Tammy and JoAnn celebrate Christmas with Teena in 1990. Little did they know it would be one of their last with her.
(courtesy JoAnn Brandon)

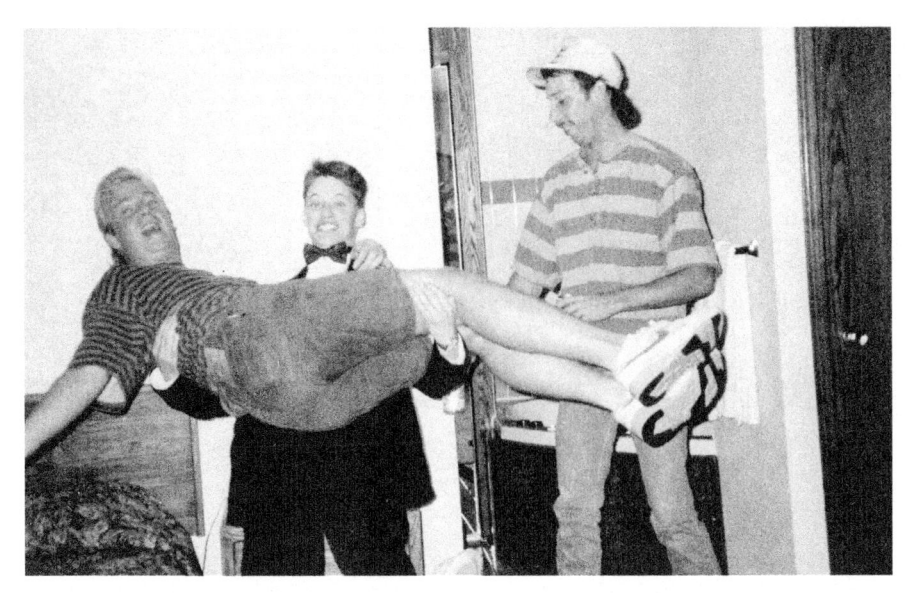

Brandon rented a room at the Harvester Hotel to celebrate his engagement to Gina Bartu. Here, he shows Gina just how much of a man he is, lifting someone twice his size without flinching. *(courtesy Gina Bartu)*

Even in the privacy of Brandon and Gina's bedroom, he covered his chest with a towel.
(courtesy Gina Bartu)

Little Johnny Lotter had a tough childhood.
(courtesy Lana Tisdel)

Lana, at eighteen had very little experience in dating, and says she had never been taken to dinner and a movie until Brandon came along.
(courtesy Lana Tisdel)

John Lotter and Lana Tisdel were still friends in 1992 though their relationship was strained.
(courtesy Lana Tisdel)

Lana and Brandon in happier times
(courtesy Lana Tisdel)

Just days before the depantsing, John and Brandon are the best of buddies. *(courtesy Lana Tisdel)*

Lana and Leslie Tisdel open gifts on Christmas Eve, 1993. That night, Brandon asked Lana not to leave his side, and she promised to get the festivities over with quickly. *(courtesy Lana Tisdel)*

Tom Nissen on Christmas Day after a long, brutal night
(author's collection)

Teena Brandon after the rape
(courtesy Lana Tisdel)

Lisa Lambert in her senior high school portrait, before she changed her hair and started to wear funky clothes
(author's collection)

Phillip DeVine in 1991, before he went on to represent the
Job Corps in Washington, D.C.
(courtesy Edith DeVine)

The boarded-up Humbolt farmhouse, scene of the triple homicide *(photo by author)*

The day after the massacre, Richardson County Attorney Doug Merz (at right) holds a press conference along with Sheriff Charles Laux. It would be the first of many media encounters for both men.
(The Falls City Journal)

John Lotter, escorted by Sheriff Laux enters the courtroom in a T-shirt, jeans, and handcuffs. During his first appearance, he waved to family members, smiled, and got smug with the press.
(The Falls City Journal)

Tom Nissen appears in court in jail-issue clothing, accompanied by Richardson County Deputy Tom Olberding. Nissen's confession led lawmen to the gun and knife deposited in the Nemaha River. (The Falls City Journal)

Transgender activism was born, in part from the "Brandon Teena" case. Here, a handful of protesters stand outside the courthouse at the Lotter trial. (The Falls City Journal)

Printed in Great Britain
by Amazon